Compositions Book 4

Music for
Various Voicings

by
Ken Langer

Compositions Book 4

Original Music
for Various Voicings

by
Ken Langer

Compositions Book 4
Music for Various Voicings
by Ken Langer

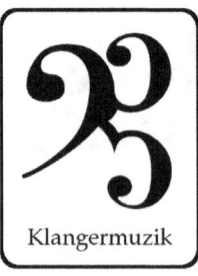

Klangermuzik
http://www.klangermuzik.com

First Edition (Softcover)

Copyright © 2013, Ken Langer

ISBN: 978-1-300-72707-1

Produced in the United States of America

The author may be contacted at ken@kenlanger.com.

Table of Contents

Introduction

This is a collection of vocal works for various parts including mixed chorus, women's chorus, men's chorus, and a variety of instrumental accompaniments. Some of these were written specifically for these groups while others are arrangements of mixed choir compositions found in my other collections.

Recordings of all the works can be found on my website: http:// kenlanger.com. Some of the recordings are live while others are MIDI transcriptions which may help you become familiar with each work.

Dickinson's Day
I. At Twilight

Emily Dickinson

Ken Langer

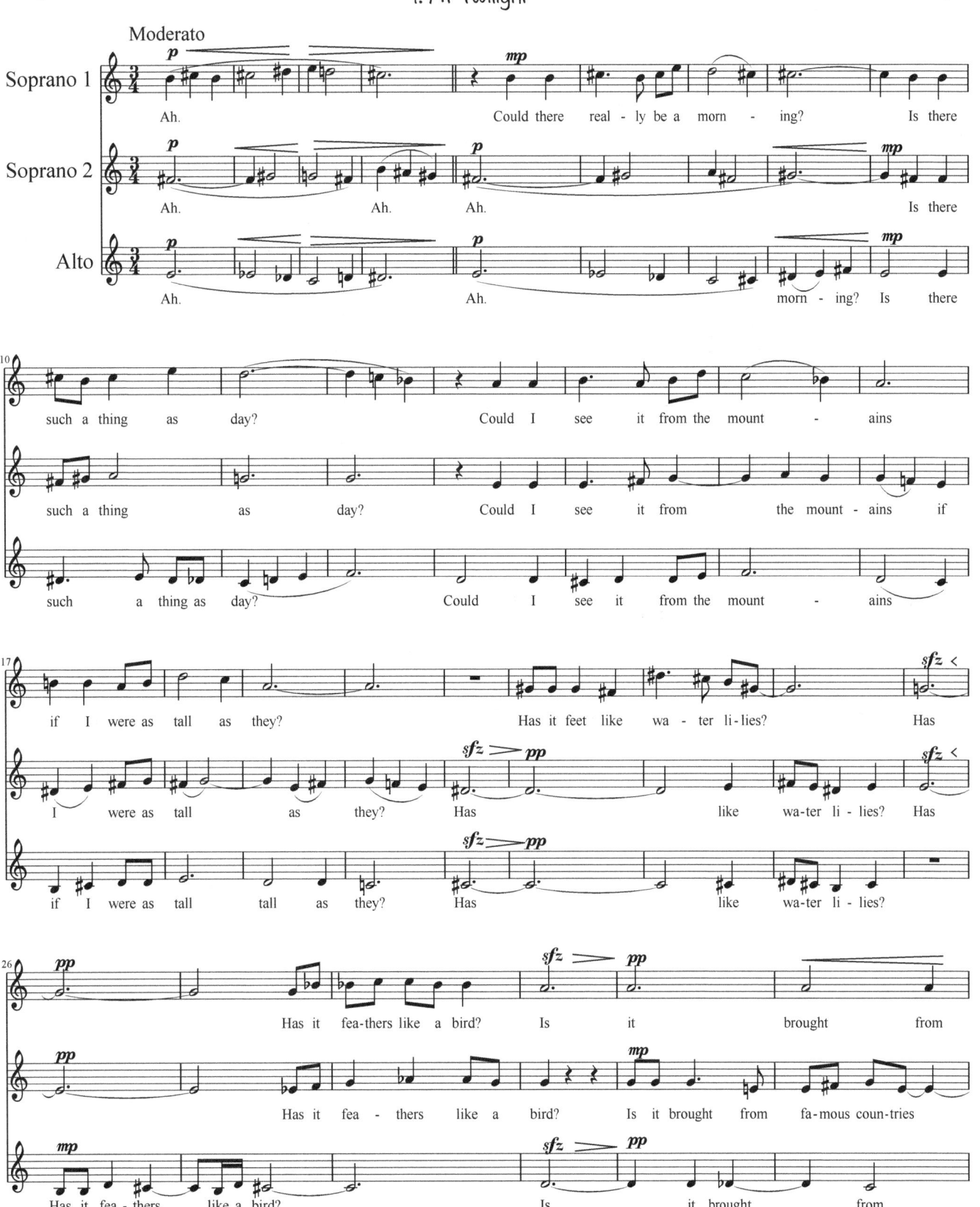

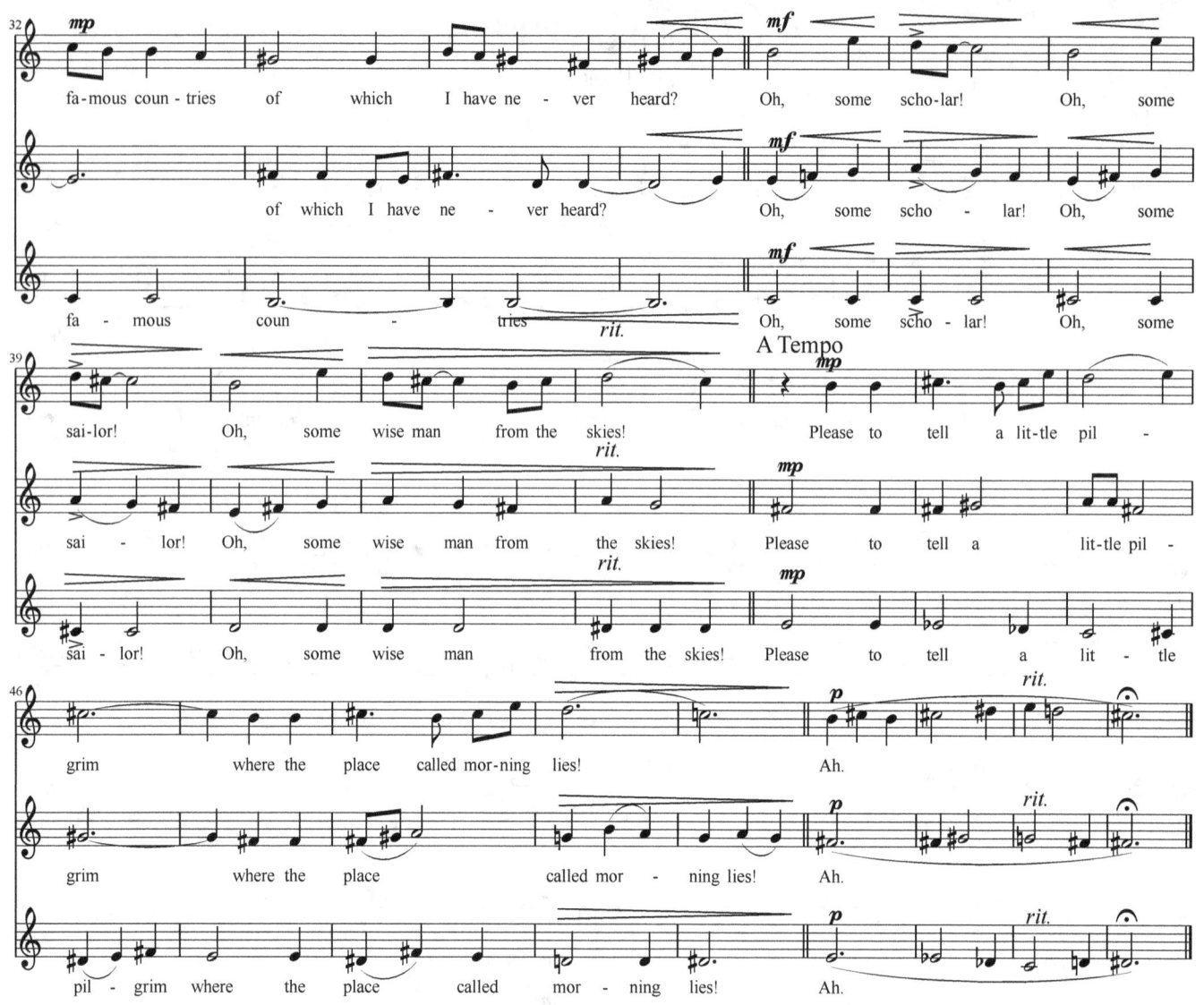

famous coun - tries of which I have ne - ver heard? Oh, some scho - lar! Oh, some

of which I have ne - ver heard? Oh, some scho - lar! Oh, some

fa - mous coun - tries Oh, some scho - lar! Oh, some

sai-lor! Oh, some wise man from the skies! Please to tell a lit-tle pil -

sai - lor! Oh, some wise man from the skies! Please to tell a lit-tle pil -

sai - lor! Oh, some wise man from the skies! Please to tell a li - tle

grim where the place called mor-ning lies! Ah.

grim where the place called mor - ning lies! Ah.

pil - grim where the place called mor - ning lies! Ah.

Dickinson's Day
2. At Dawn

Emily Dickinson

Ken Langer

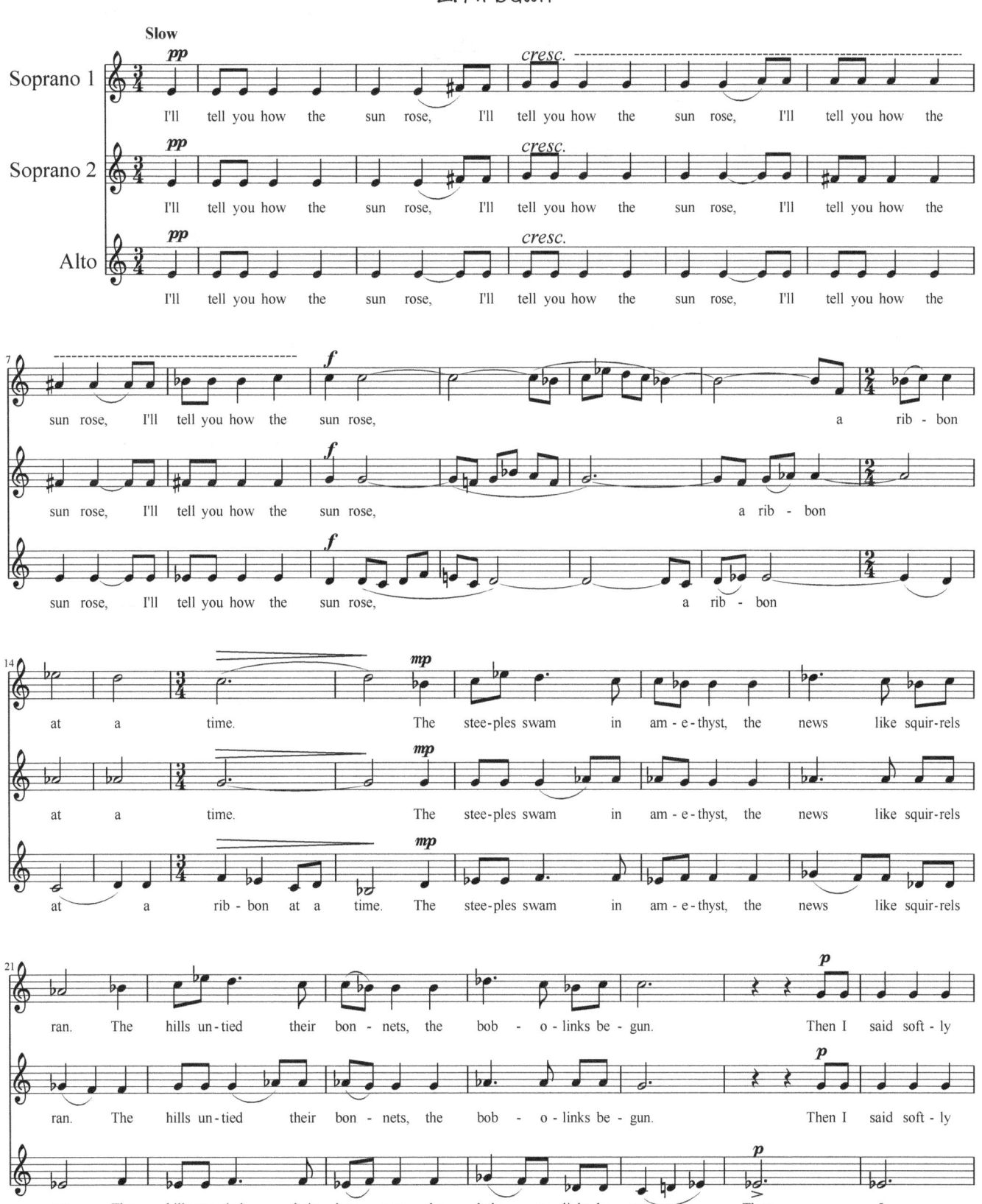

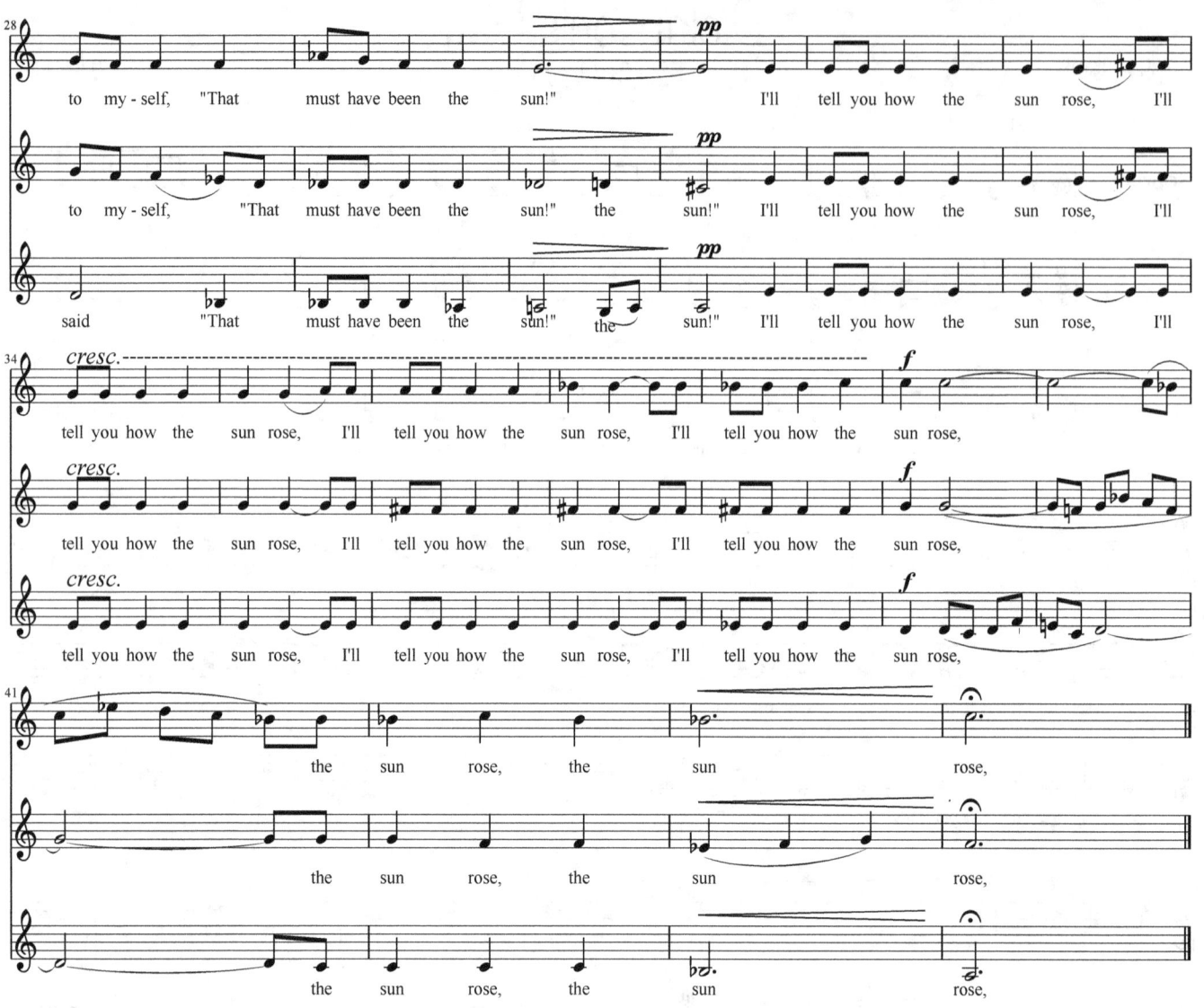

to my-self, "That must have been the sun!" I'll tell you how the sun rose, I'll

to my-self, "That must have been the sun!" the sun!" I'll tell you how the sun rose, I'll

said "That must have been the sun!" the sun!" I'll tell you how the sun rose, I'll

cresc.

tell you how the sun rose, I'll tell you how the sun rose, I'll tell you how the sun rose,

cresc.

tell you how the sun rose, I'll tell you how the sun rose, I'll tell you how the sun rose,

cresc.

tell you how the sun rose, I'll tell you how the sun rose, I'll tell you how the sun rose,

the sun rose, the sun rose,

the sun rose, the sun rose,

the sun rose, the sun rose,

12

Dickinson's Day
3. At Morning

Emily Dickinson

Ken Langer

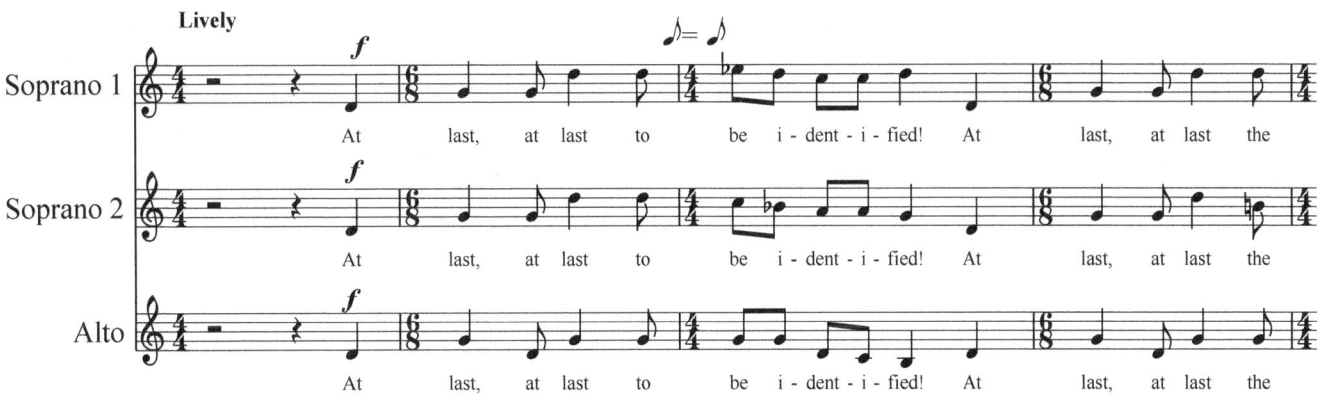

Lively

Soprano 1: At last, at last to be i - dent - i - fied! At last, at last the

Soprano 2: At last, at last to be i - dent - i - fied! At last, at last the

Alto: At last, at last to be i - dent - i - fied! At last, at last the

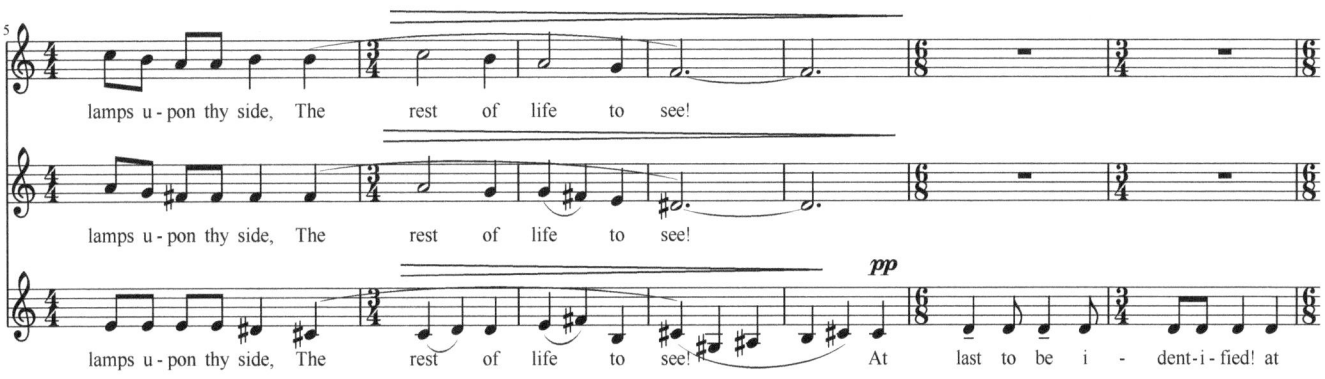

Soprano 1: lamps u - pon thy side, The rest of life to see!

Soprano 2: lamps u - pon thy side, The rest of life to see!

Alto: lamps u - pon thy side, The rest of life to see! At last to be i - dent-i-fied! at

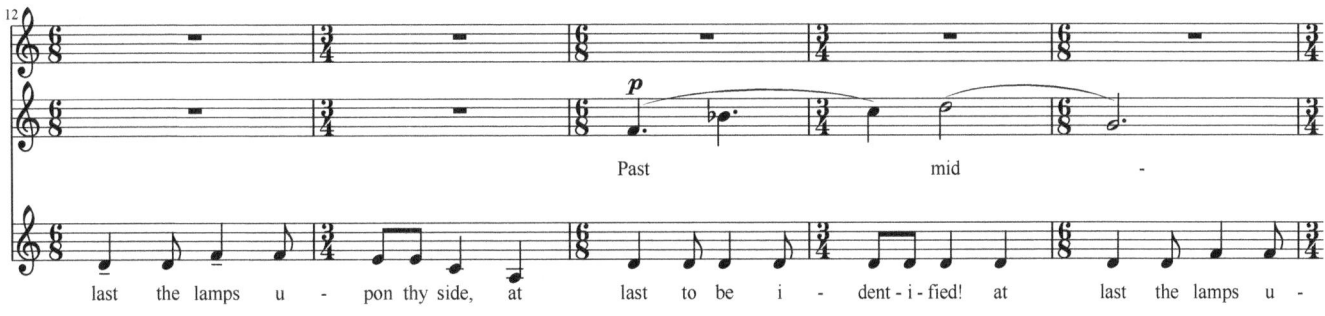

Soprano 2: Past mid -

Alto: last the lamps u - pon thy side, at last to be i - dent - i - fied! at last the lamps u -

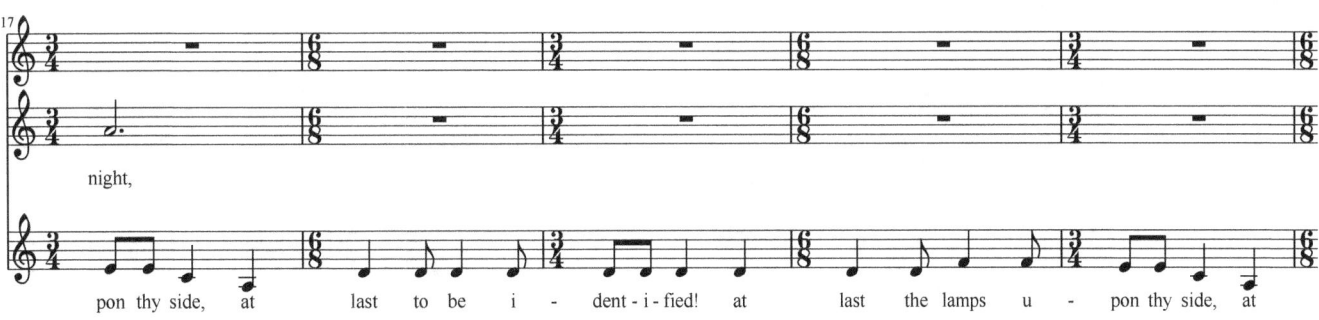

Soprano 2: night,

Alto: pon thy side, at last to be i - dent - i - fied! at last the lamps u - pon thy side, at

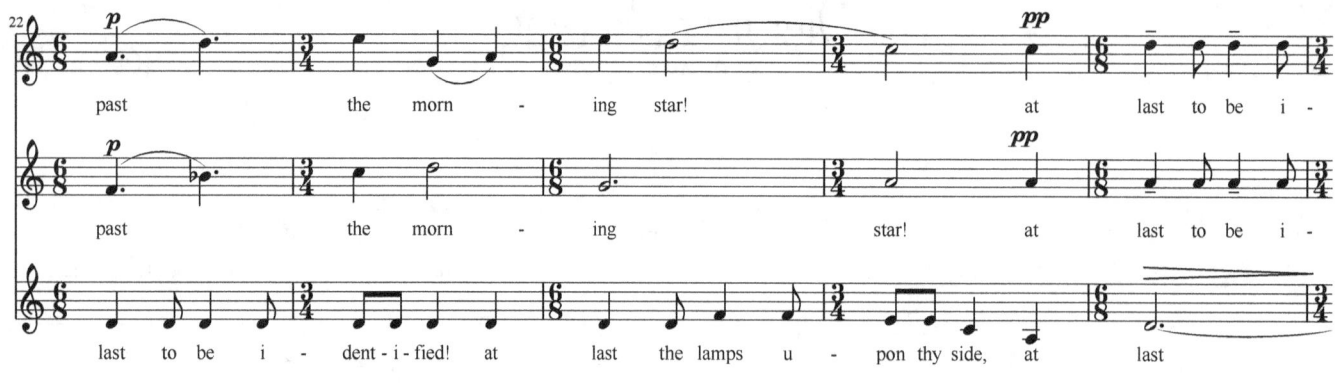

past   the morn - ing star!   at last to be i-

past   the morn - ing   star!   at last to be i-

last to be i - dent - i - fied! at   last the lamps u - pon thy side, at   last

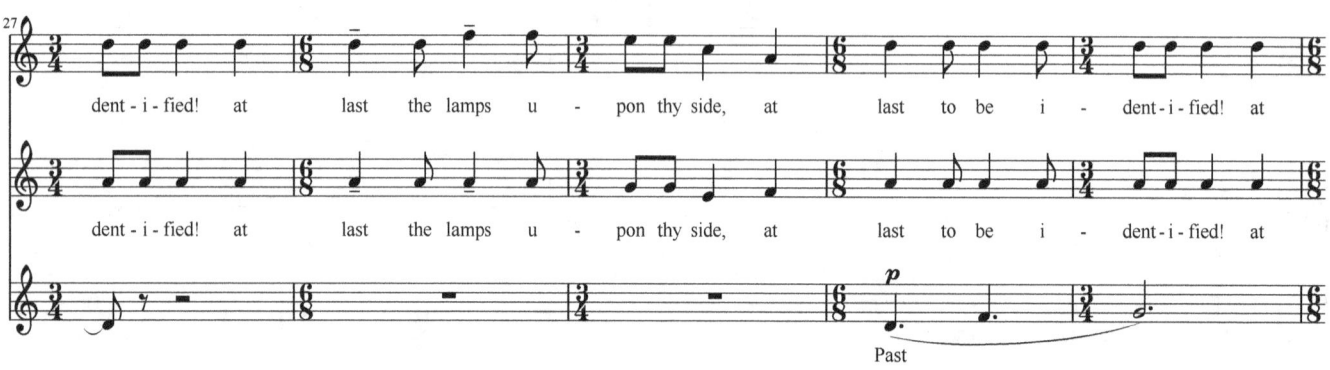

dent - i - fied! at   last the lamps u - pon thy side, at   last to be i - dent - i - fied! at

dent - i - fied! at   last the lamps u - pon thy side, at   last to be i - dent - i - fied! at

Past

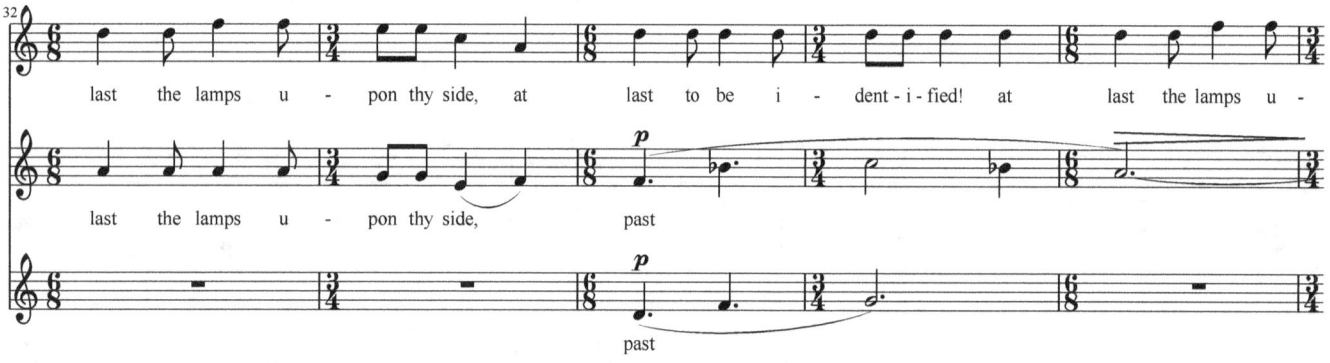

last the lamps u - pon thy side, at   last to be i - dent - i - fied! at   last the lamps u-

last the lamps u - pon thy side,   past

past

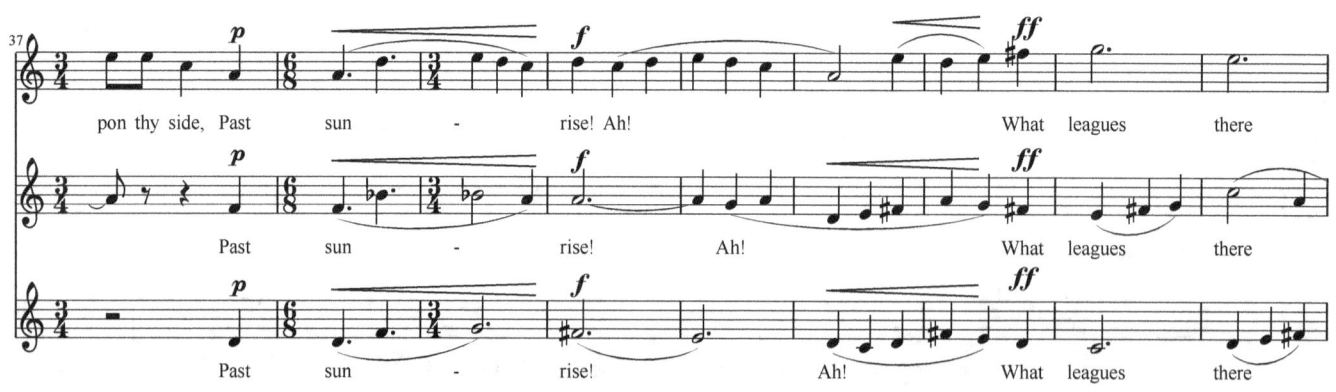

pon thy side, Past sun - rise! Ah!   What leagues there

Past sun - rise! Ah!   What leagues there

Past sun - rise! Ah!   What leagues there

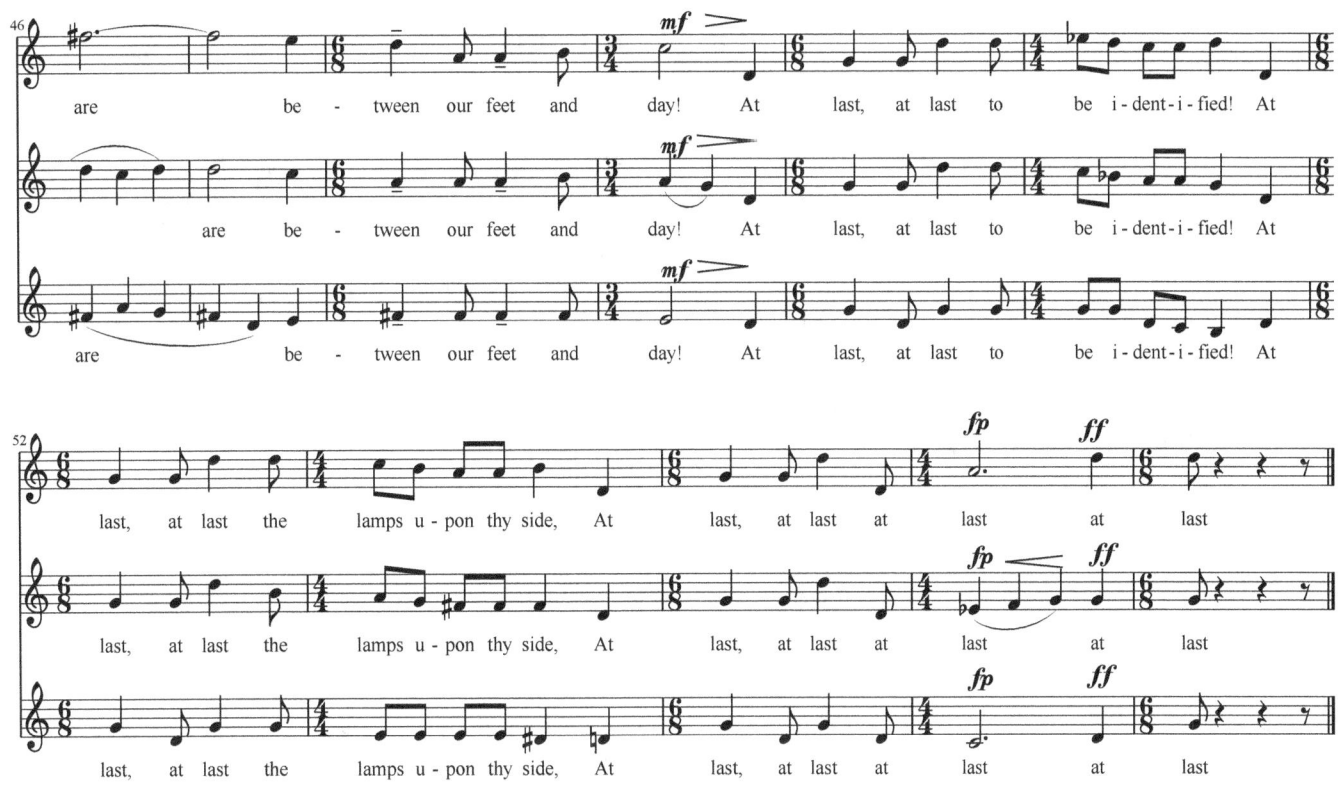

Dickinson's Day

4. At Afternoon

Emily Dickinson

Ken Langer

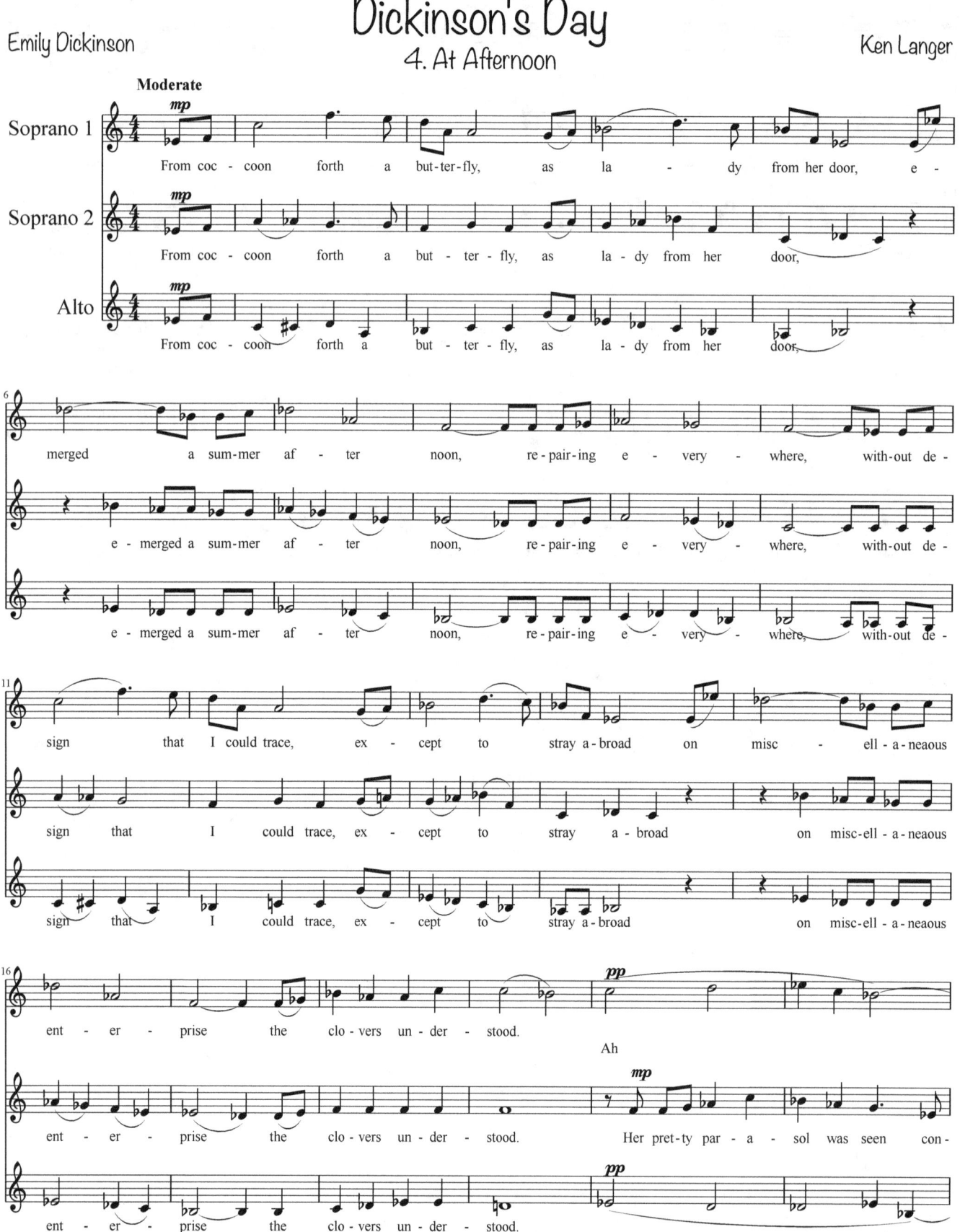

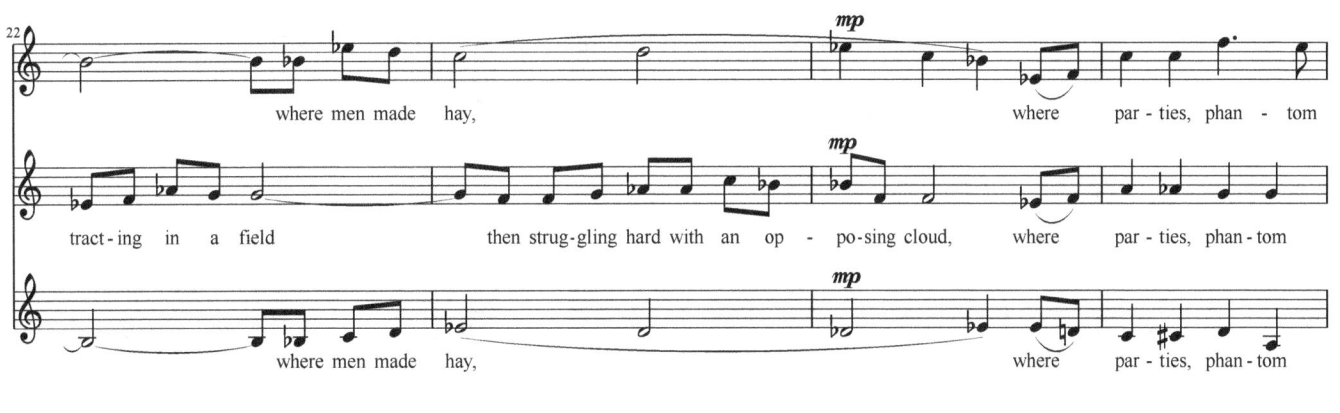

where men made hay, where par - ties, phan - tom

tract - ing in a field then strug - gling hard with an op - po - sing cloud, where par - ties, phan - tom

where men made hay, where par - ties, phan - tom

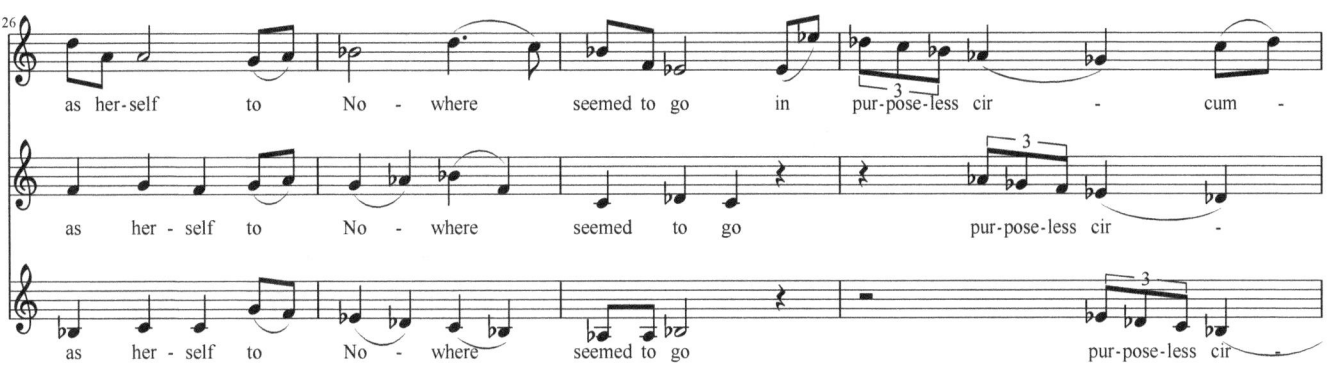

as her - self to No - where seemed to go in pur - pose - less cir - cum -

as her - self to No - where seemed to go pur - pose - less cir -

as her - self to No - where seemed to go pur - pose - less cir -

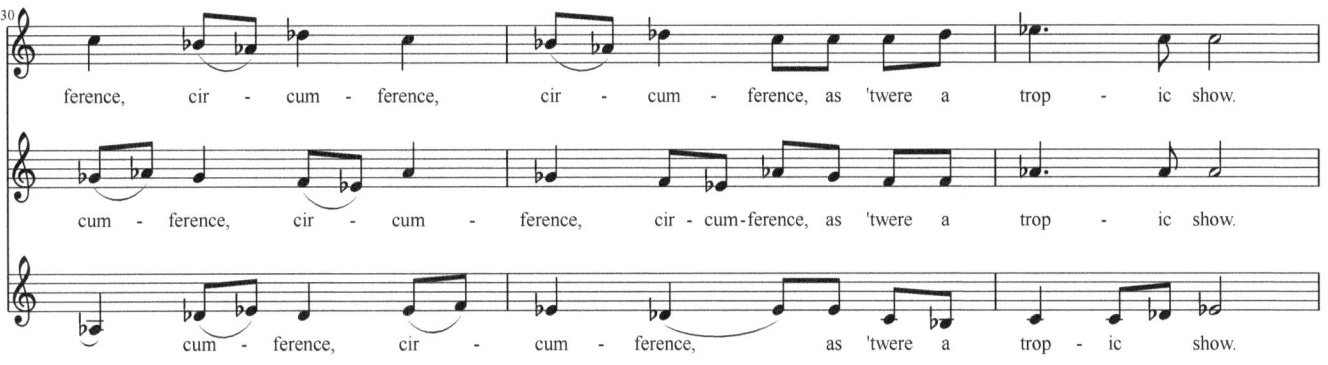

ference, cir - cum - ference, cir - cum - ference, as 'twere a trop - ic show.

cum - ference, cir - cum - ference, cir - cum - ference, as 'twere a trop - ic show.

cum - ference, cir - cum - ference, as 'twere a trop - ic show.

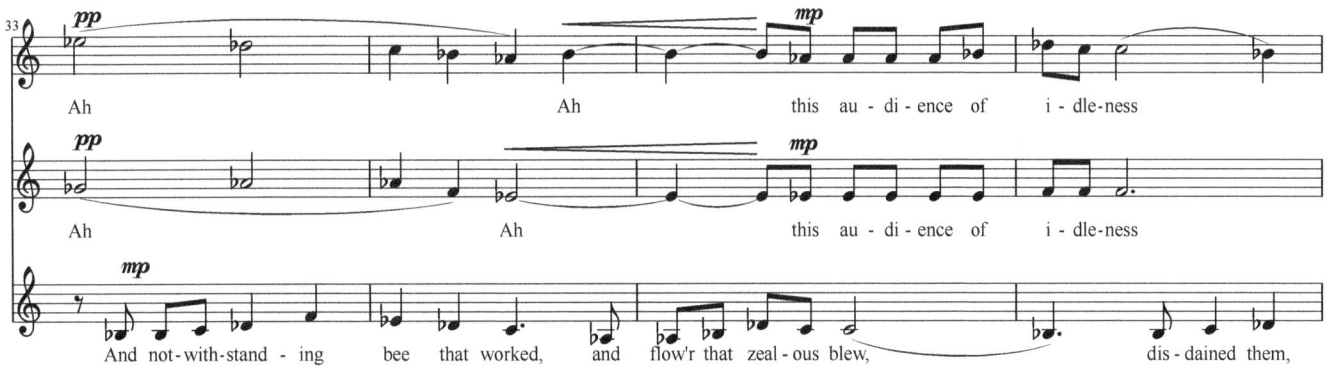

Ah Ah this au - di - ence of i - dle - ness

Ah Ah this au - di - ence of i - dle - ness

And not - with - stand - ing bee that worked, and flow'r that zeal - ous blew, dis - dained them,

17

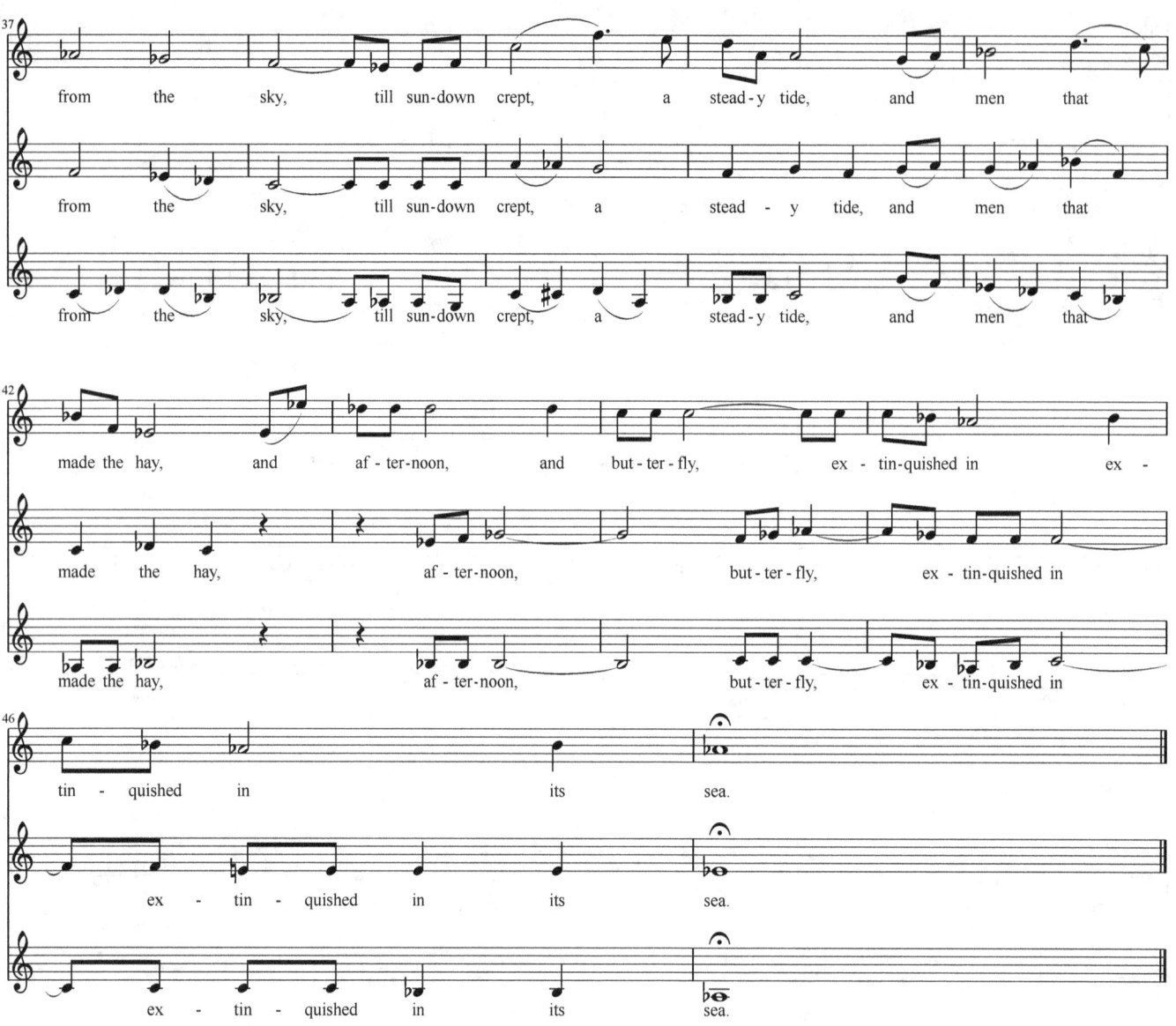

Dickinson's Day
5. At Sunset

Emily Dickinson

Ken Langer

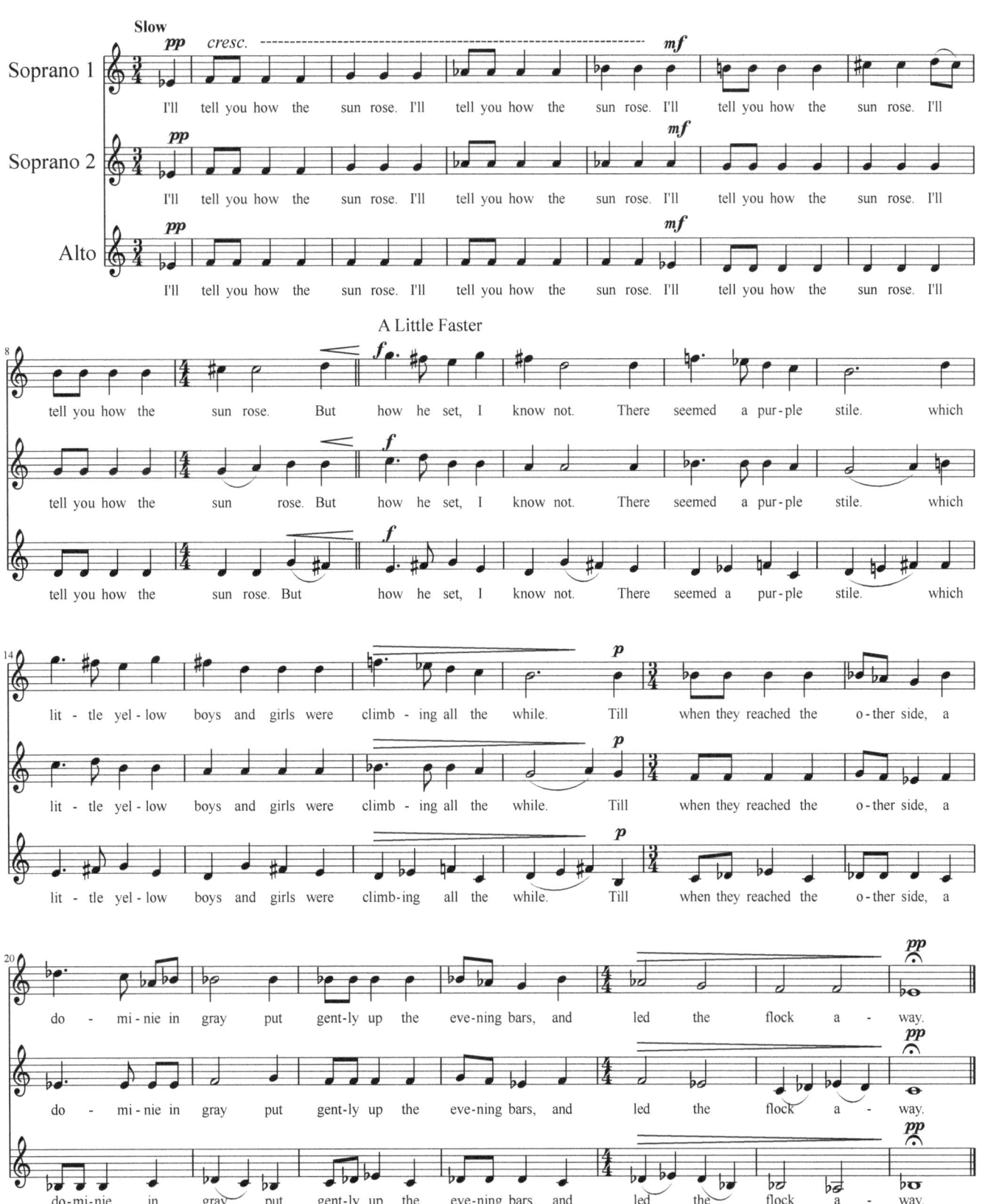

Divine Wisdom

adapted from Hildegard of Bingen

Ken Langer

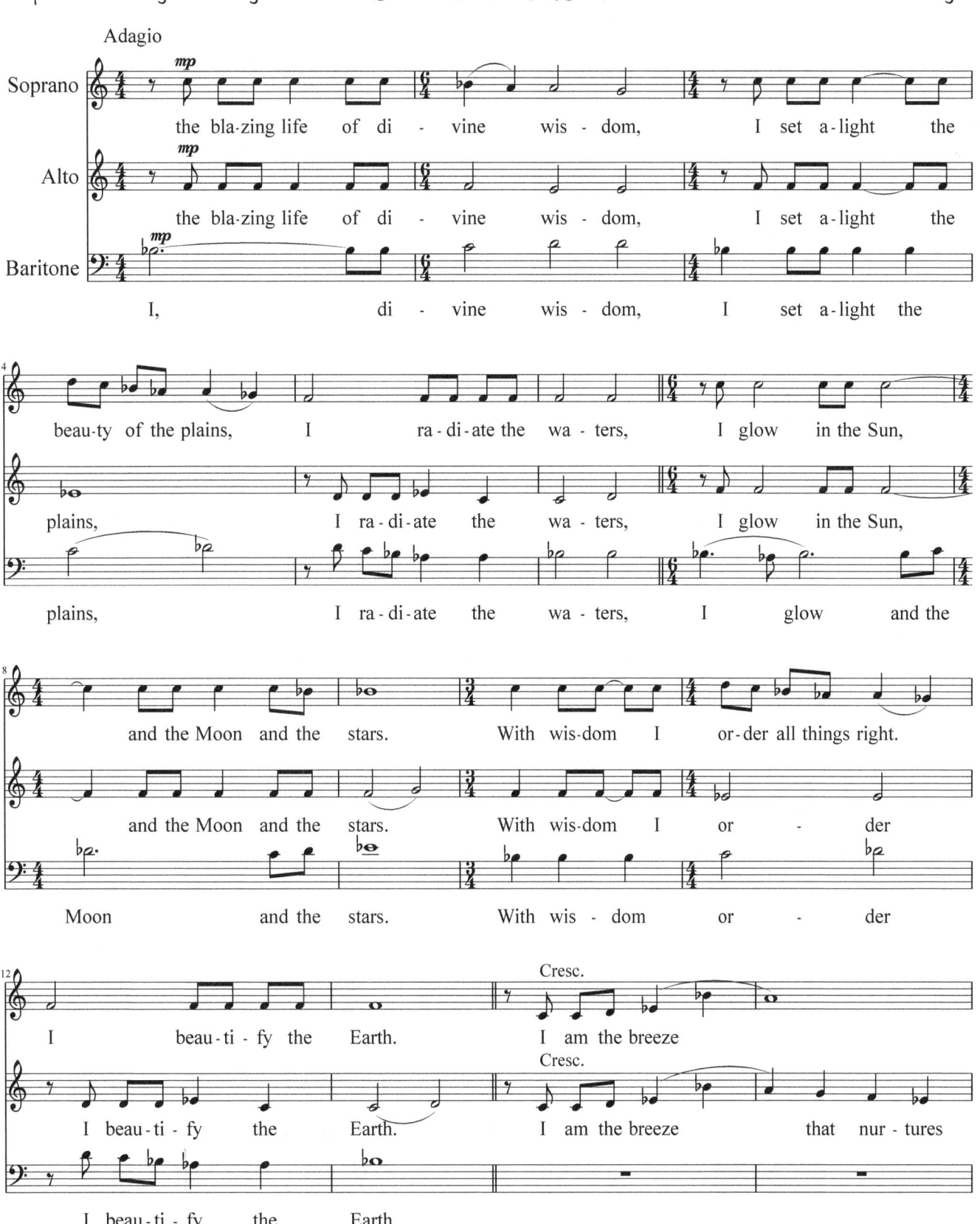

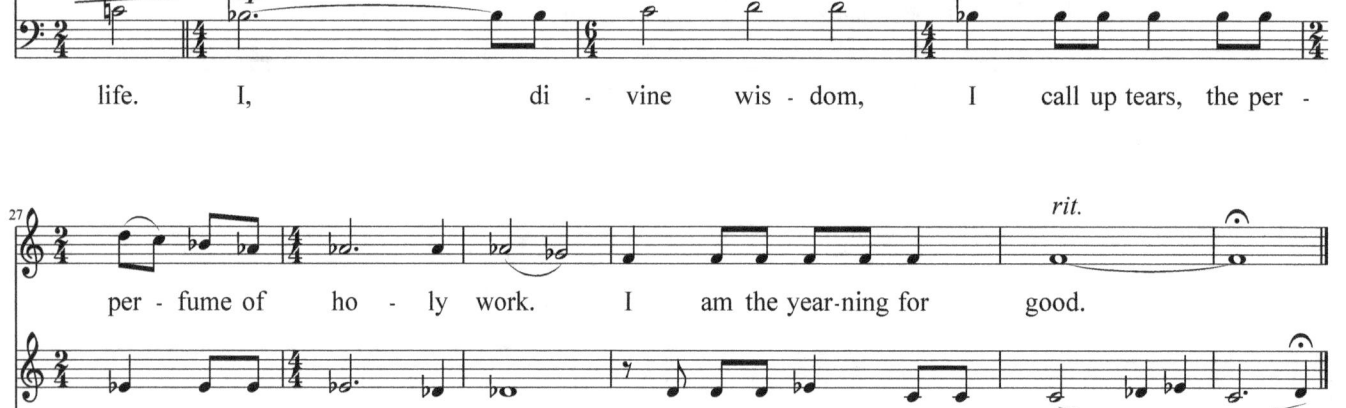

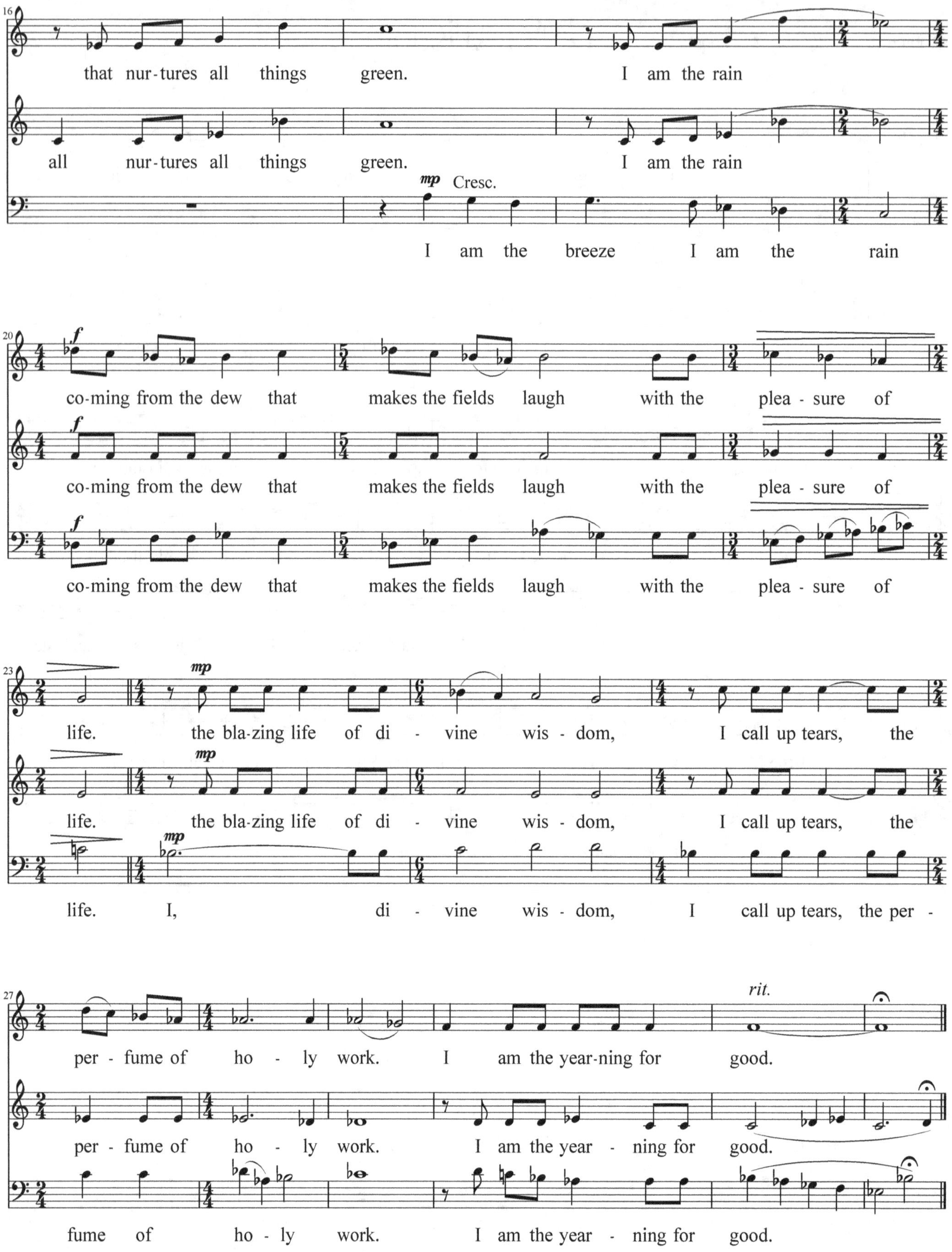

Festival Alleluia

Ken Langer

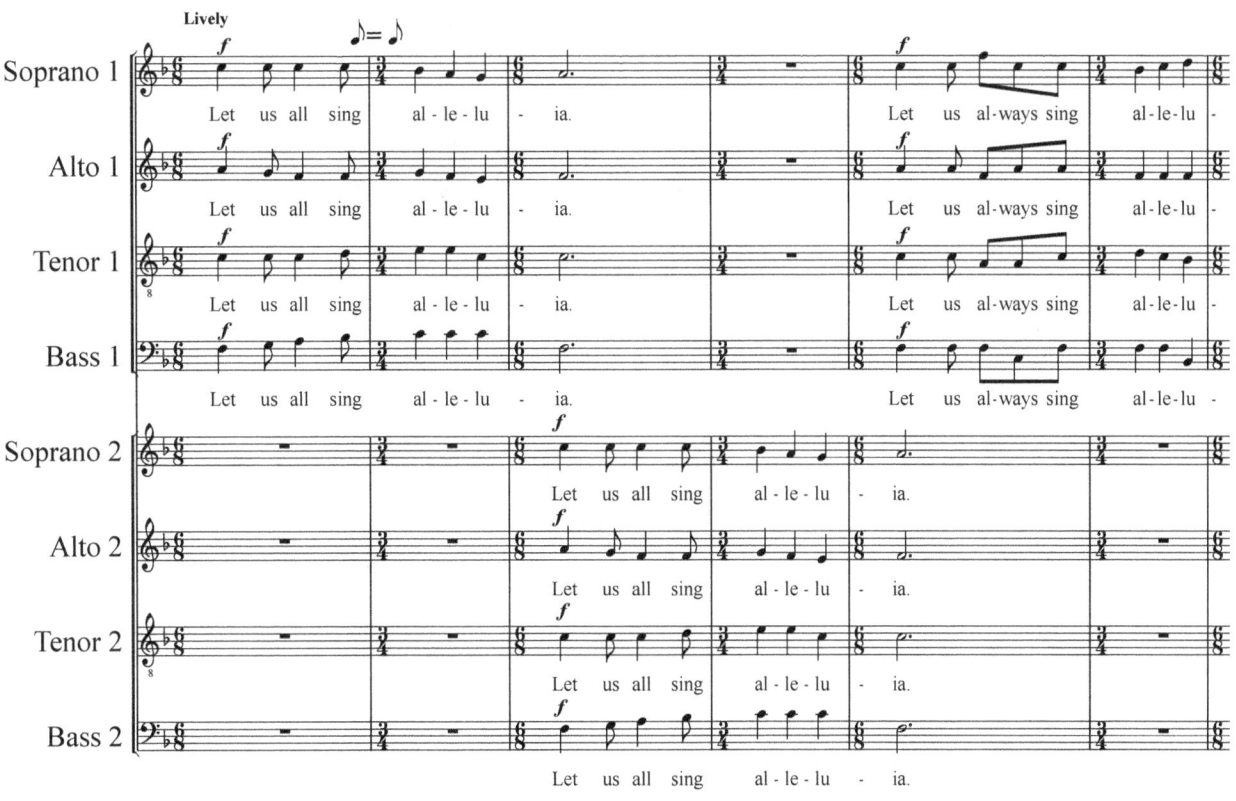

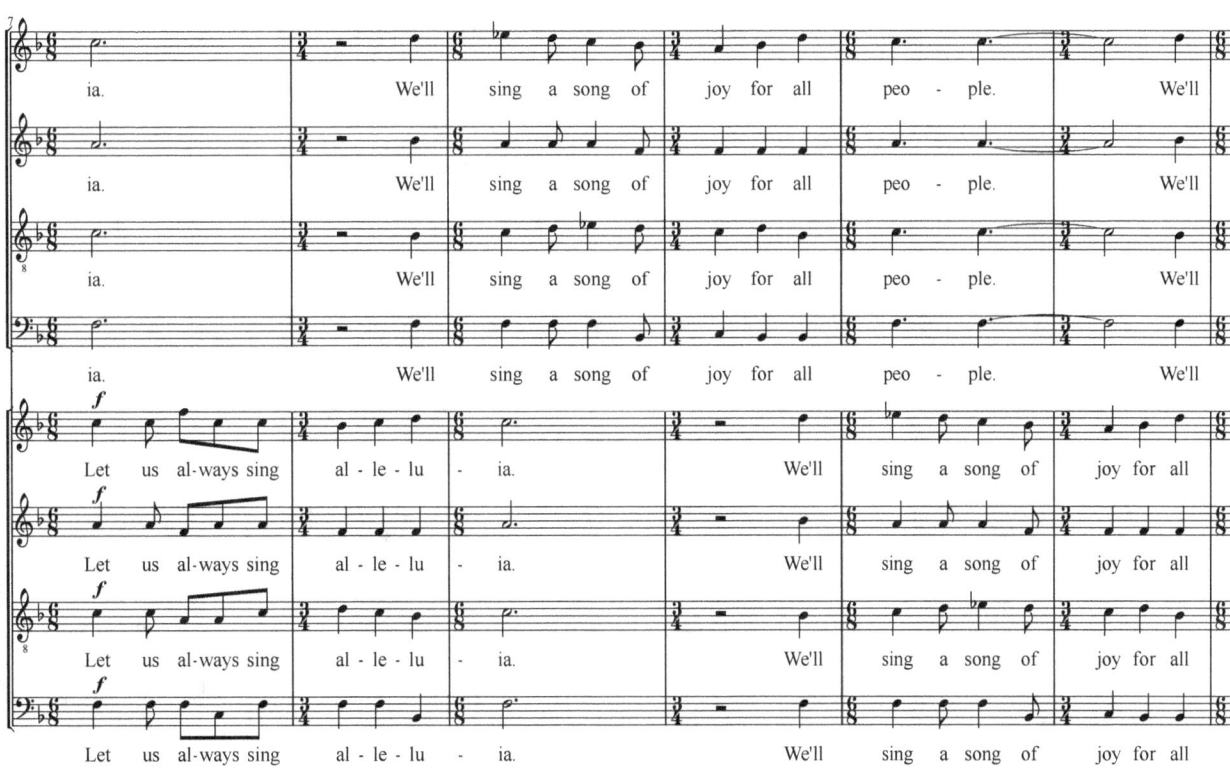

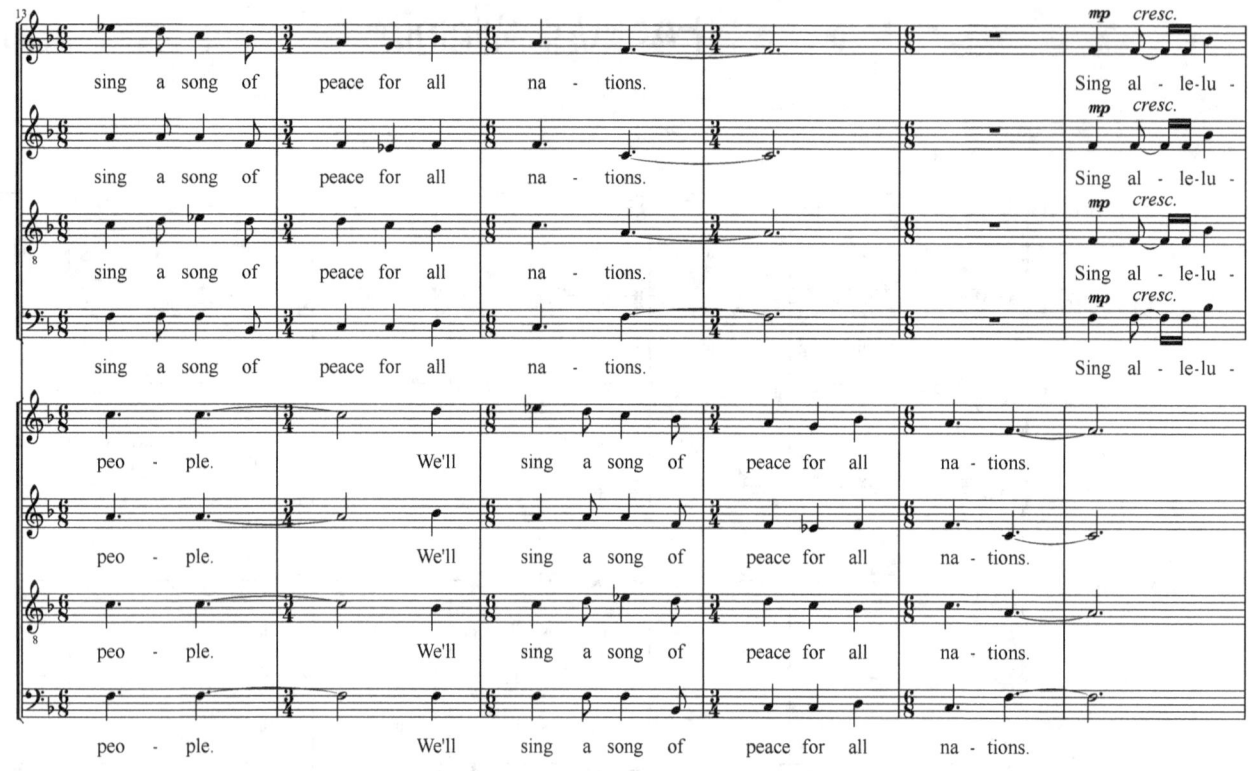

sing a song of peace for all na - tions.
Sing al - le - lu -

sing a song of peace for all na - tions.
Sing al - le - lu -

sing a song of peace for all na - tions.
Sing al - le - lu -

sing a song of peace for all na - tions.
Sing al - le - lu -

peo - ple. We'll sing a song of peace for all na - tions.

peo - ple. We'll sing a song of peace for all na - tions.

peo - ple. We'll sing a song of peace for all na - tions.

peo - ple. We'll sing a song of peace for all na - tions.

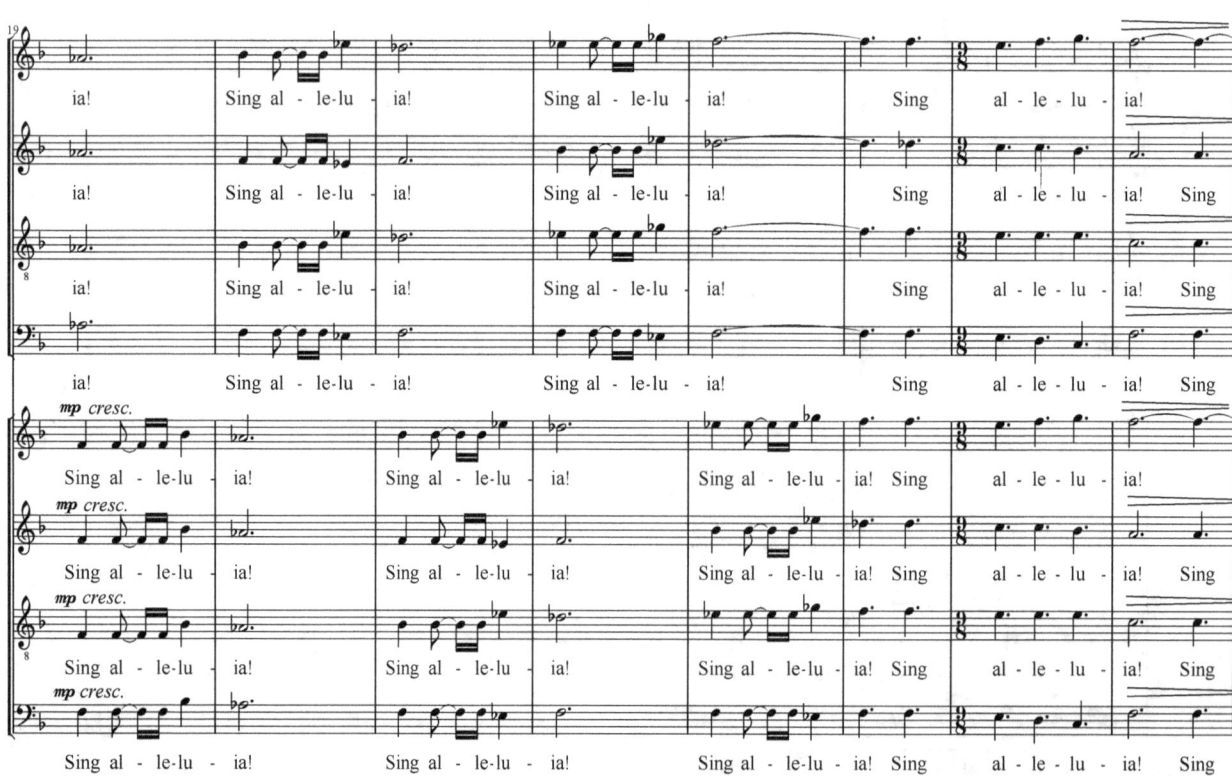

ia! Sing al - le-lu - ia! Sing al - le-lu - ia! Sing al - le - lu - ia!

ia! Sing al - le-lu - ia! Sing al - le-lu - ia! Sing al - le - lu - ia! Sing

ia! Sing al - le-lu - ia! Sing al - le-lu - ia! Sing al - le - lu - ia! Sing

ia! Sing al - le-lu - ia! Sing al - le-lu - ia! Sing al - le - lu - ia! Sing

Sing al - le-lu - ia! Sing al - le-lu - ia! Sing al - le-lu - ia! Sing al - le - lu - ia!

Sing al - le-lu - ia! Sing al - le-lu - ia! Sing al - le-lu - ia! Sing al - le - lu - ia! Sing

Sing al - le-lu - ia! Sing al - le-lu - ia! Sing al - le-lu - ia! Sing al - le - lu - ia! Sing

Sing al - le-lu - ia! Sing al - le-lu - ia! Sing al - le-lu - ia! Sing al - le - lu - ia! Sing

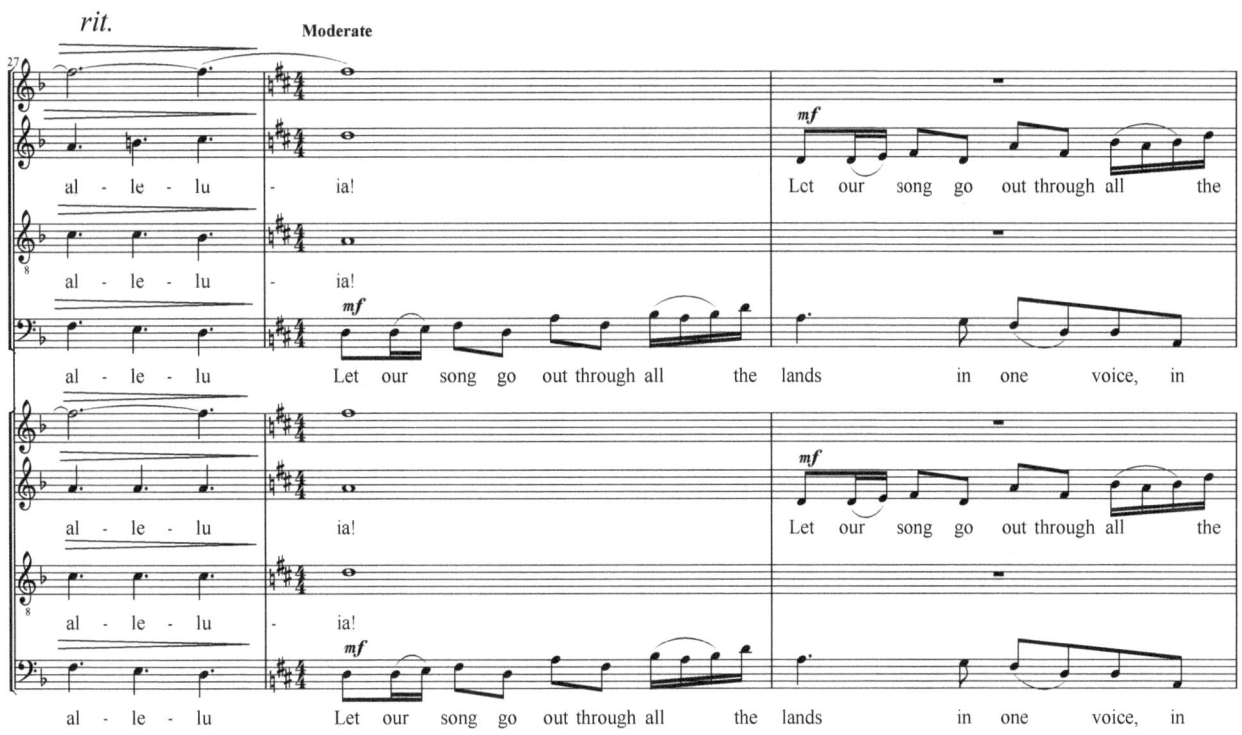

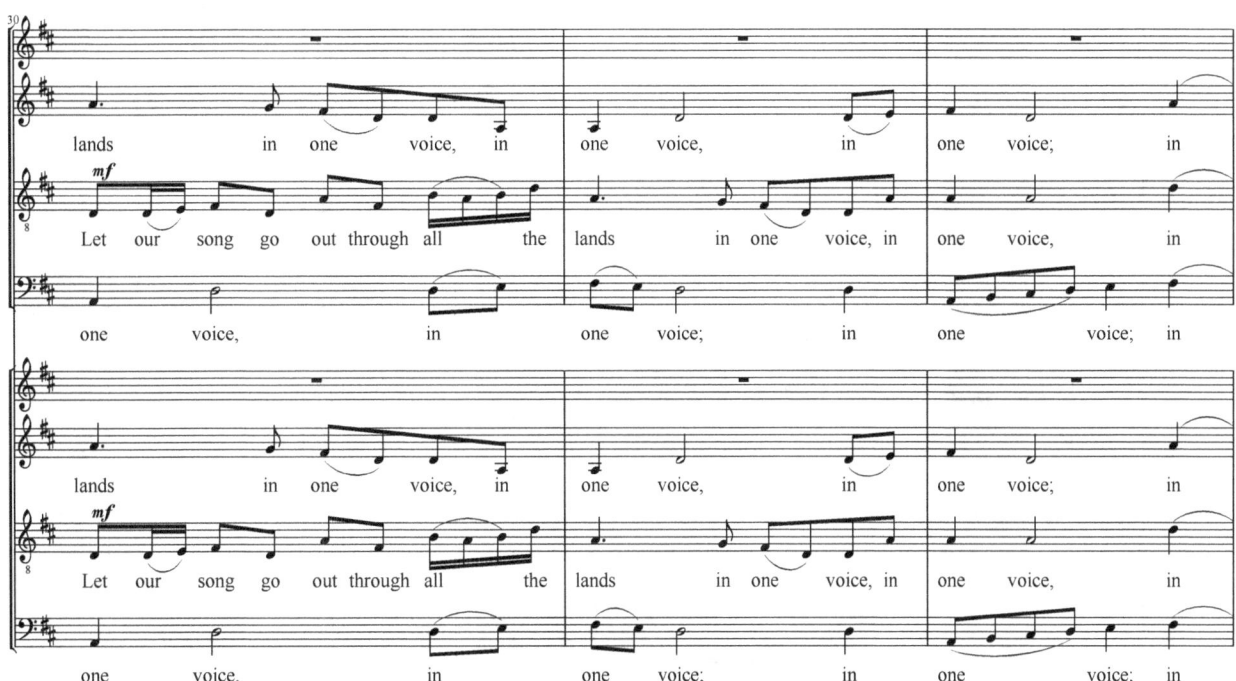

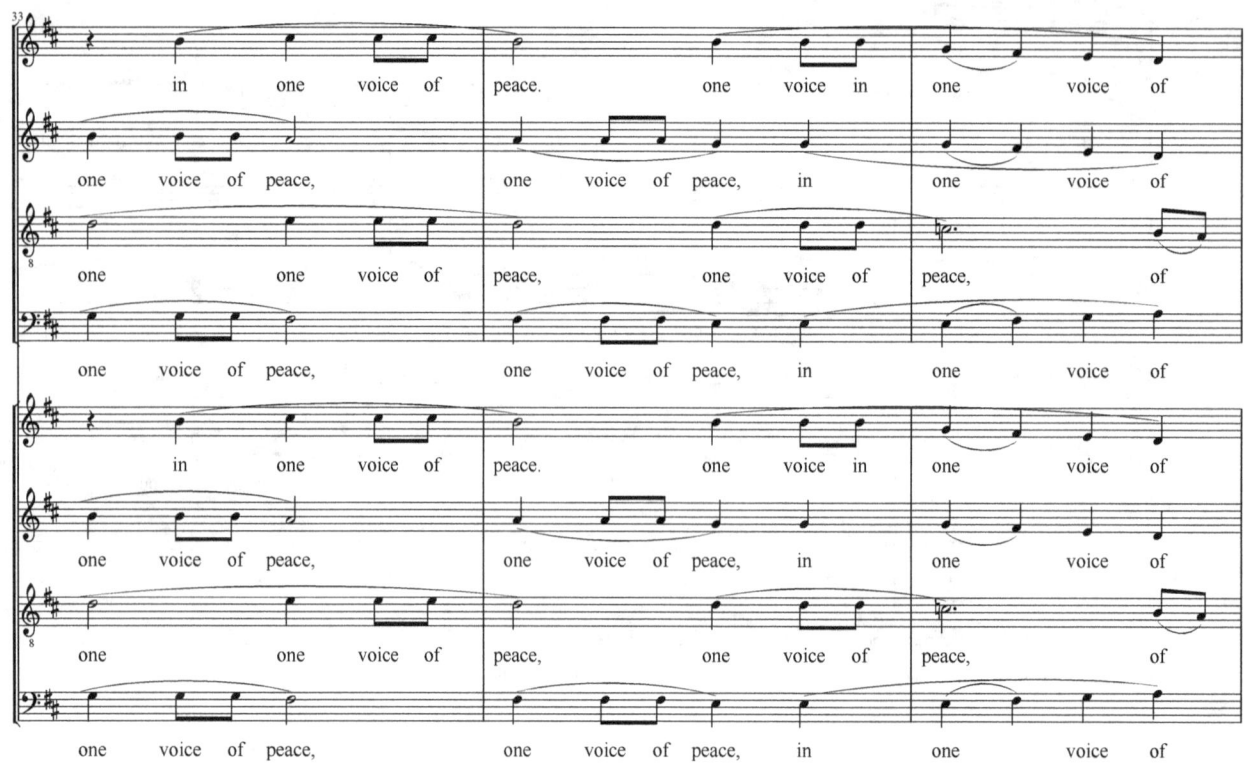

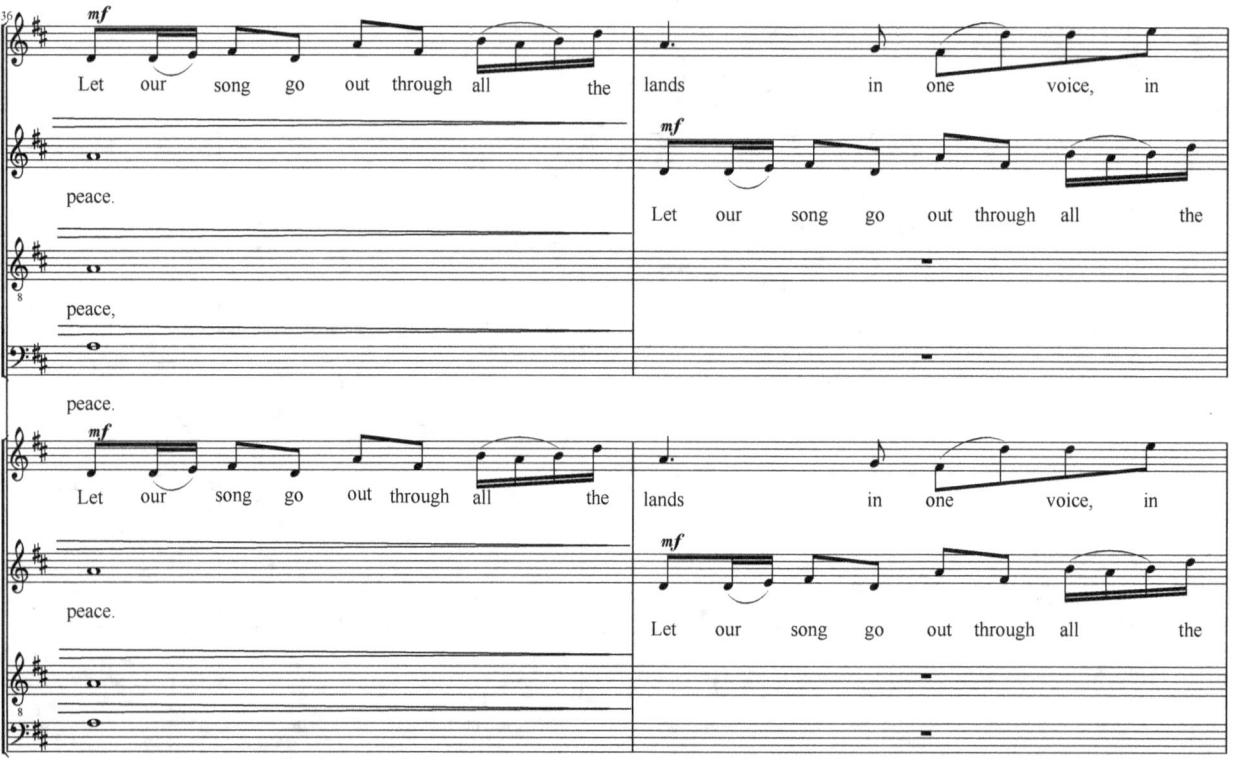

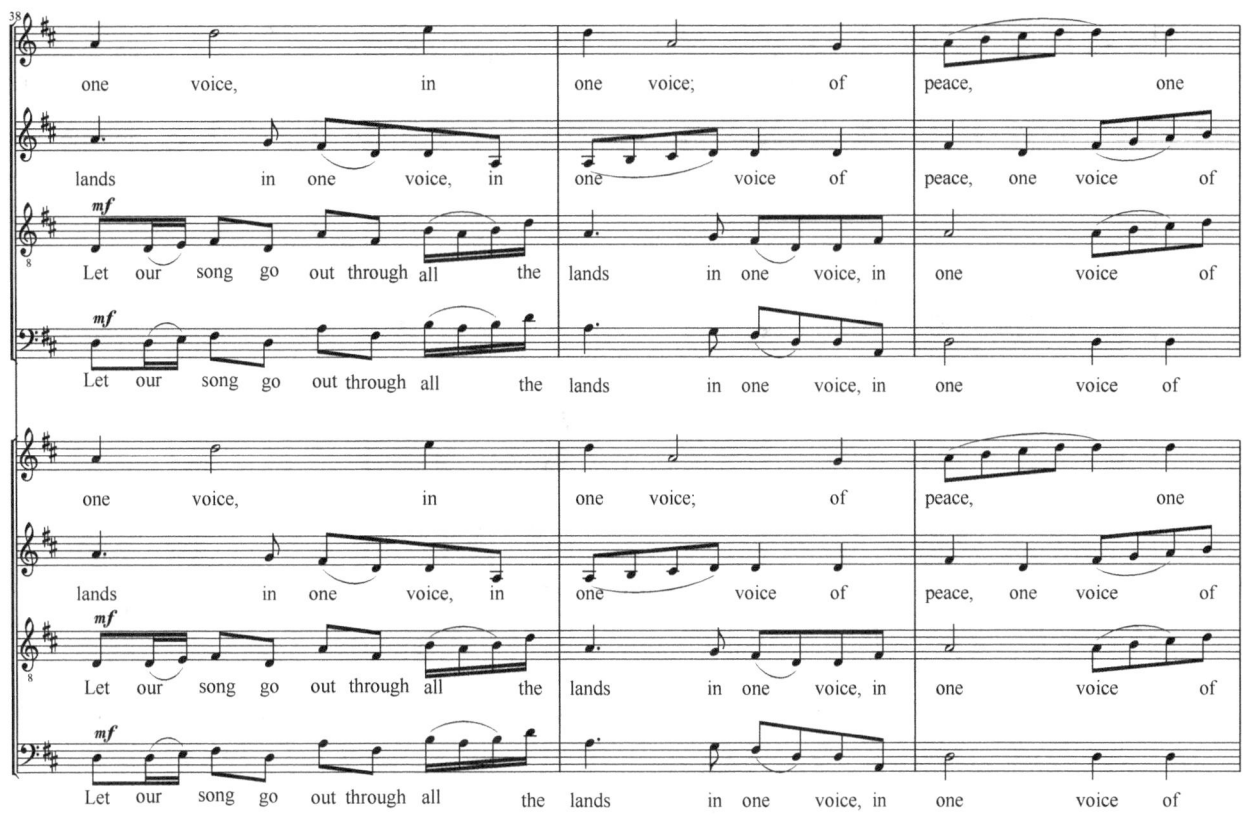

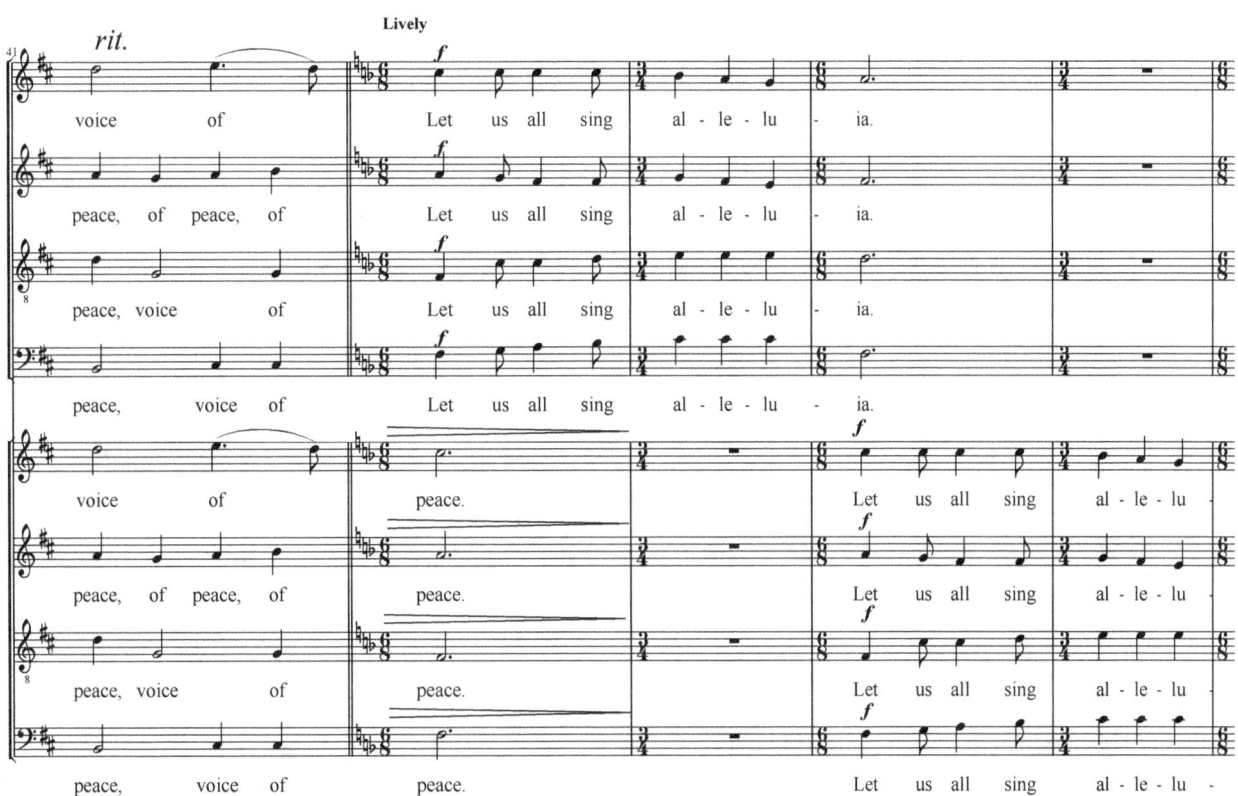

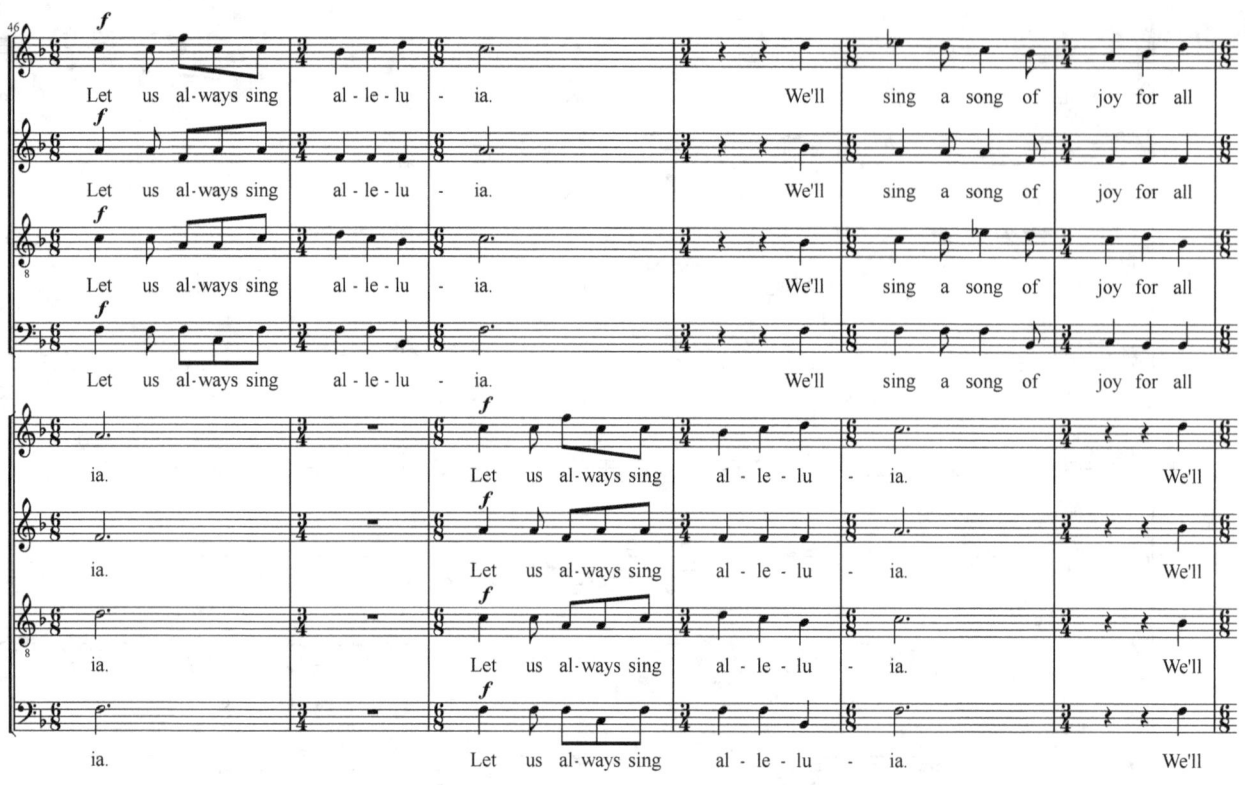

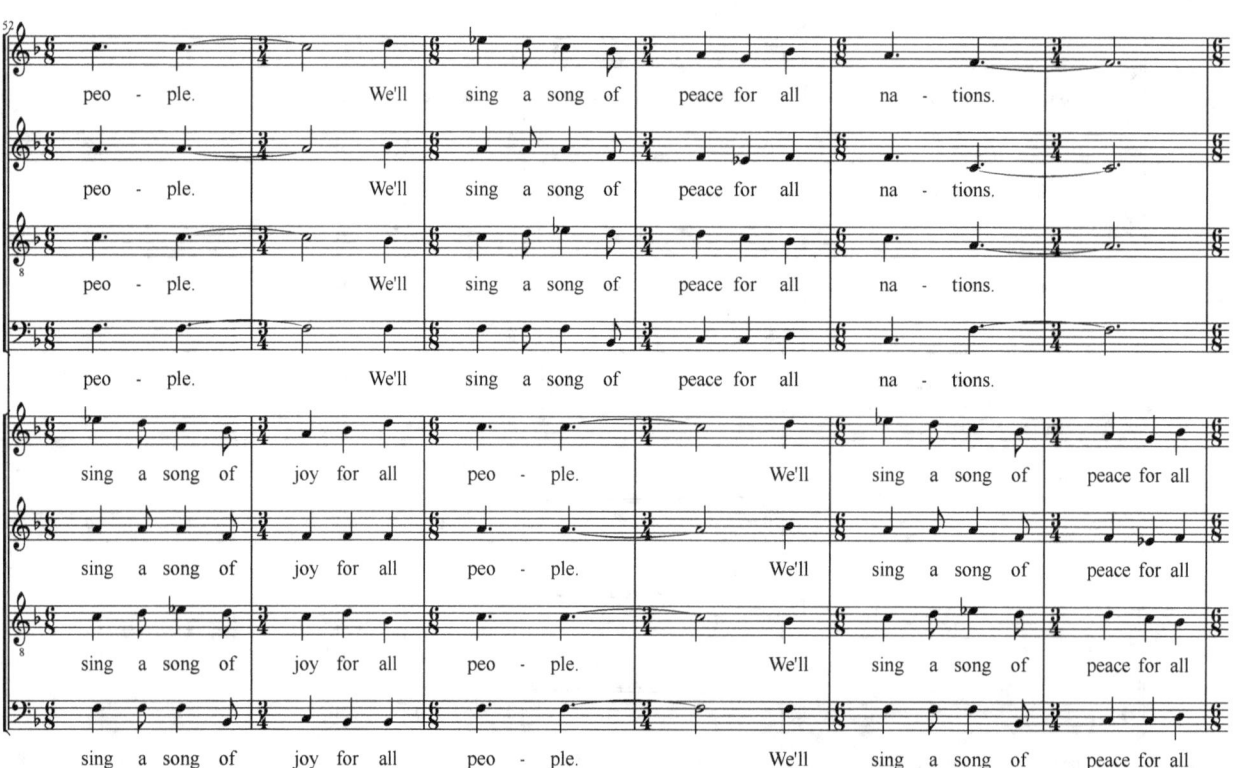

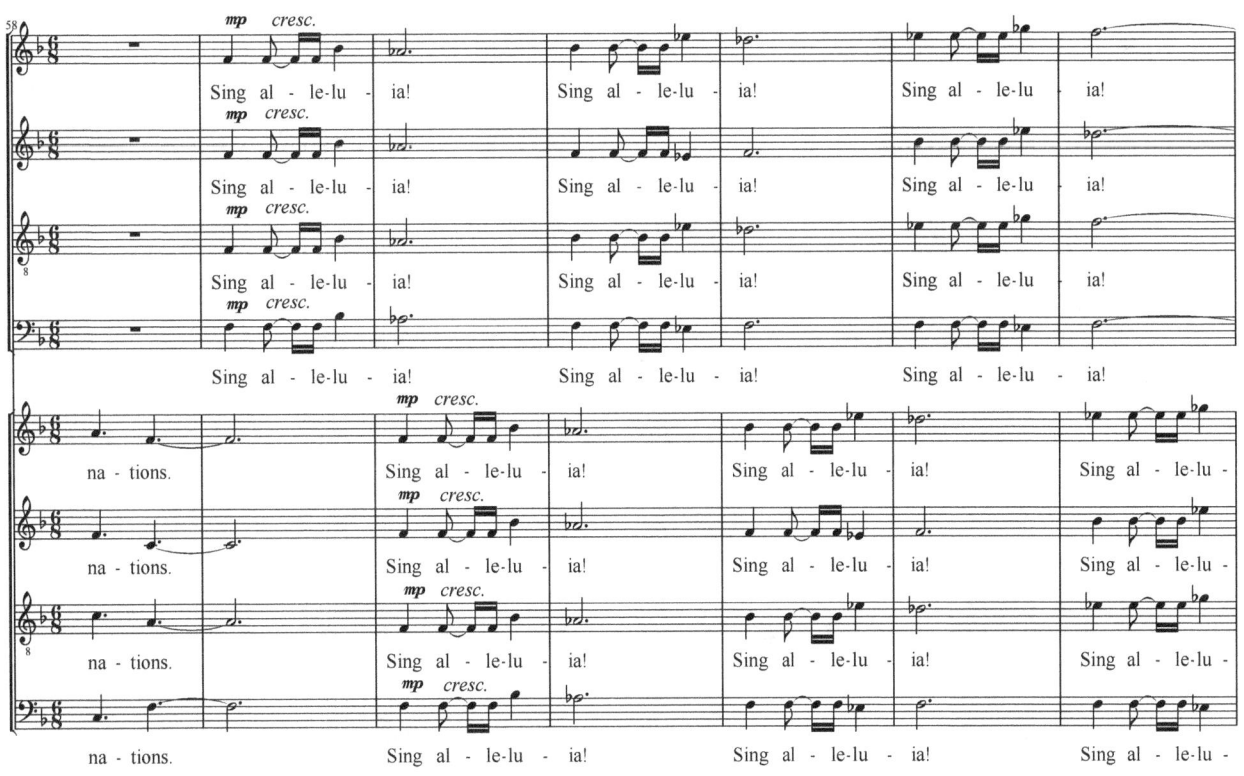

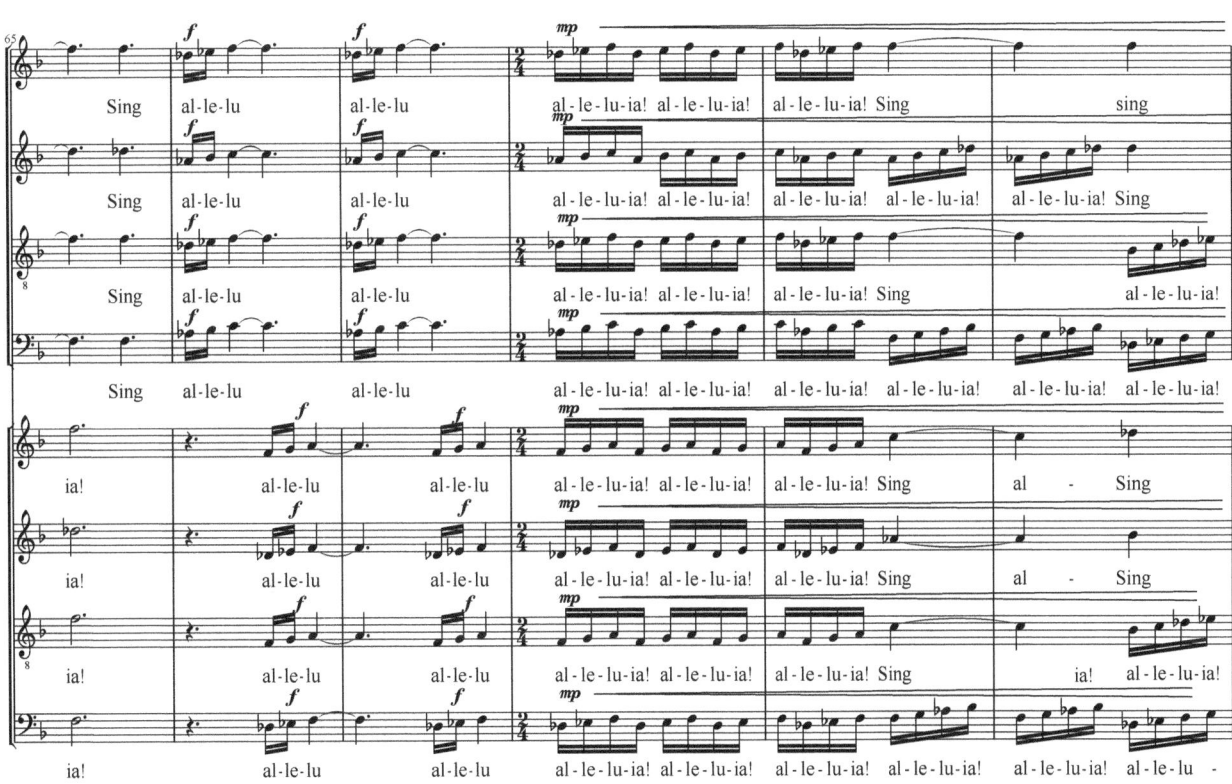

29

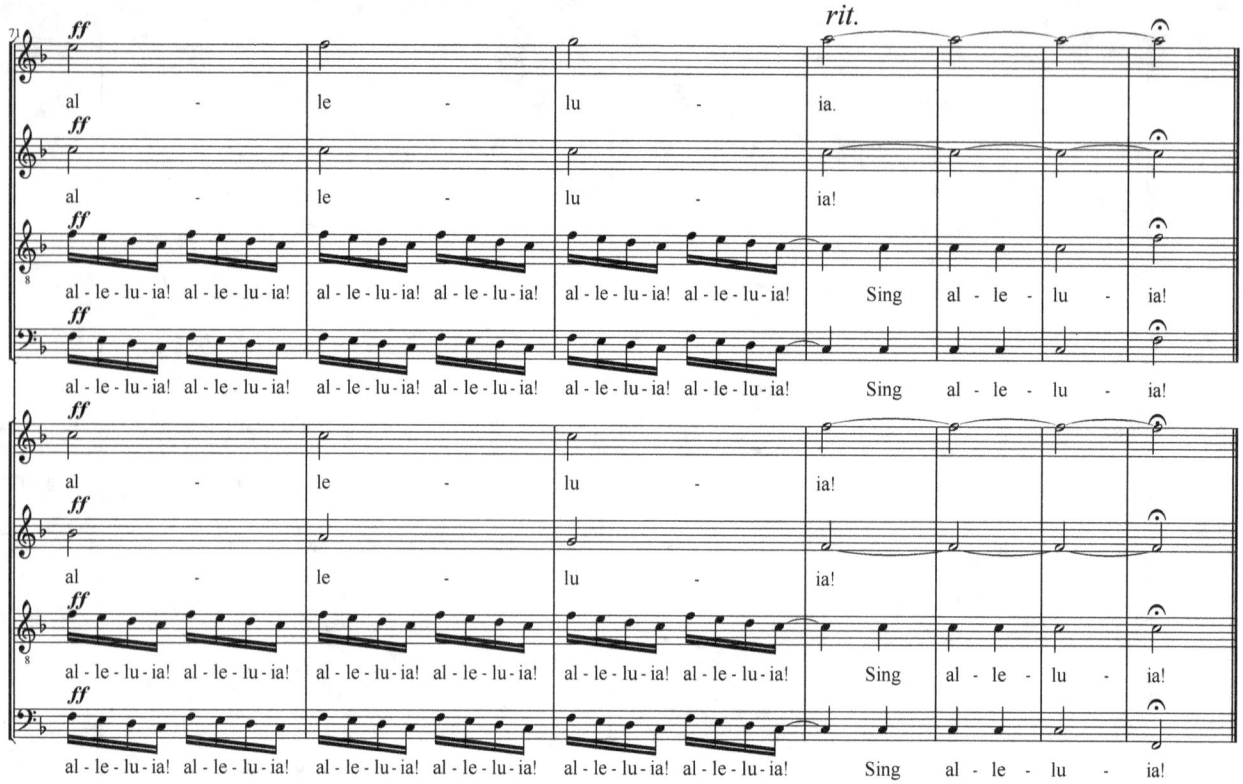

al - le - lu - ia.

al - le - lu - ia!

al - le - lu - ia! al - le - lu - ia! al - le - lu - ia! al - le - lu - ia! al - le - lu - ia! al - le - lu - ia! Sing al - le - lu - ia!

al - le - lu - ia! al - le - lu - ia! al - le - lu - ia! al - le - lu - ia! al - le - lu - ia! al - le - lu - ia! Sing al - le - lu - ia!

al - le - lu - ia!

al - le - lu - ia!

al - le - lu - ia! al - le - lu - ia! al - le - lu - ia! al - le - lu - ia! al - le - lu - ia! al - le - lu - ia! Sing al - le - lu - ia!

al - le - lu - ia! al - le - lu - ia! al - le - lu - ia! al - le - lu - ia! al - le - lu - ia! al - le - lu - ia! Sing al - le - lu - ia!

I Believe In Love

Ken Langer

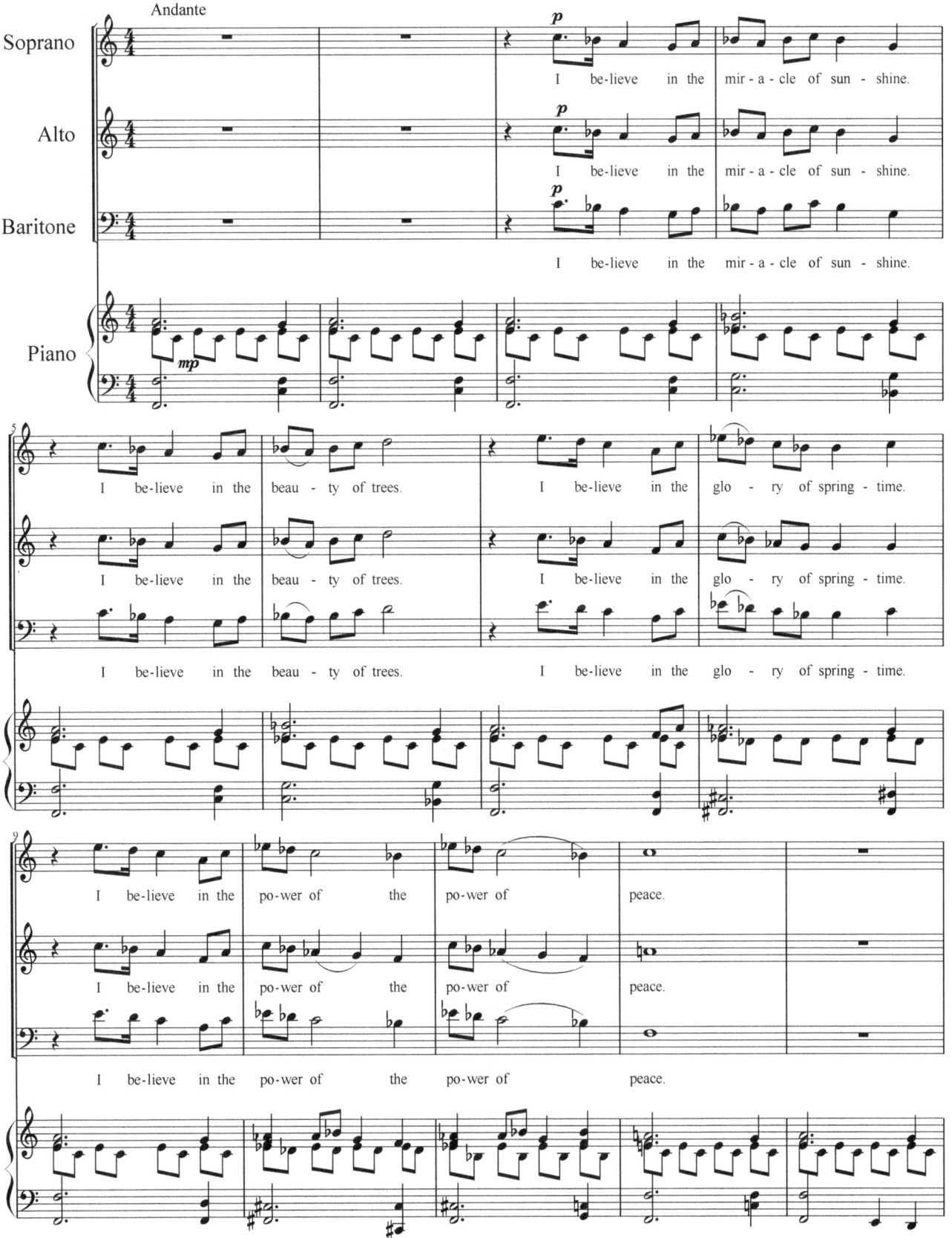

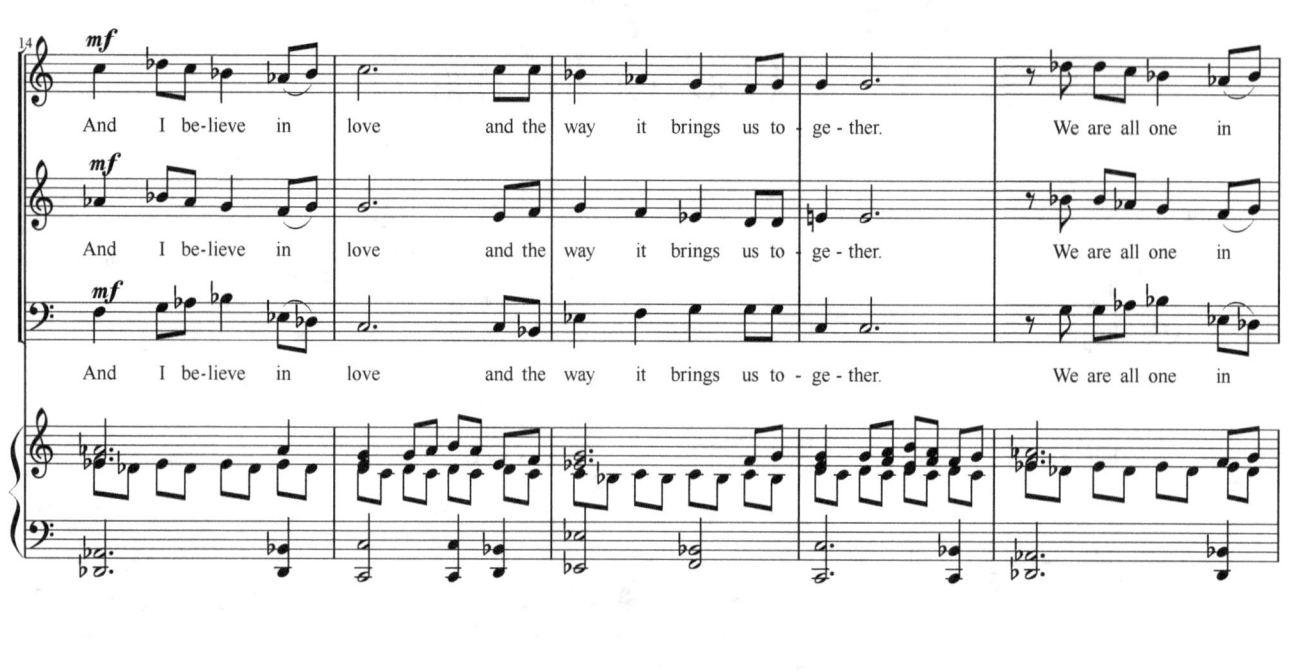

And I be-lieve in love and the way it brings us to-ge-ther. We are all one in

And I be-lieve in love and the way it brings us to-ge-ther. We are all one in

And I be-lieve in love and the way it brings us to-ge-ther. We are all one in

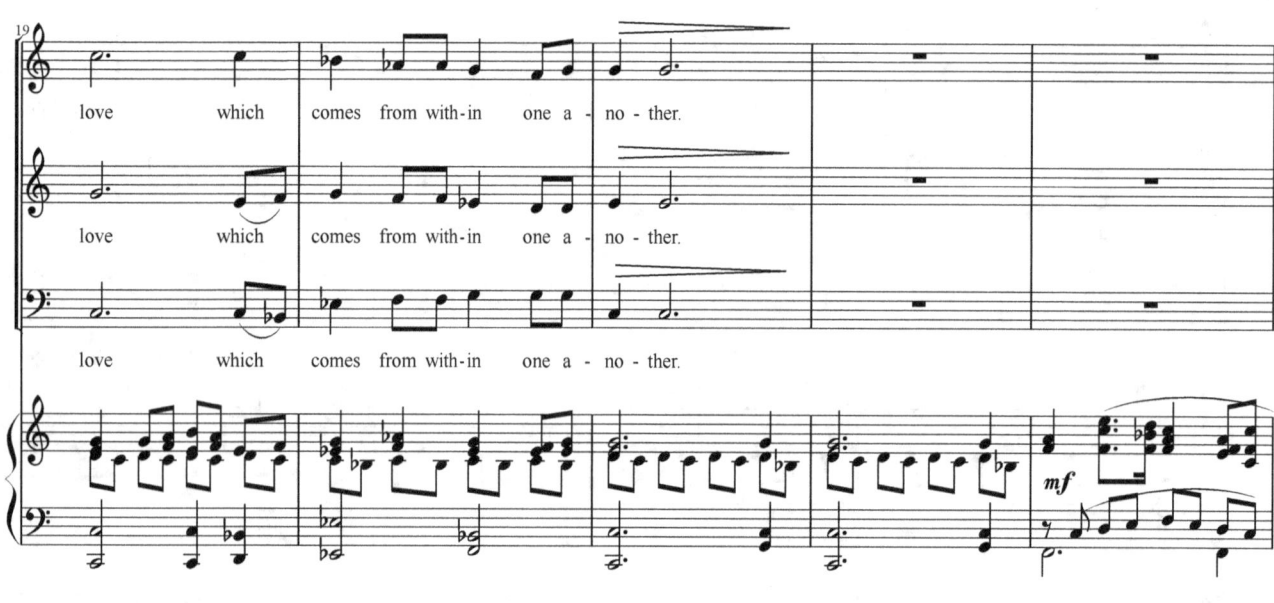

love which comes from with-in one a-no-ther.

love which comes from with-in one a-no-ther.

love which comes from with-in one a-no-ther.

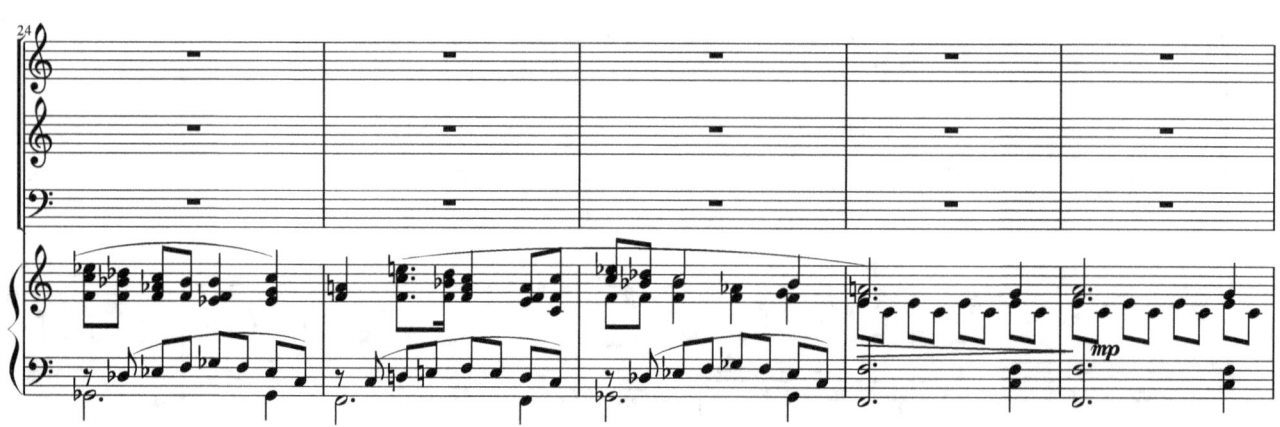

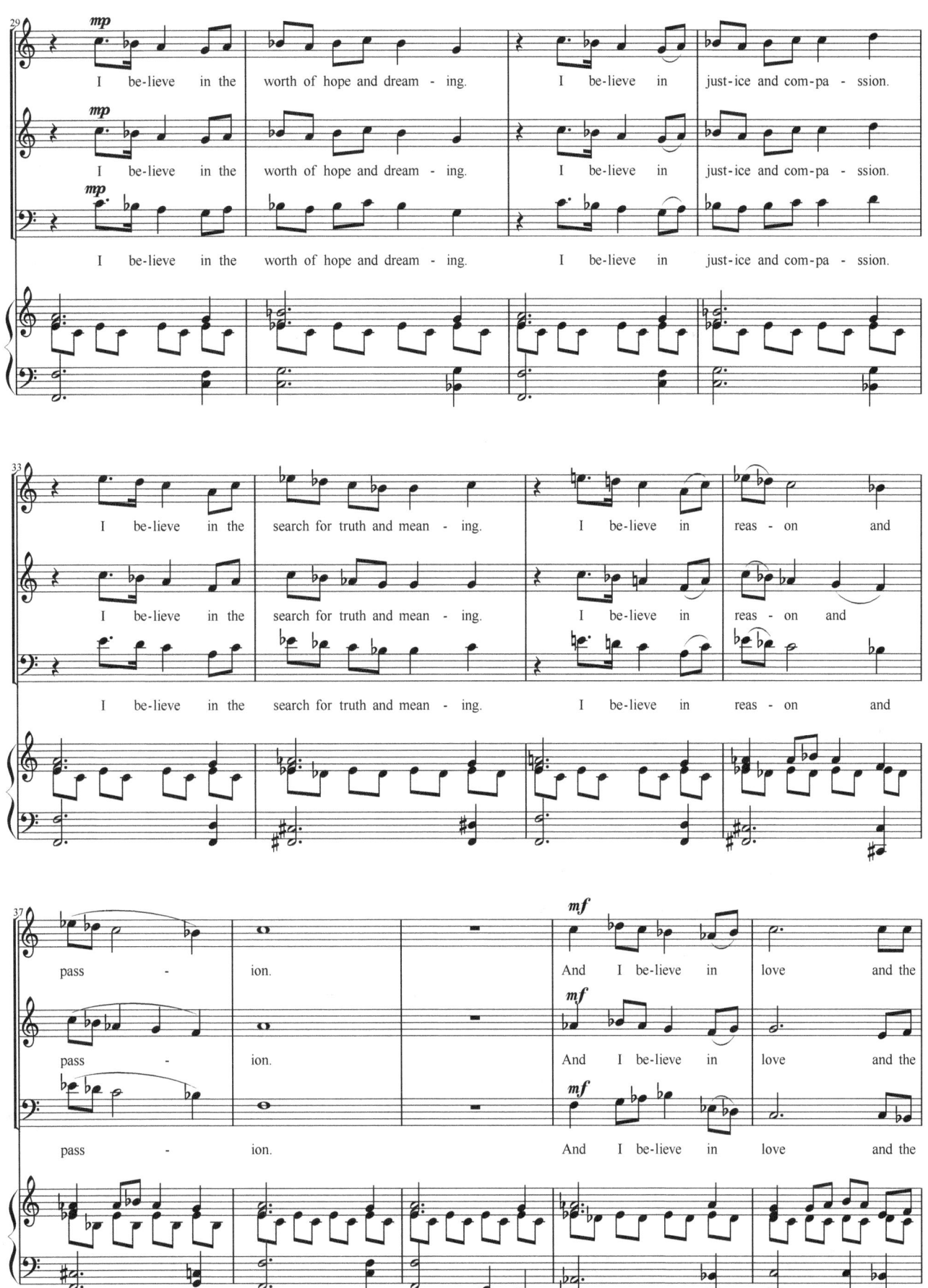

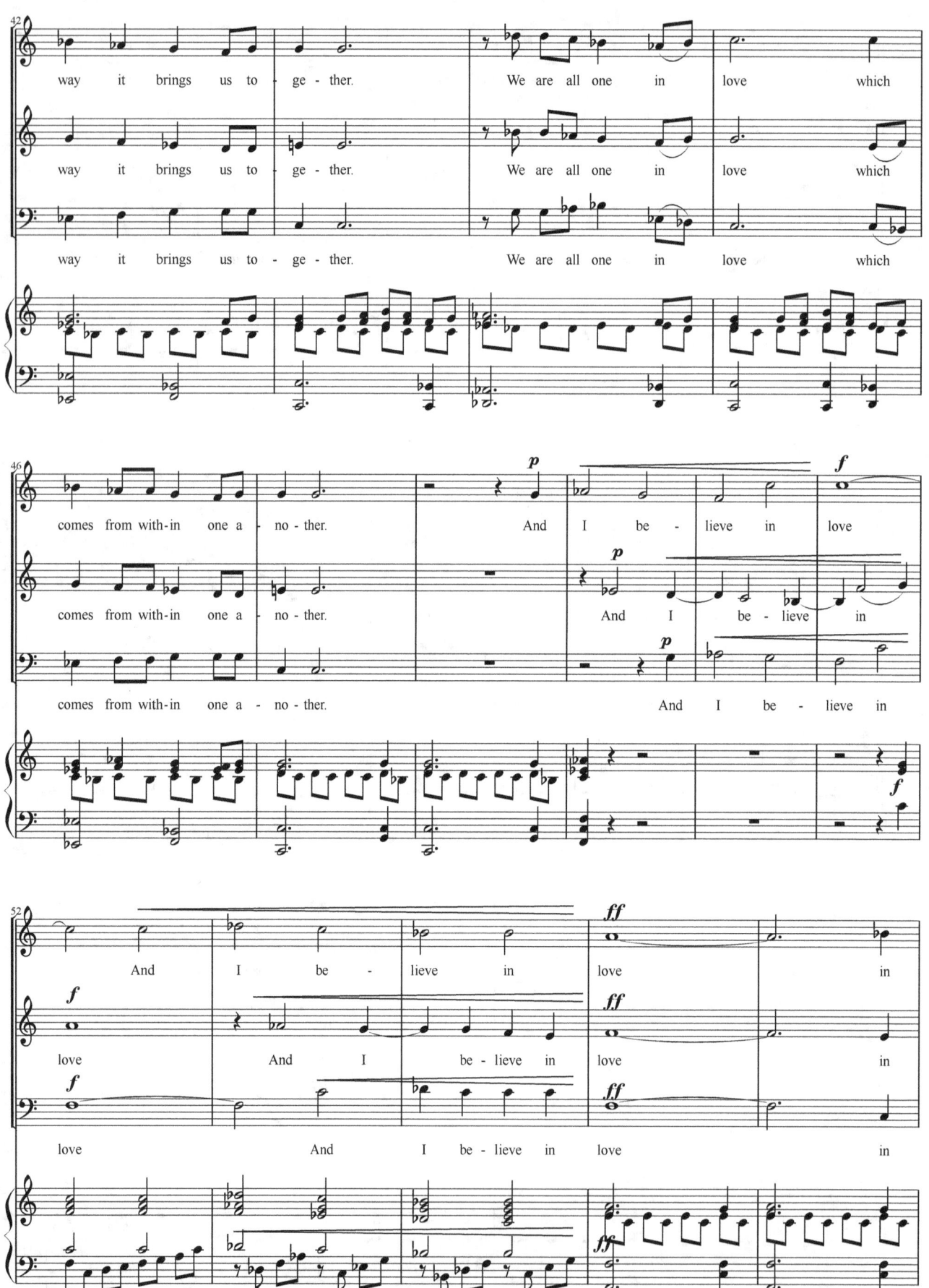

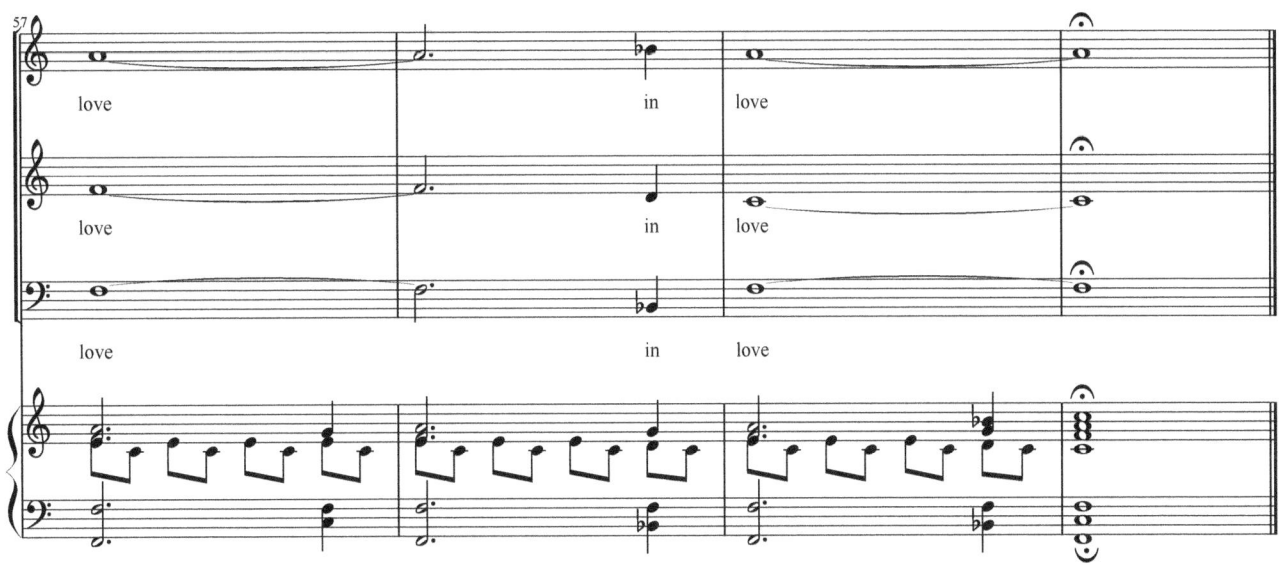

love   in love

love   in love

love   in love

If I Can Stop

Ken Langer

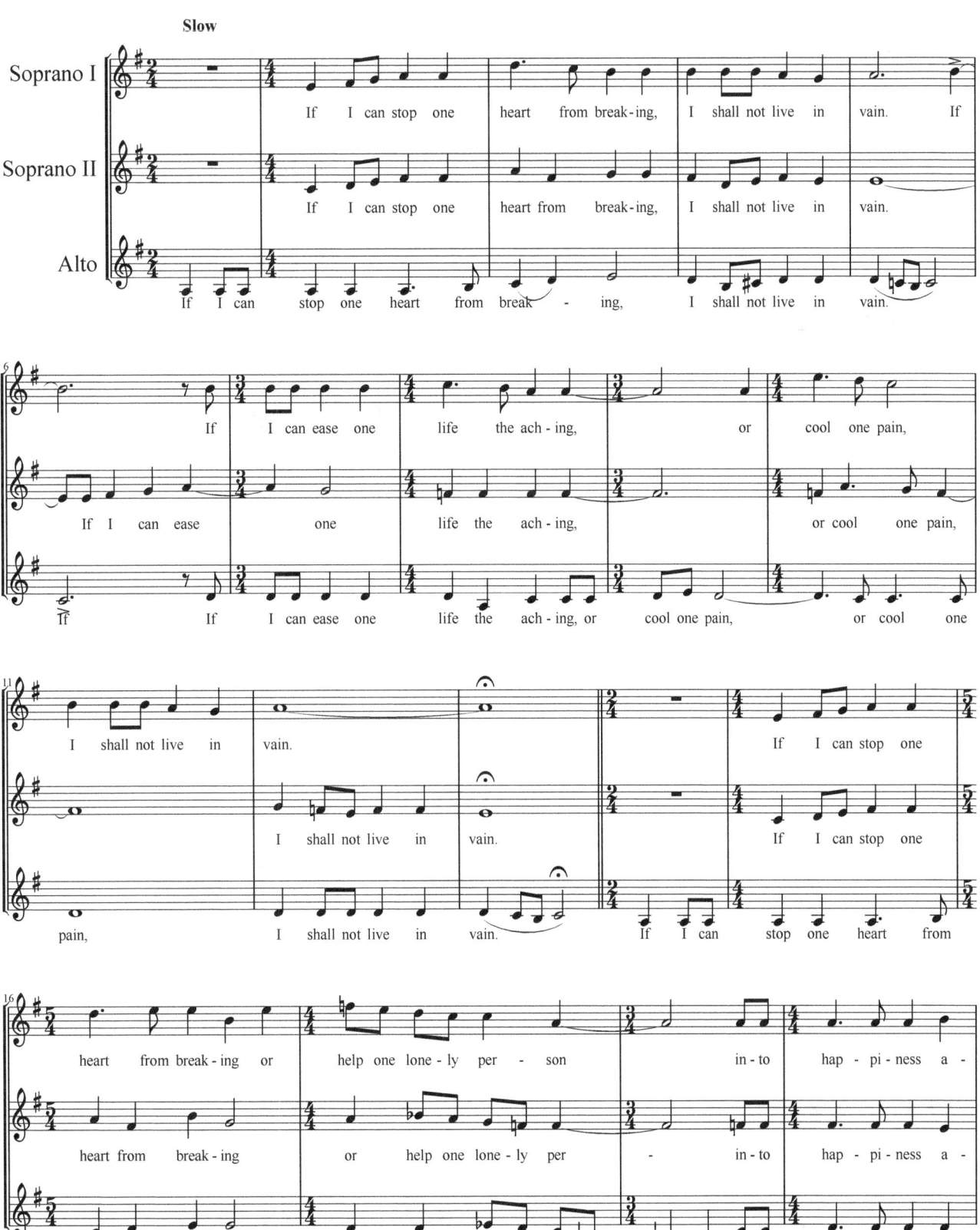

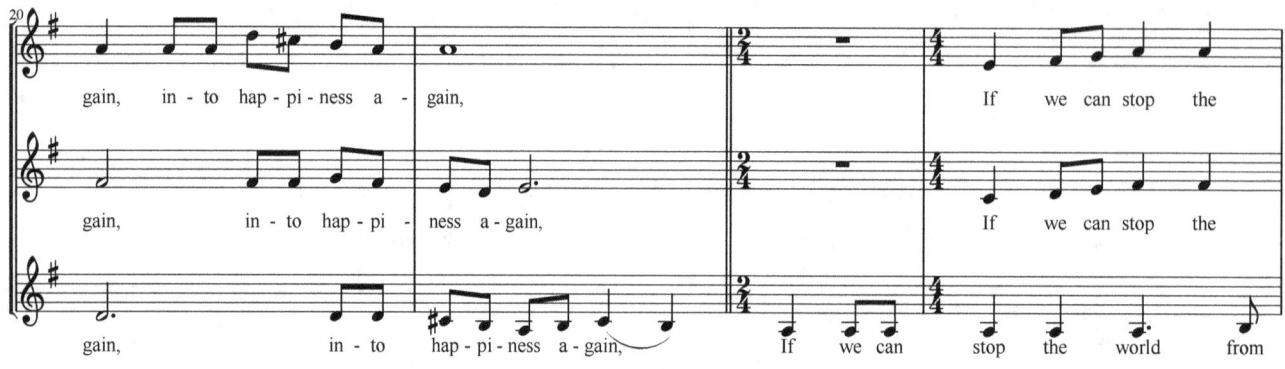

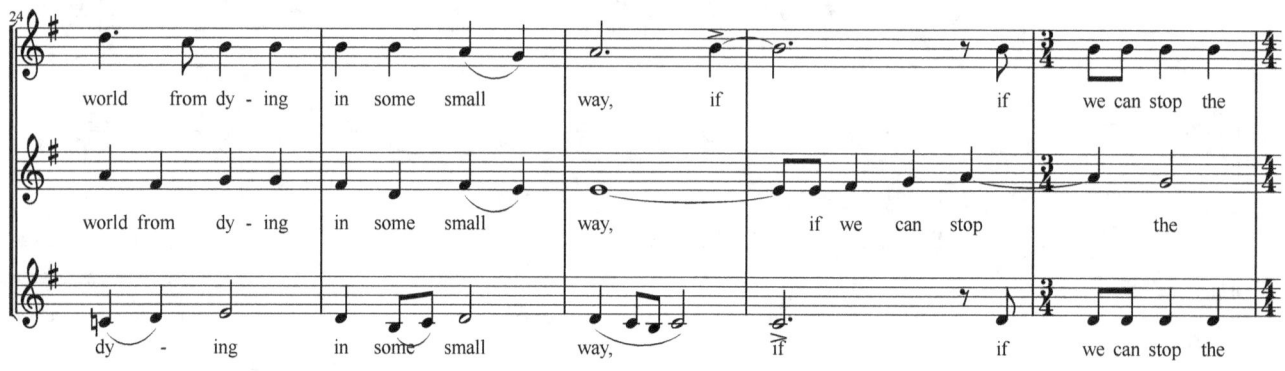

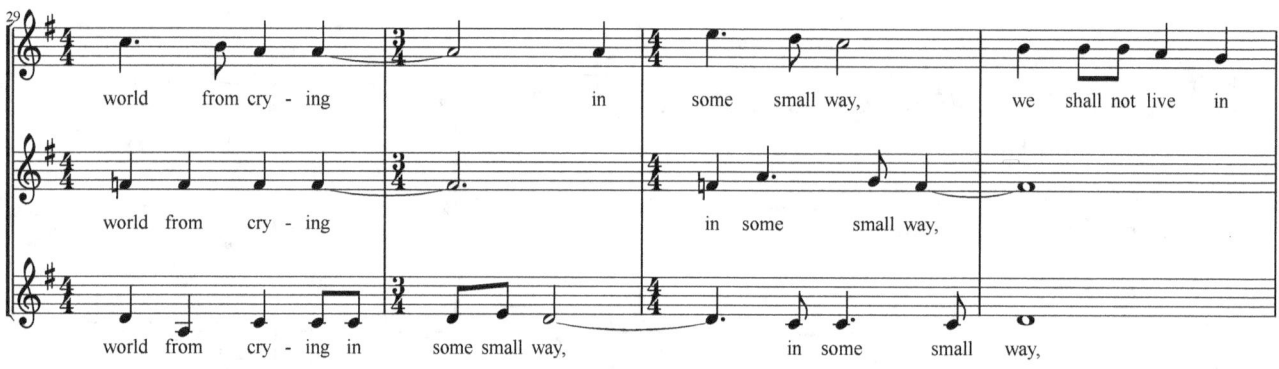

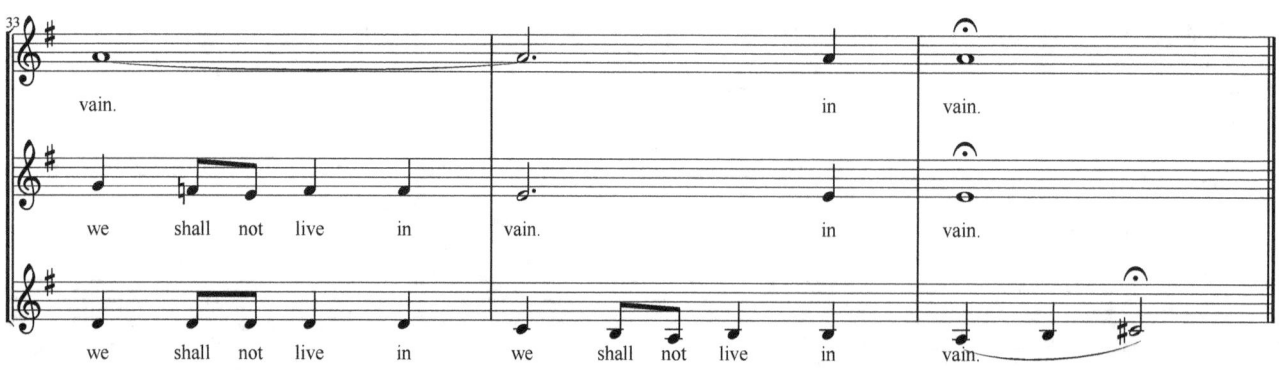

In Dream Time

Ken Langer

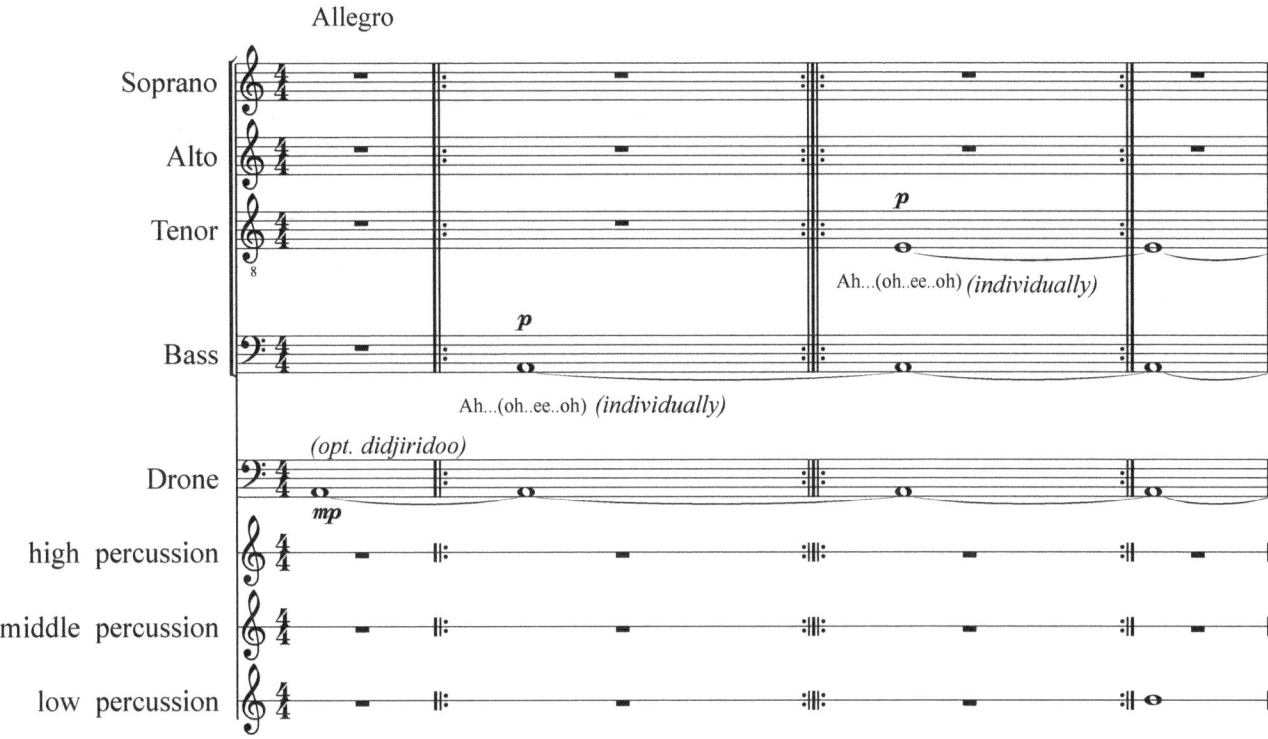

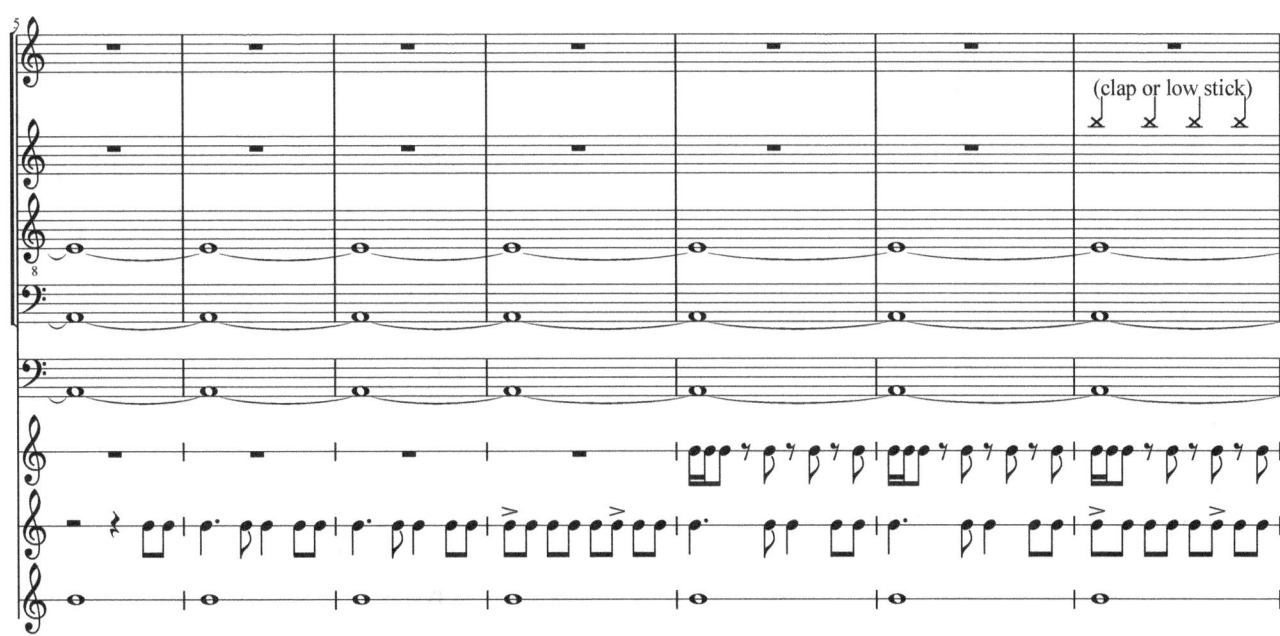

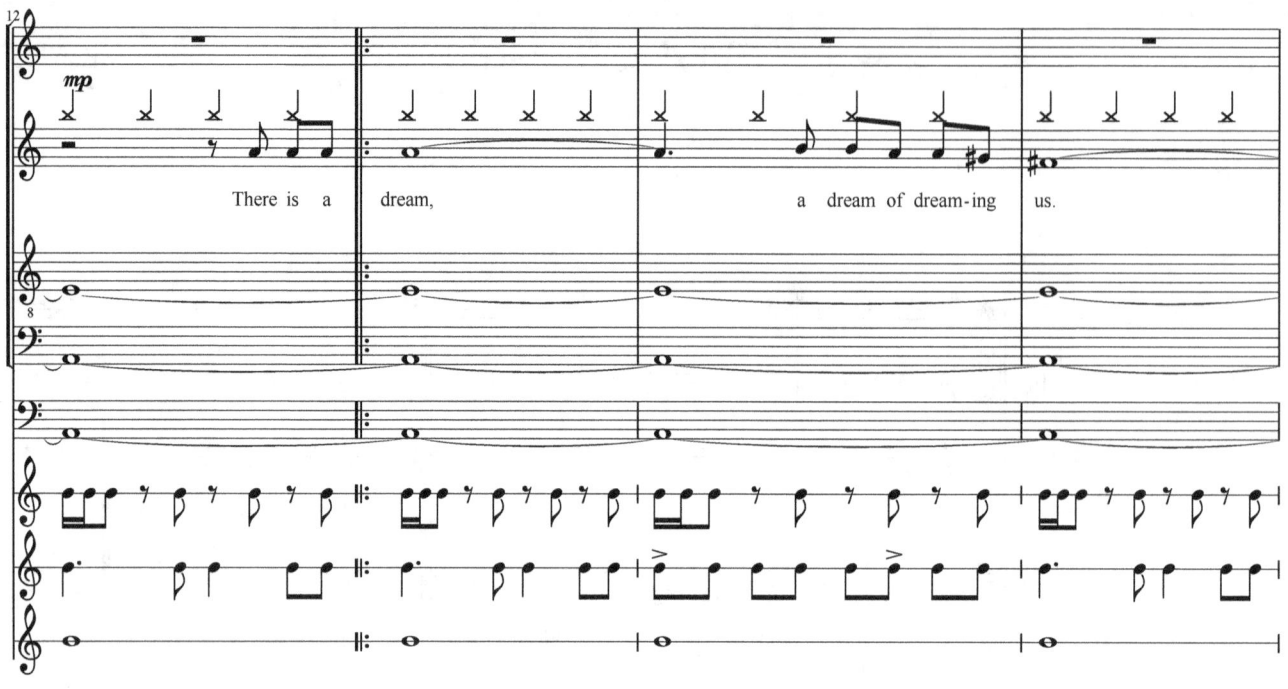

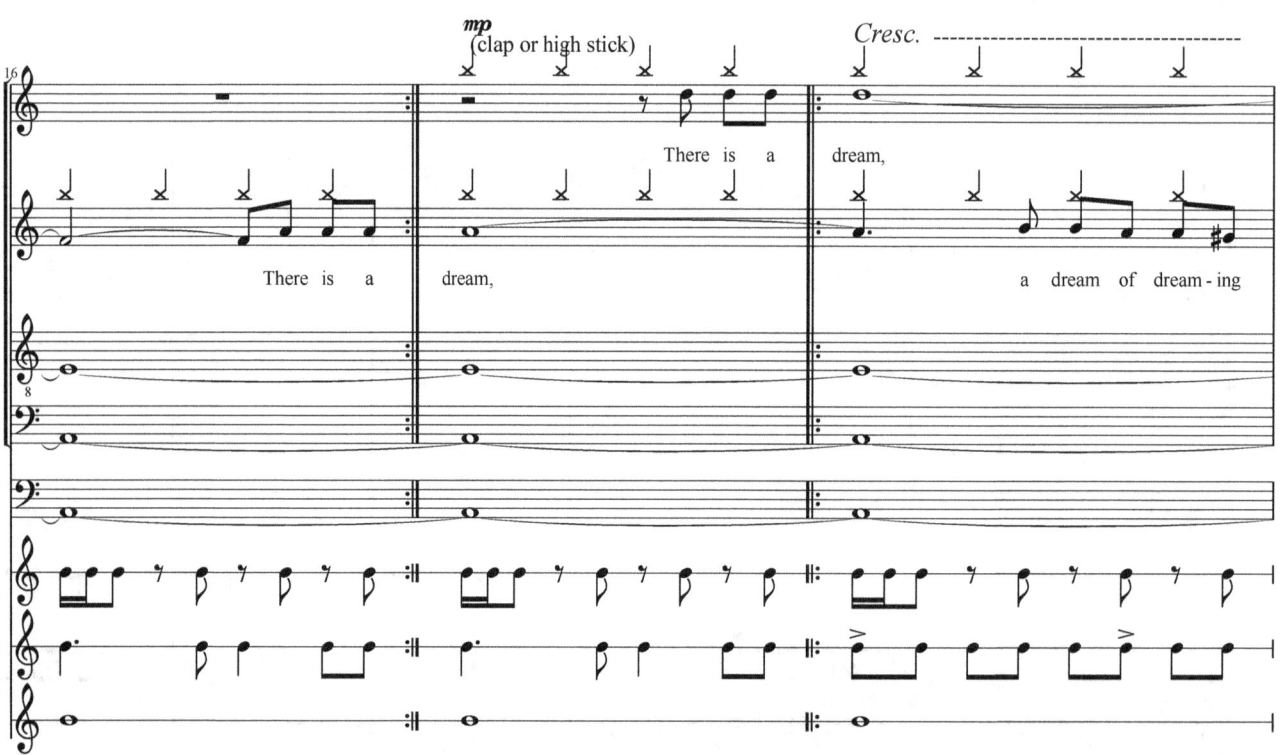

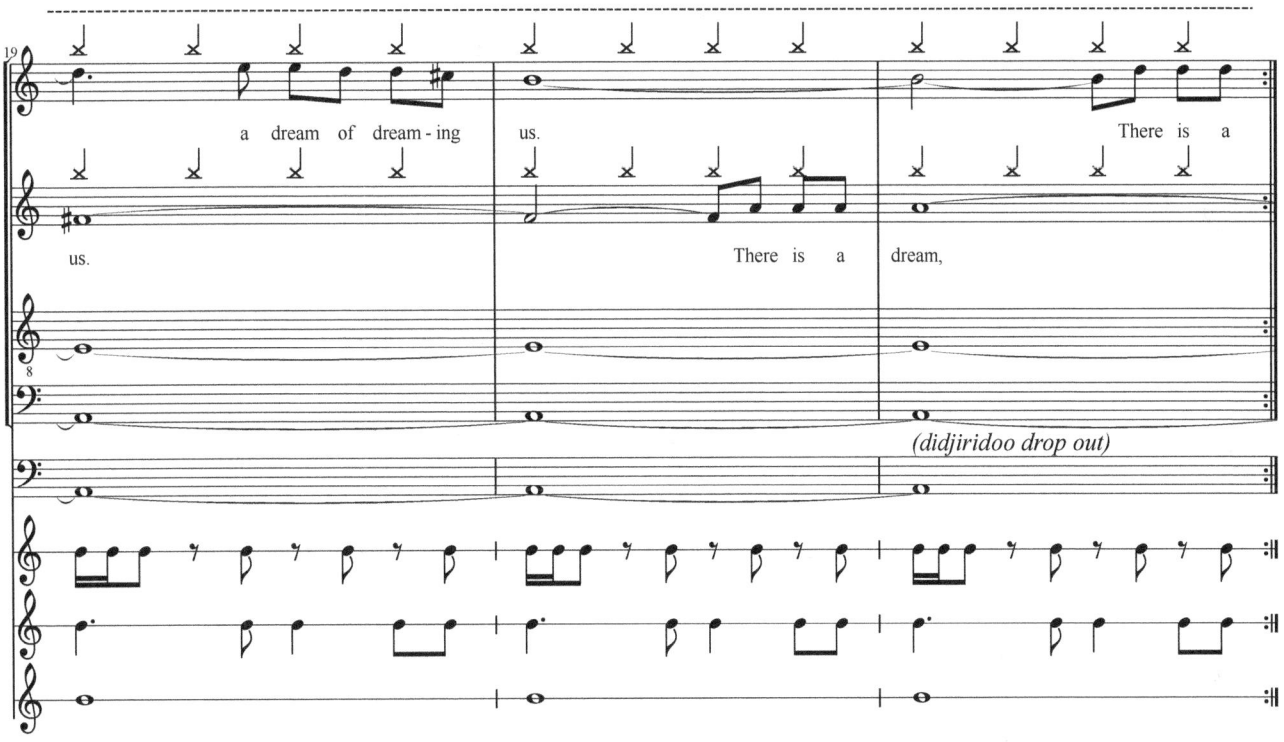

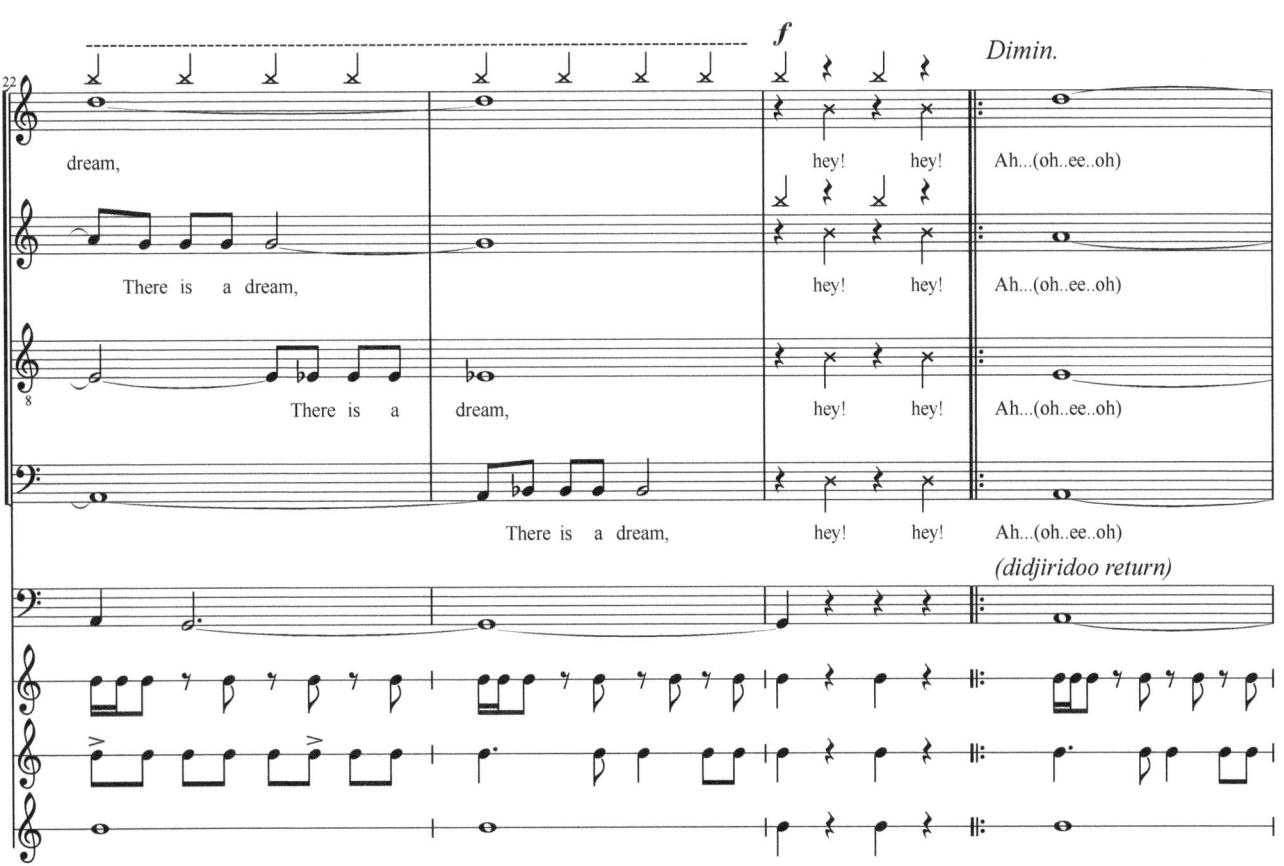

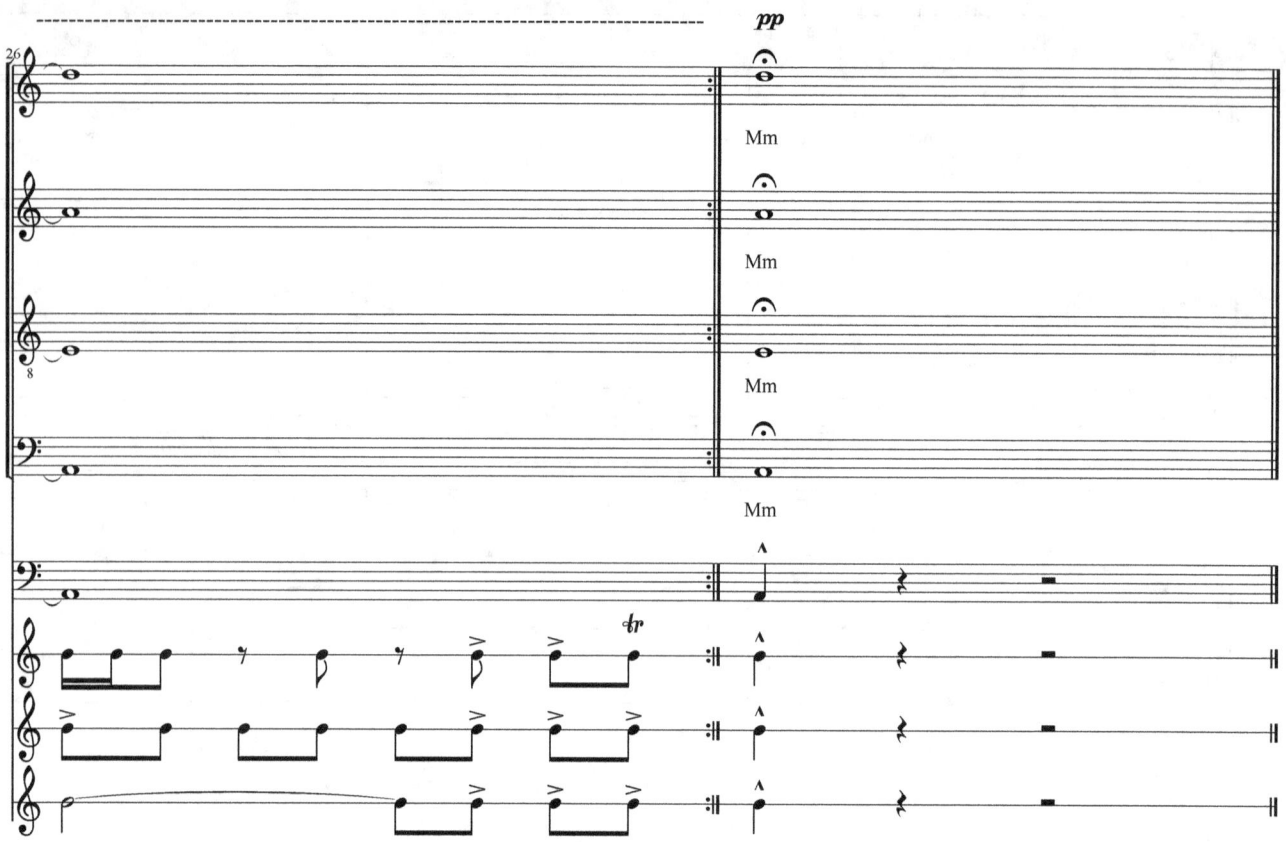

Performance Note: When the voices are directed to sing "Ah...(oh..ee..oh)" they should attempt to imitate the sound of the didjeridoo each at their own pace to create a vocal montage.

Invocation
from "Wedding Music"

Ken Langer

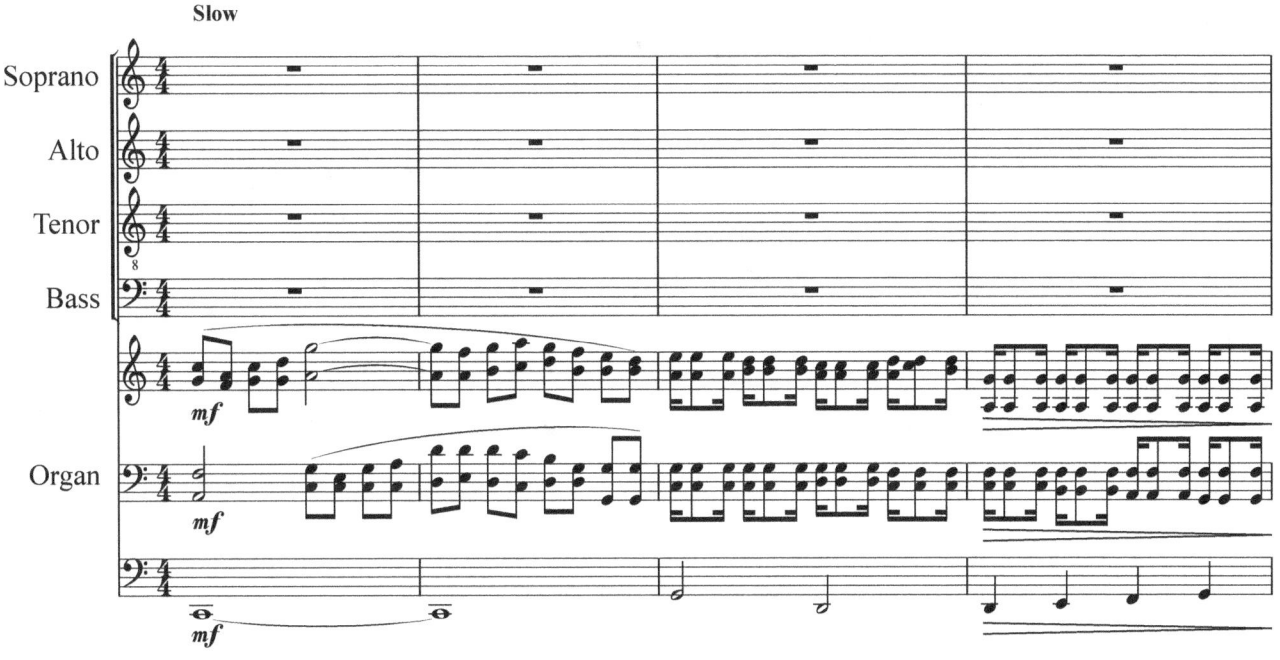

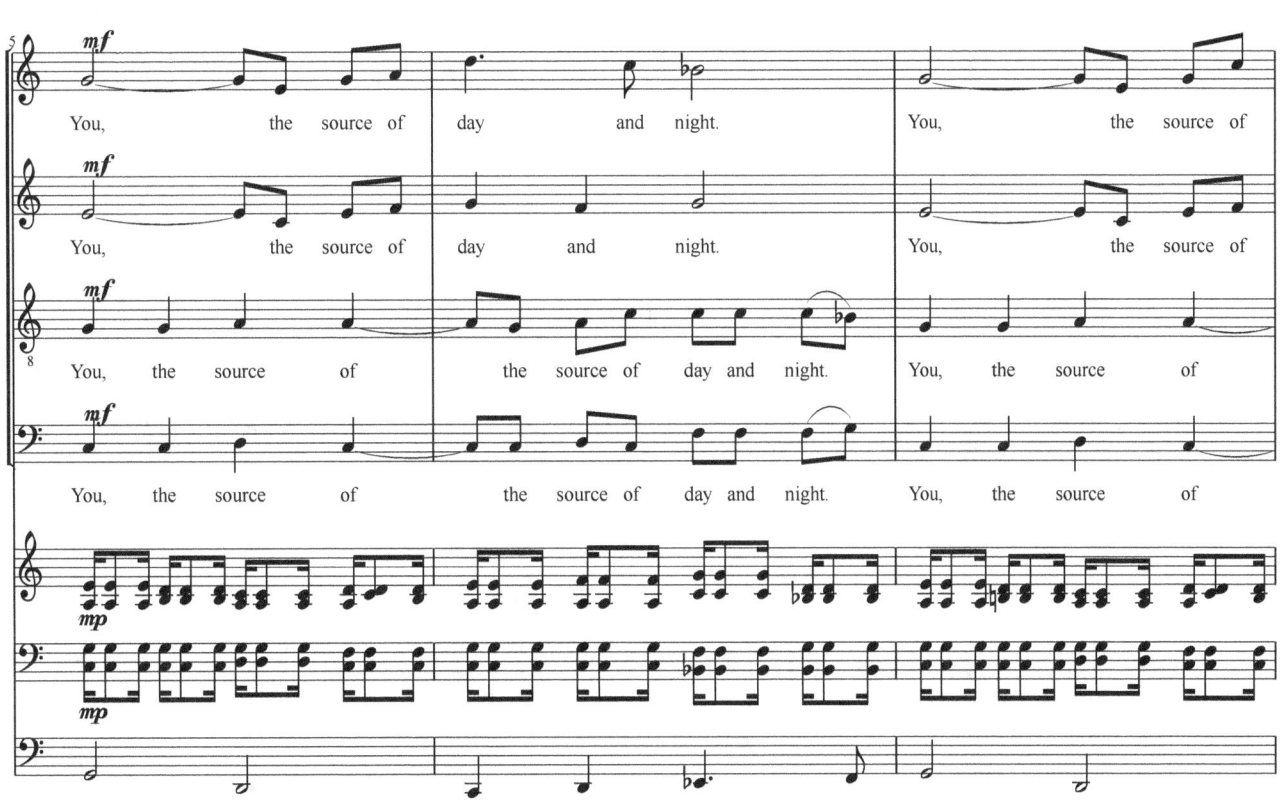

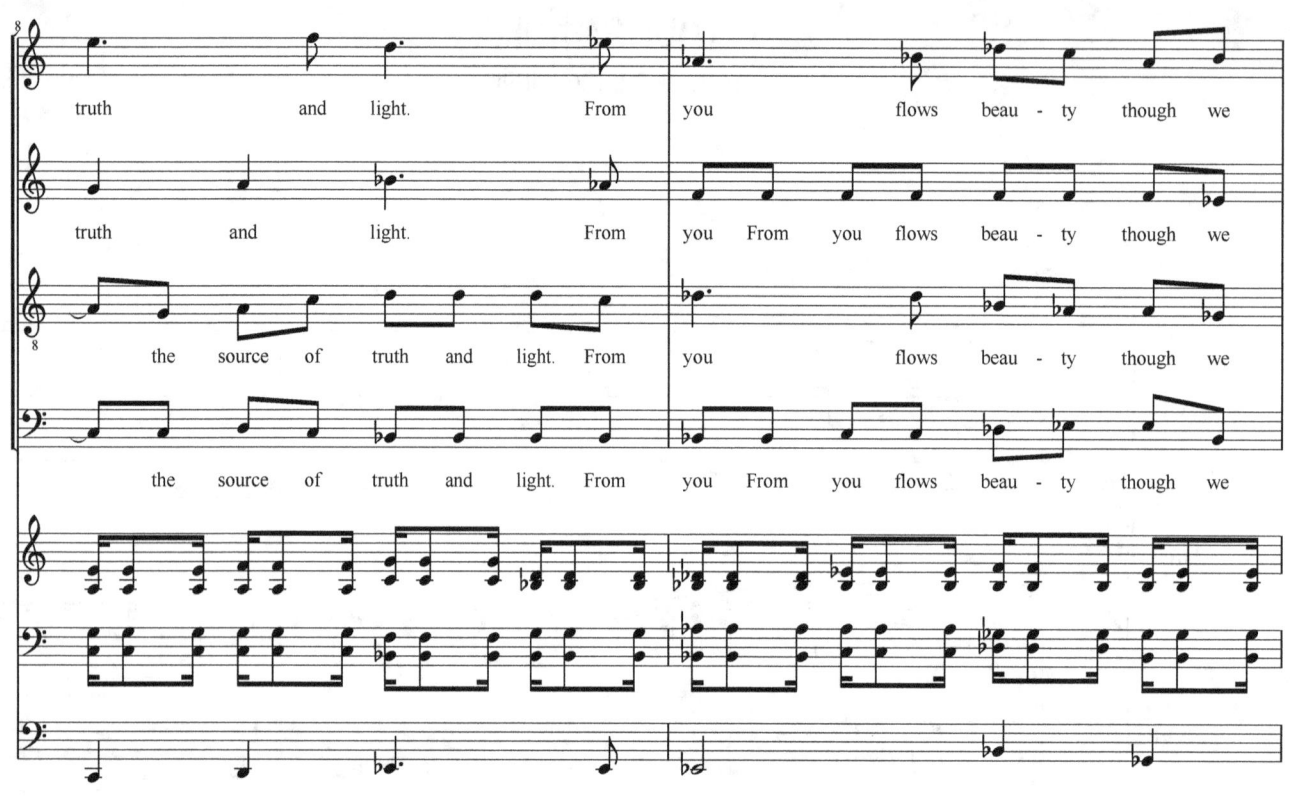

truth and light. From you flows beau - ty though we

truth and light. From you From you flows beau - ty though we

the source of truth and light. From you flows beau - ty though we

the source of truth and light. From you From you flows beau - ty though we

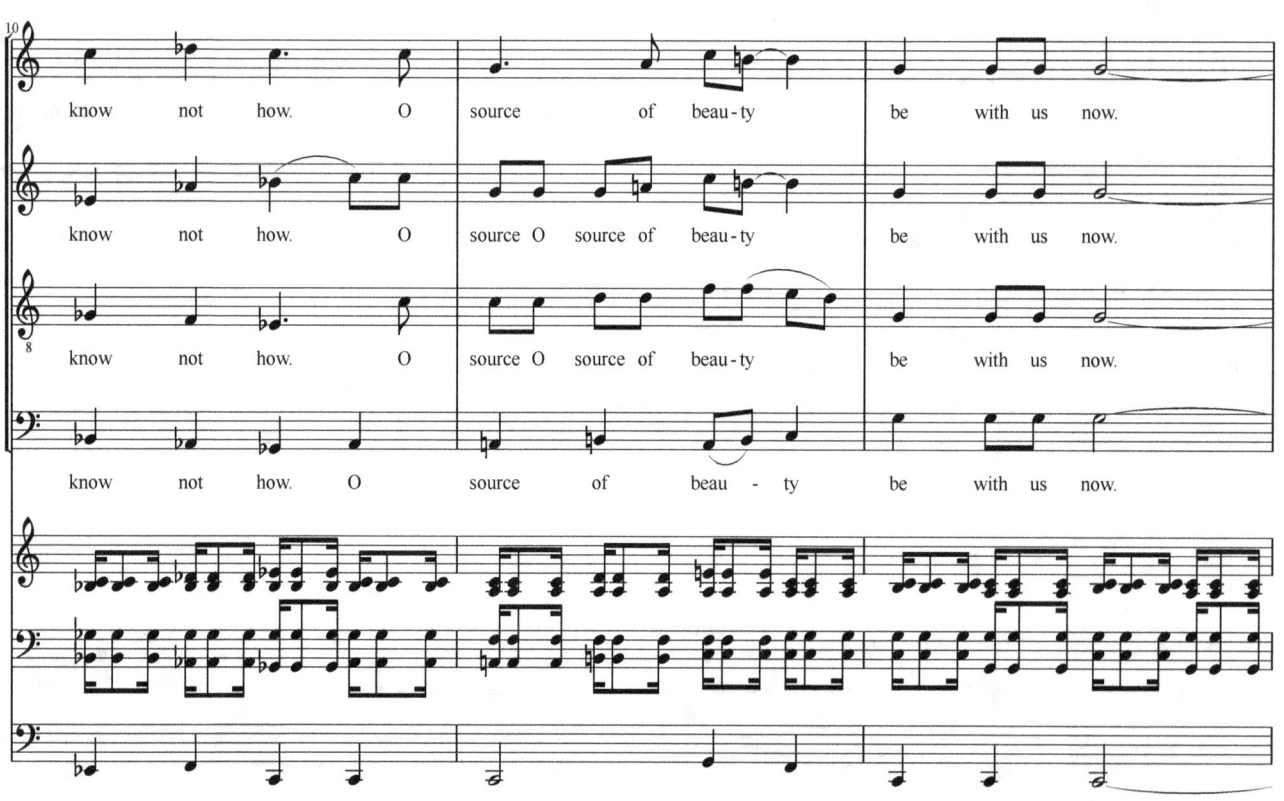

know not how. O source of beau - ty be with us now.

know not how. O source O source of beau - ty be with us now.

know not how. O source O source of beau - ty be with us now.

know not how. O source of beau - ty be with us now.

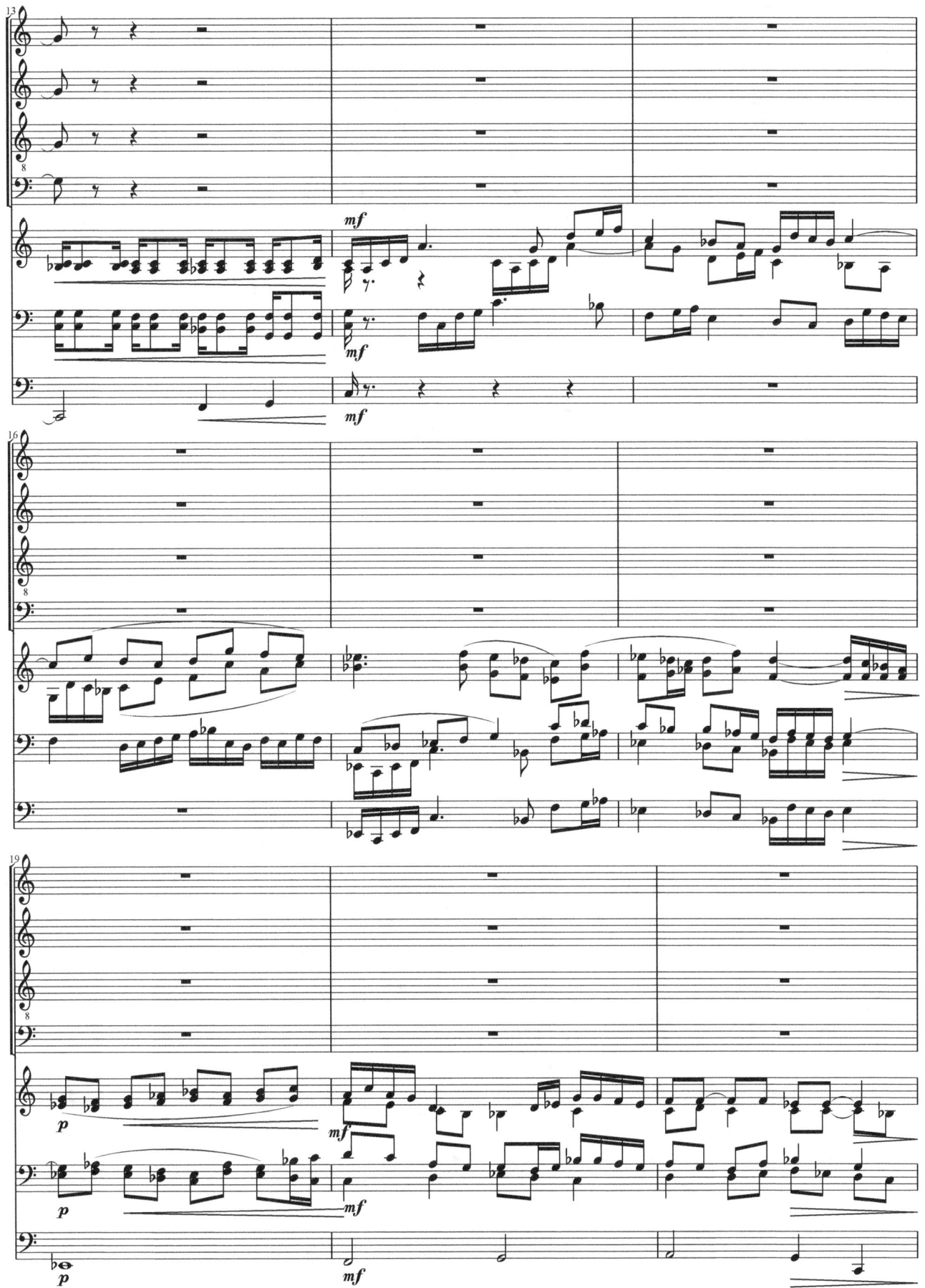

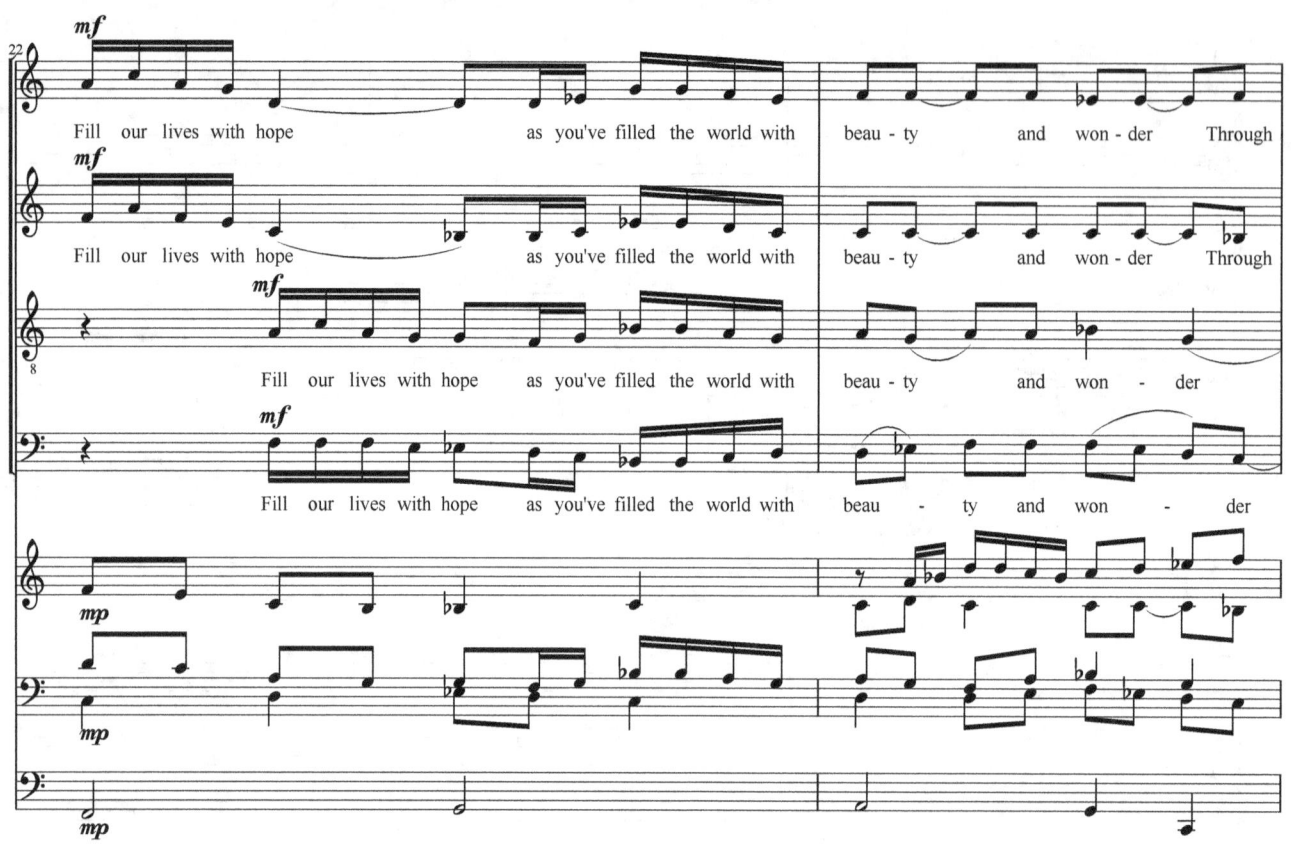

Fill our lives with hope as you've filled the world with beau-ty and won-der Through

Fill our lives with hope as you've filled the world with beau-ty and won-der Through

Fill our lives with hope as you've filled the world with beau-ty and won-der

Fill our lives with hope as you've filled the world with beau-ty and won-der

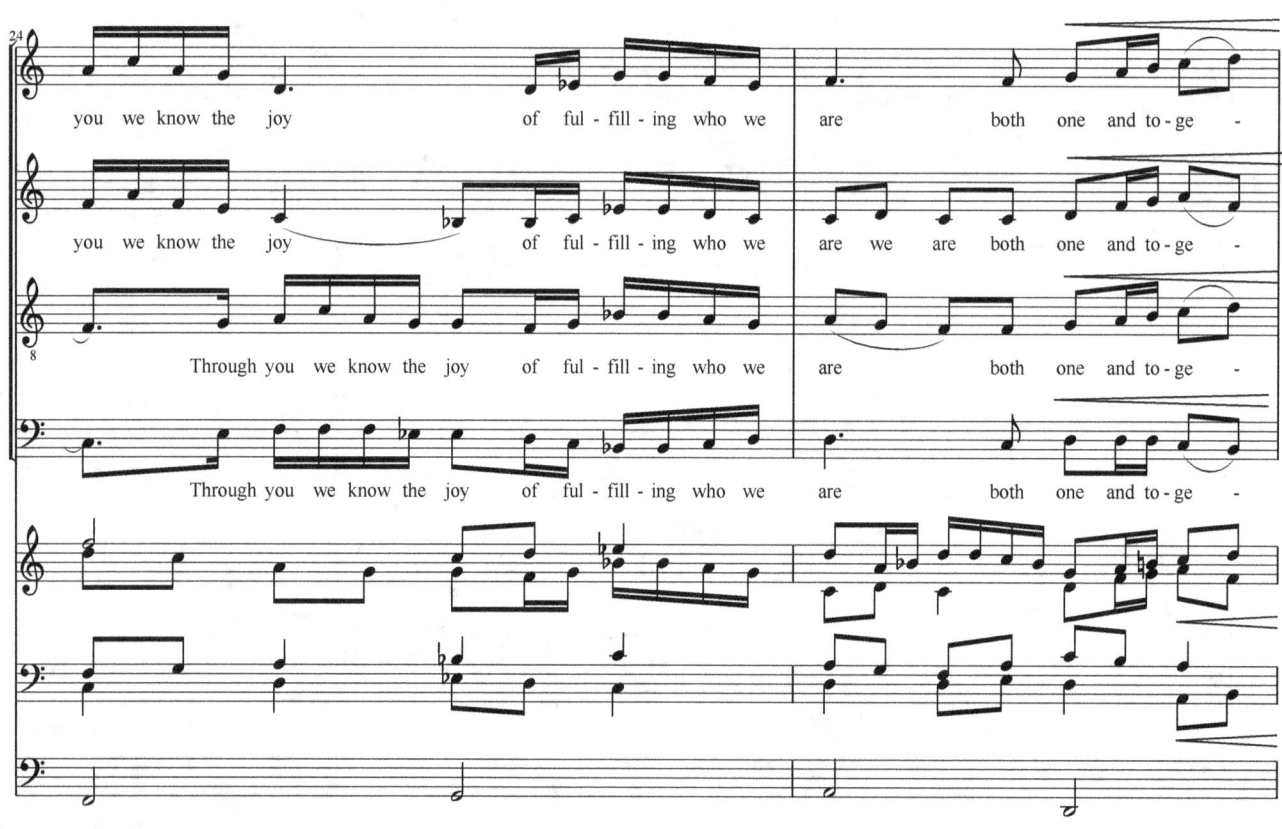

you we know the joy of ful-fill-ing who we are both one and to-ge -

you we know the joy of ful-fill-ing who we are we are both one and to-ge -

Through you we know the joy of ful-fill-ing who we are both one and to-ge -

Through you we know the joy of ful-fill-ing who we are both one and to-ge -

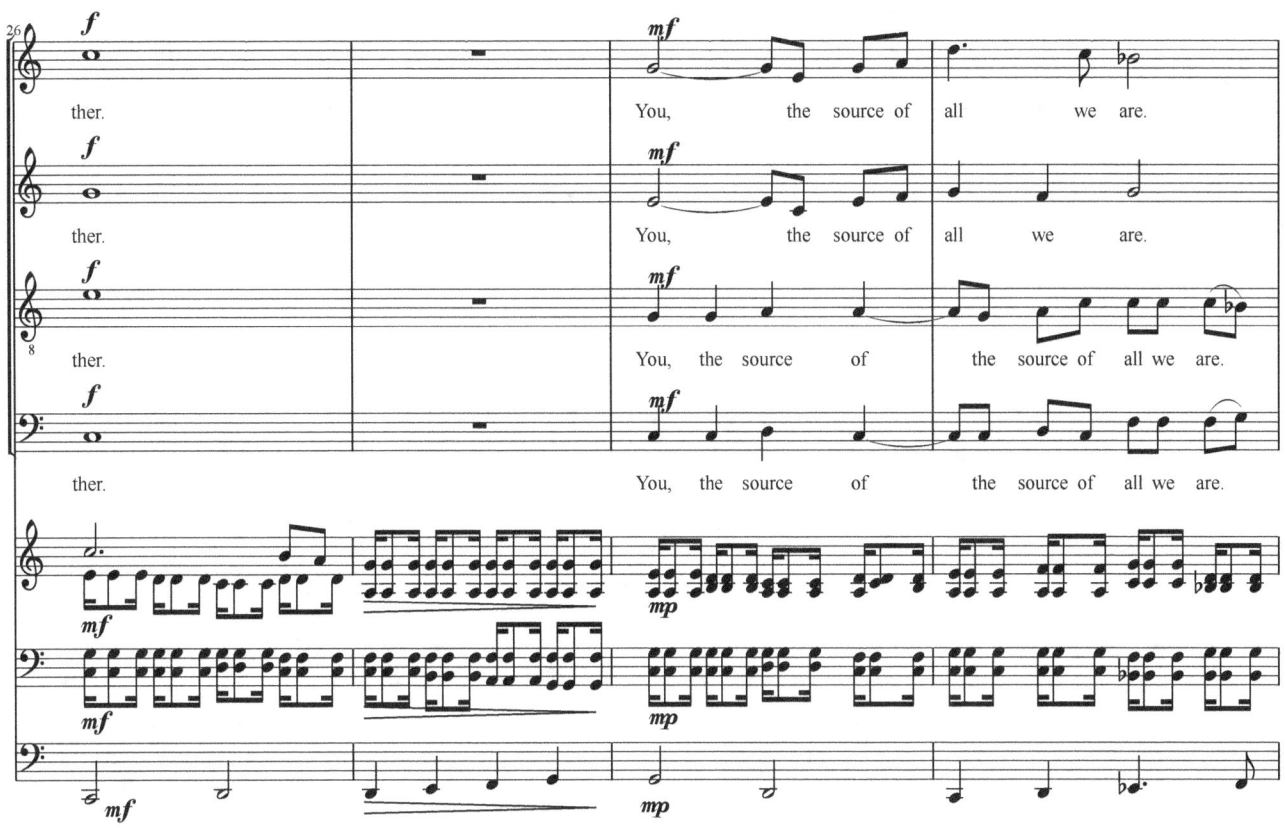

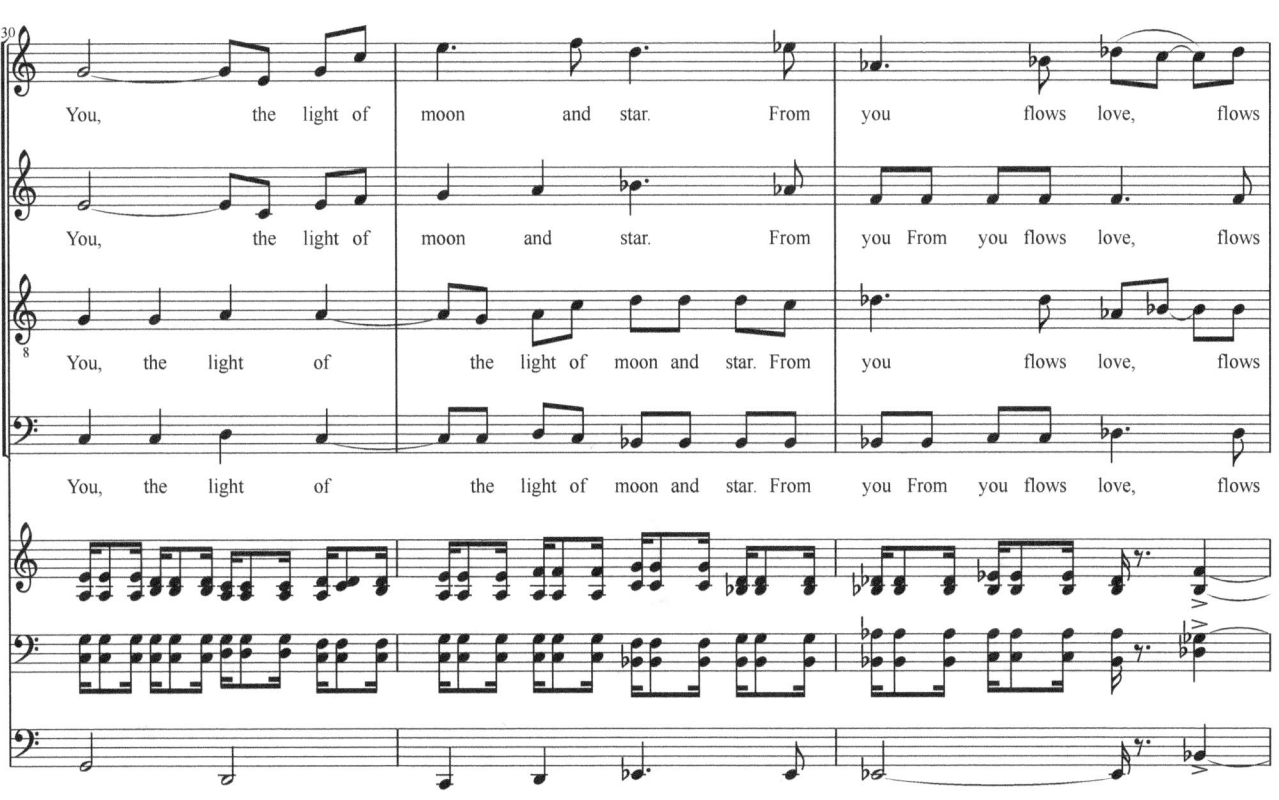

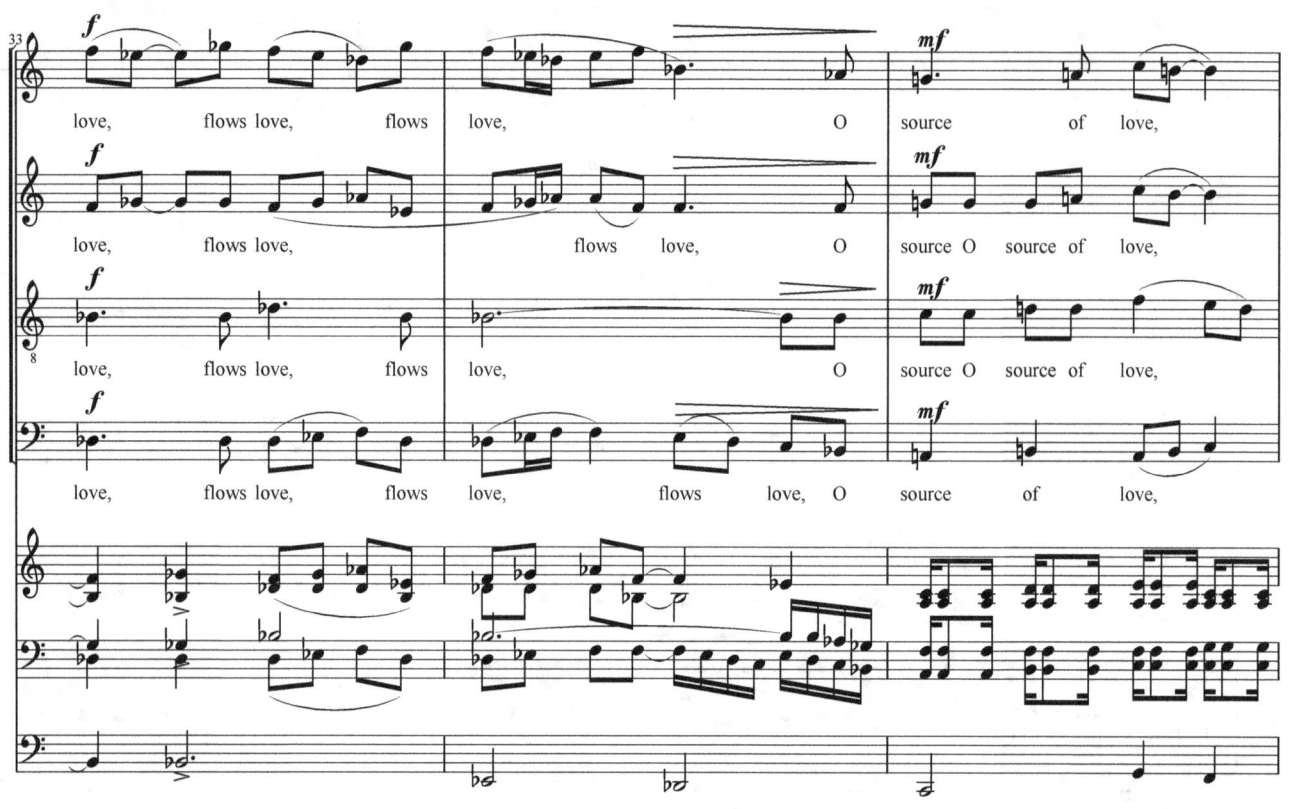

love,   flows love,   flows   love,   O   source   of   love,

love,   flows love,   flows   love,   O   source O source of   love,

love,   flows love,   flows   love,   O   source O source of   love,

love,   flows love,   flows   love,   flows   love, O source   of   love,

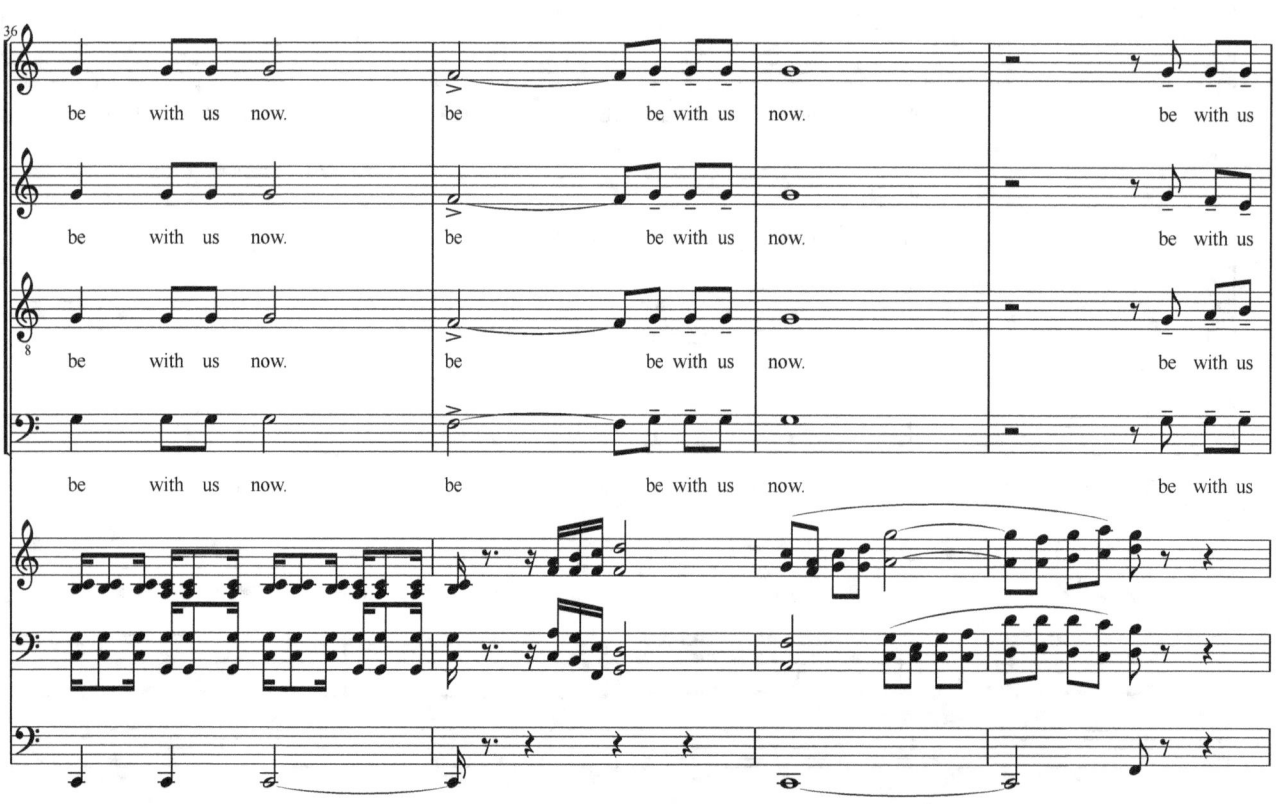

be   with   us   now.   be   be with us   now.   be   with us

be   with   us   now.   be   be with us   now.   be   with us

be   with   us   now.   be   be with us   now.   be   with us

be   with   us   now.   be   be with us   now.   be   with us

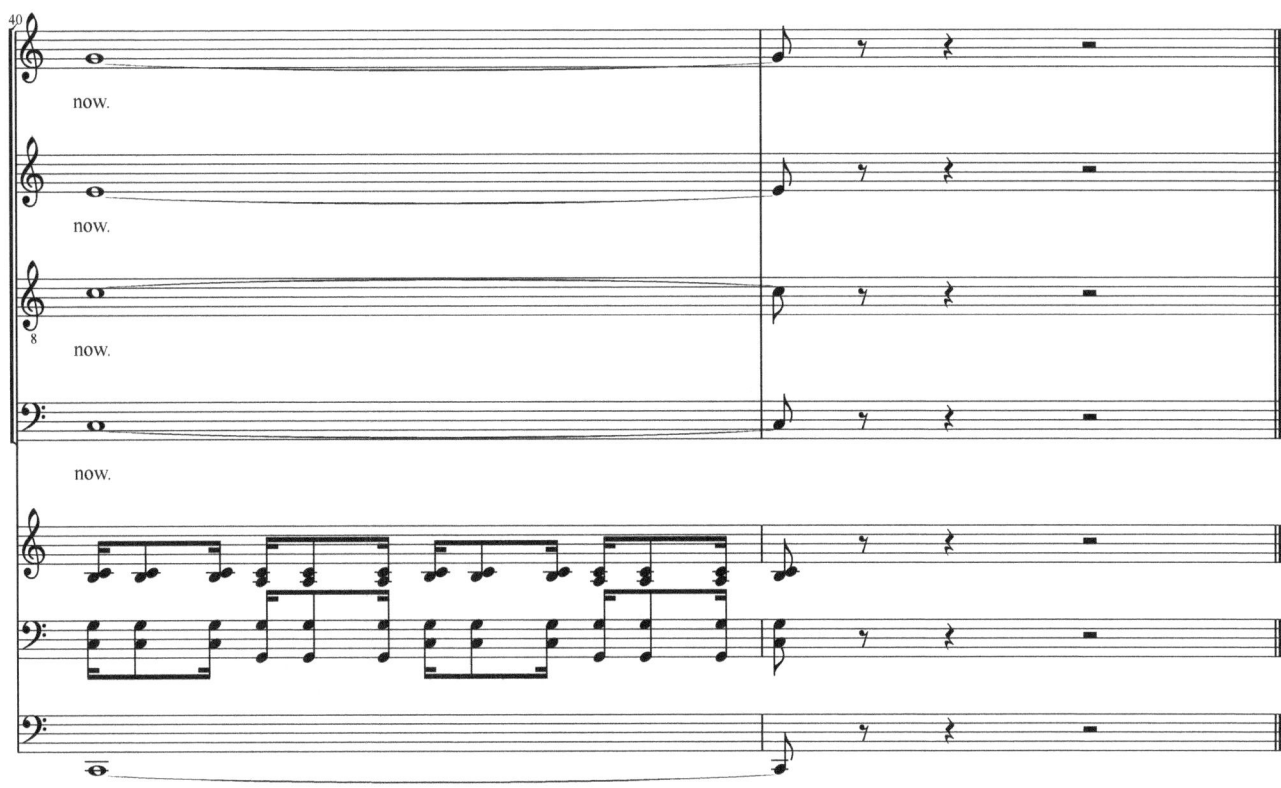

now.

now.

now.

now.

Love's Philosophy
from "Wedding Music"

Percy Bysshe Shelley

Ken Langer

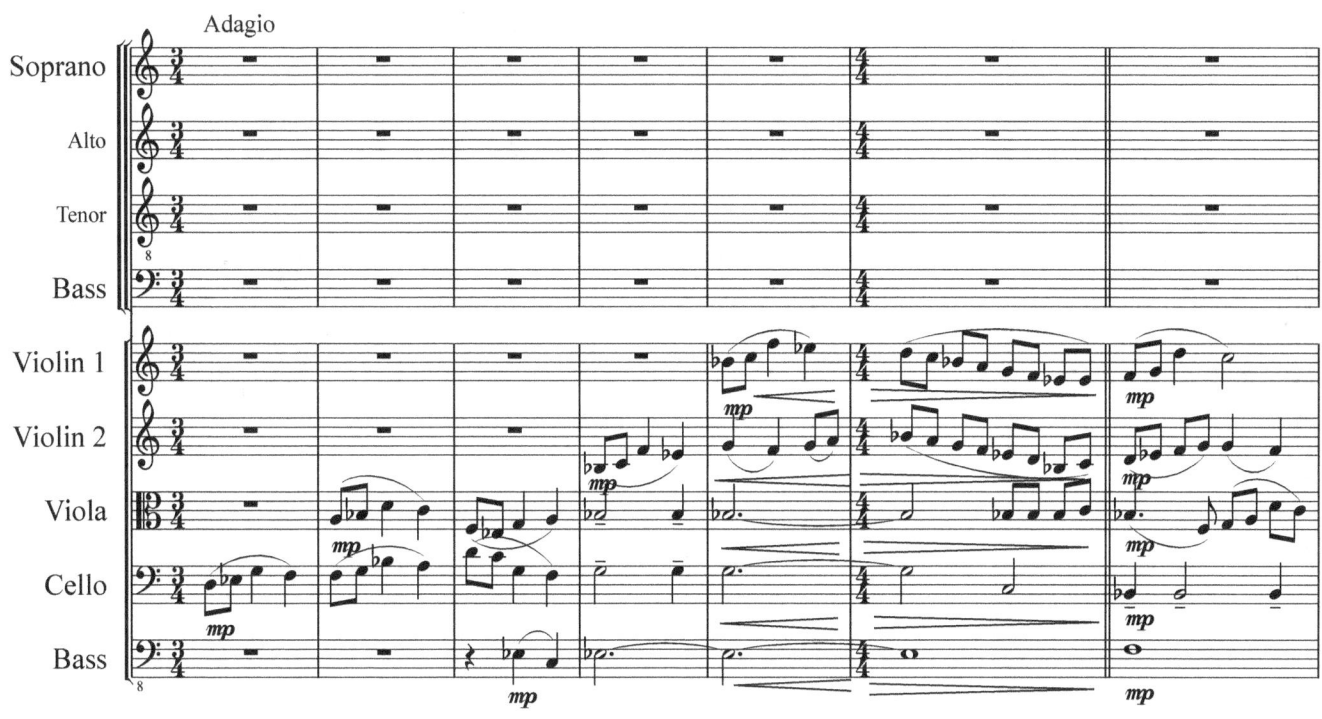

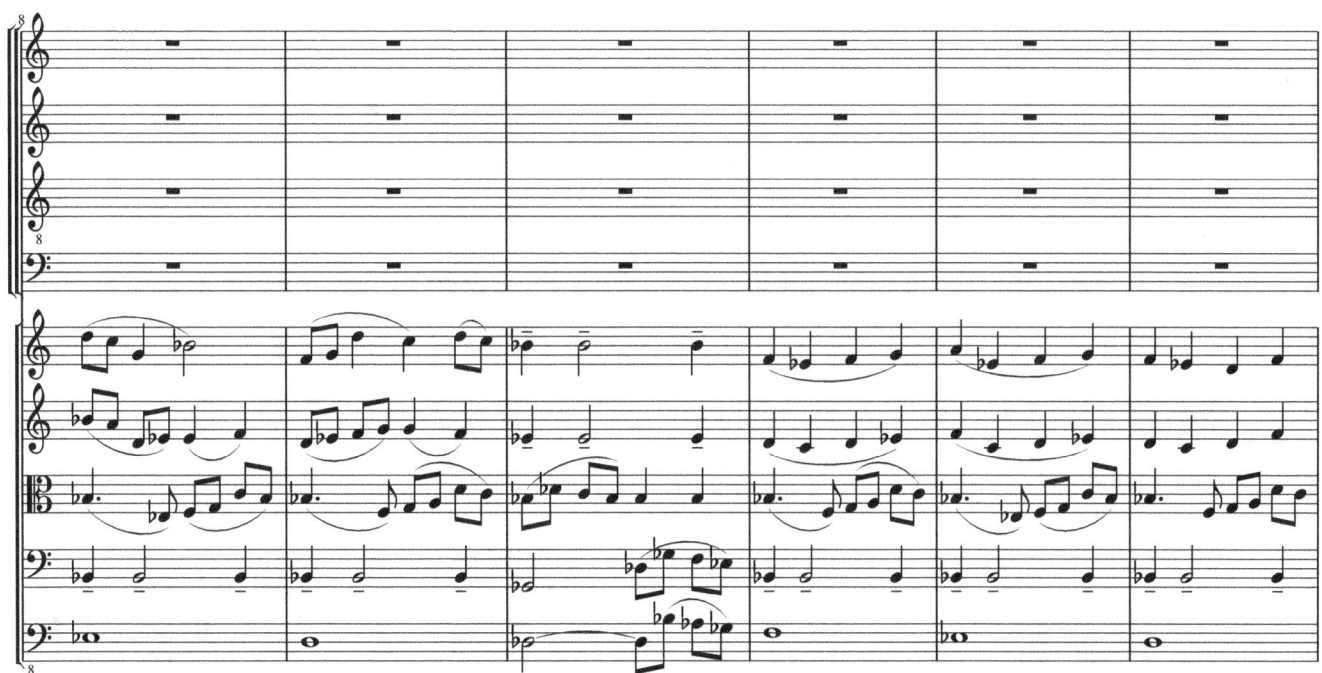

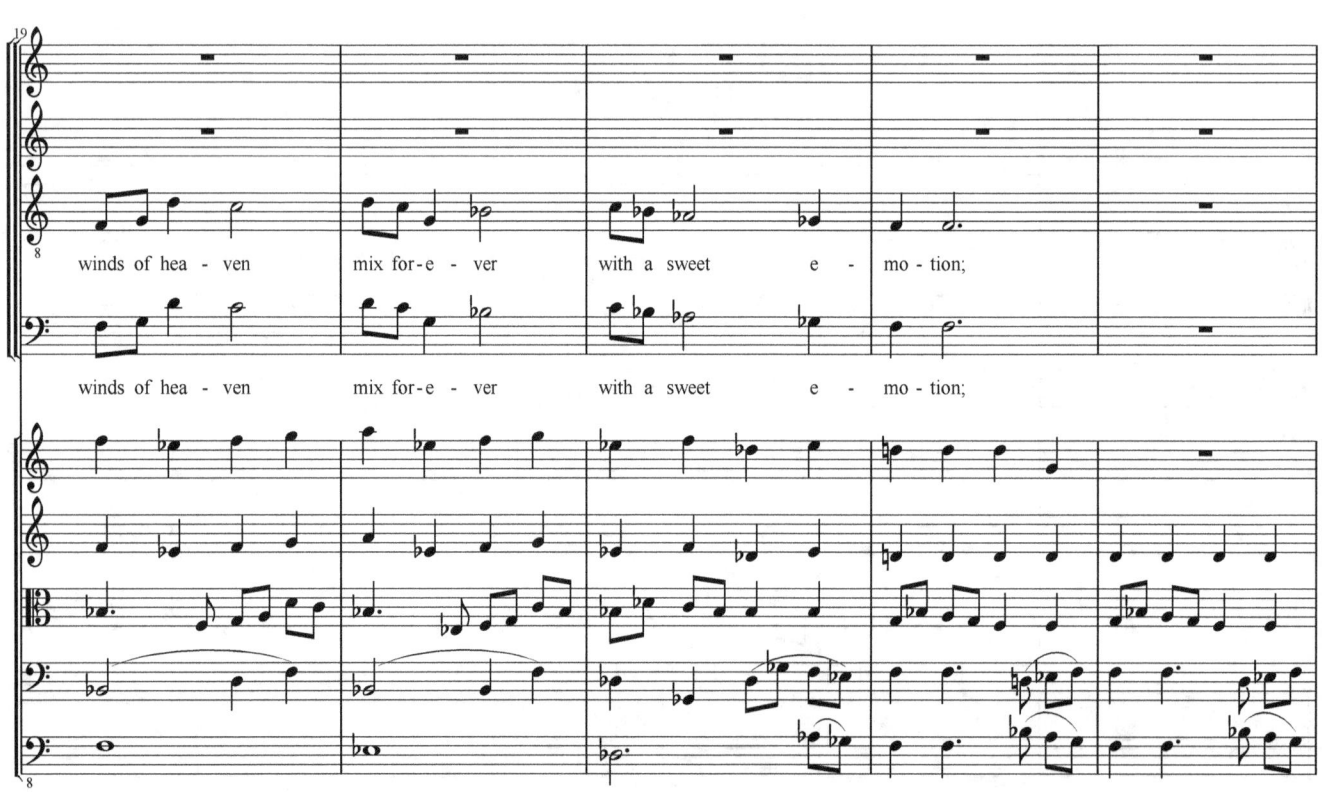

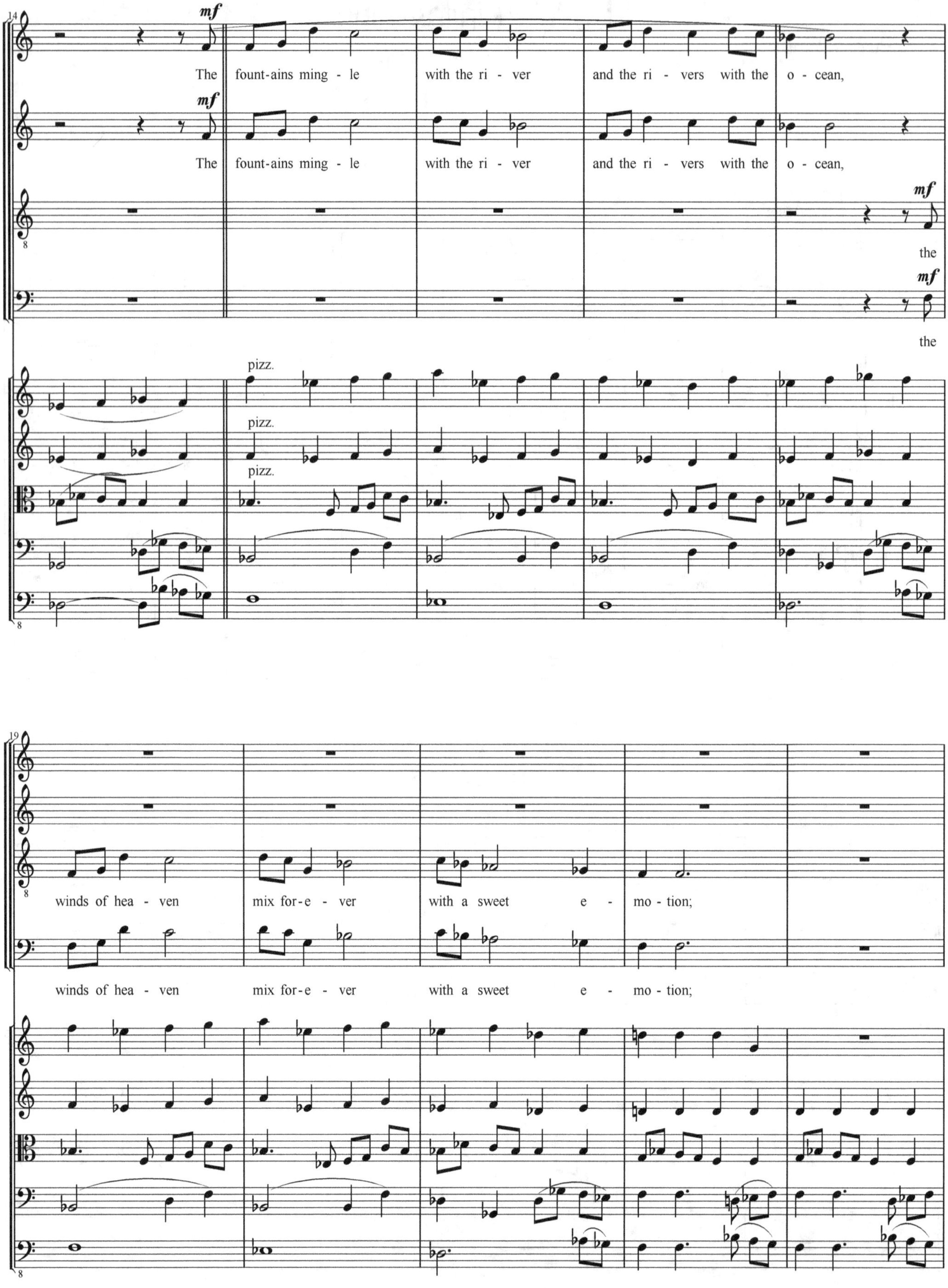

The foun-tains ming - le with the ri - ver and the ri - vers with the o - cean,

The foun-tains ming - le with the ri - ver and the ri - vers with the o - cean,

the

the

winds of hea - ven mix for-e - ver with a sweet e - mo - tion;

winds of hea - ven mix for-e - ver with a sweet e - mo - tion;

52

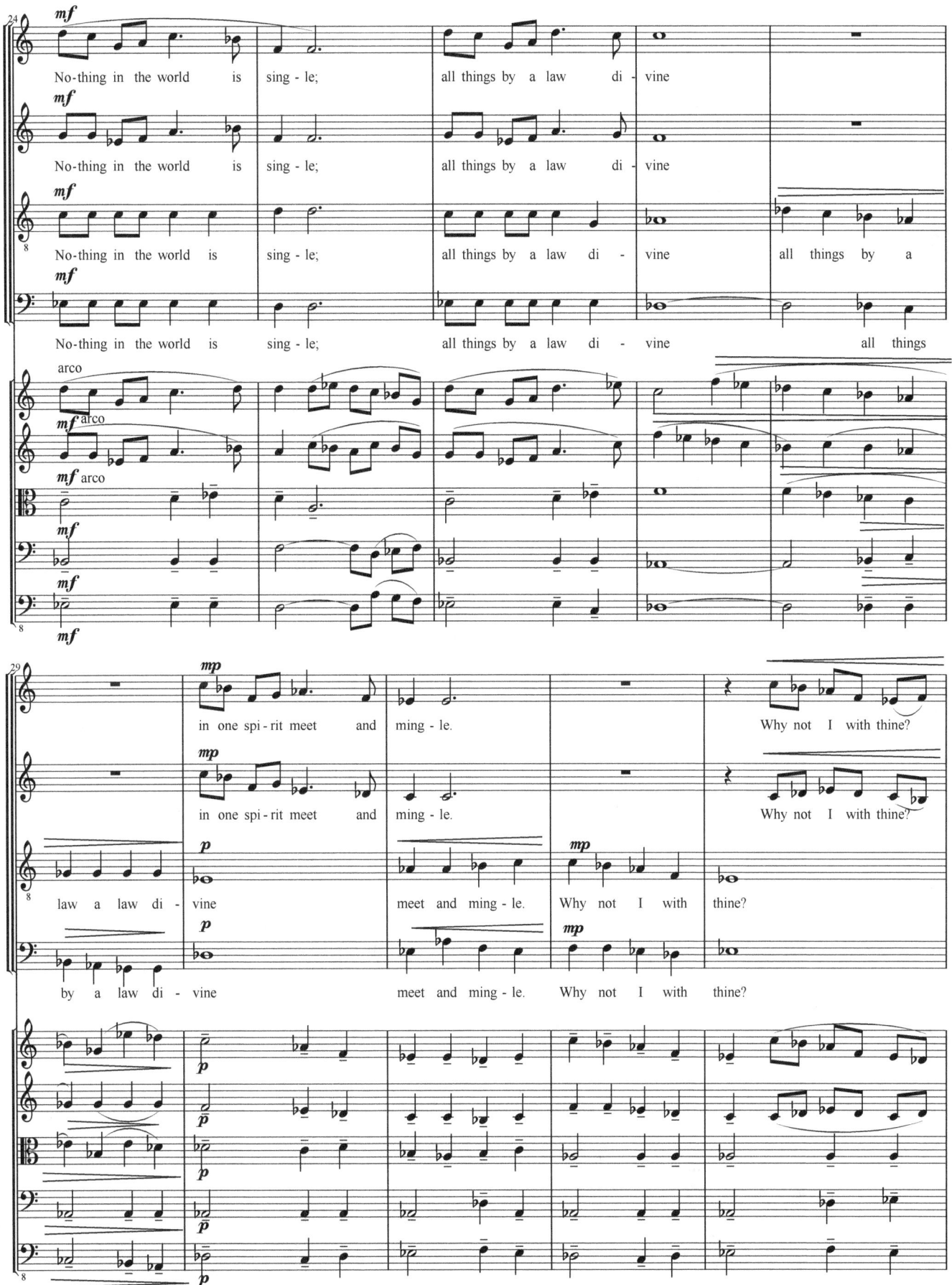

No-thing in the world is sing - le; all things by a law di - vine

No-thing in the world is sing - le; all things by a law di - vine

No-thing in the world is sing - le; all things by a law di - vine all things by a

No-thing in the world is sing - le; all things by a law di - vine all things

in one spi - rit meet and ming - le. Why not I with thine?

in one spi - rit meet and ming - le. Why not I with thine?

law a law di - vine meet and ming - le. Why not I with thine?

by a law di - vine meet and ming - le. Why not I with thine?

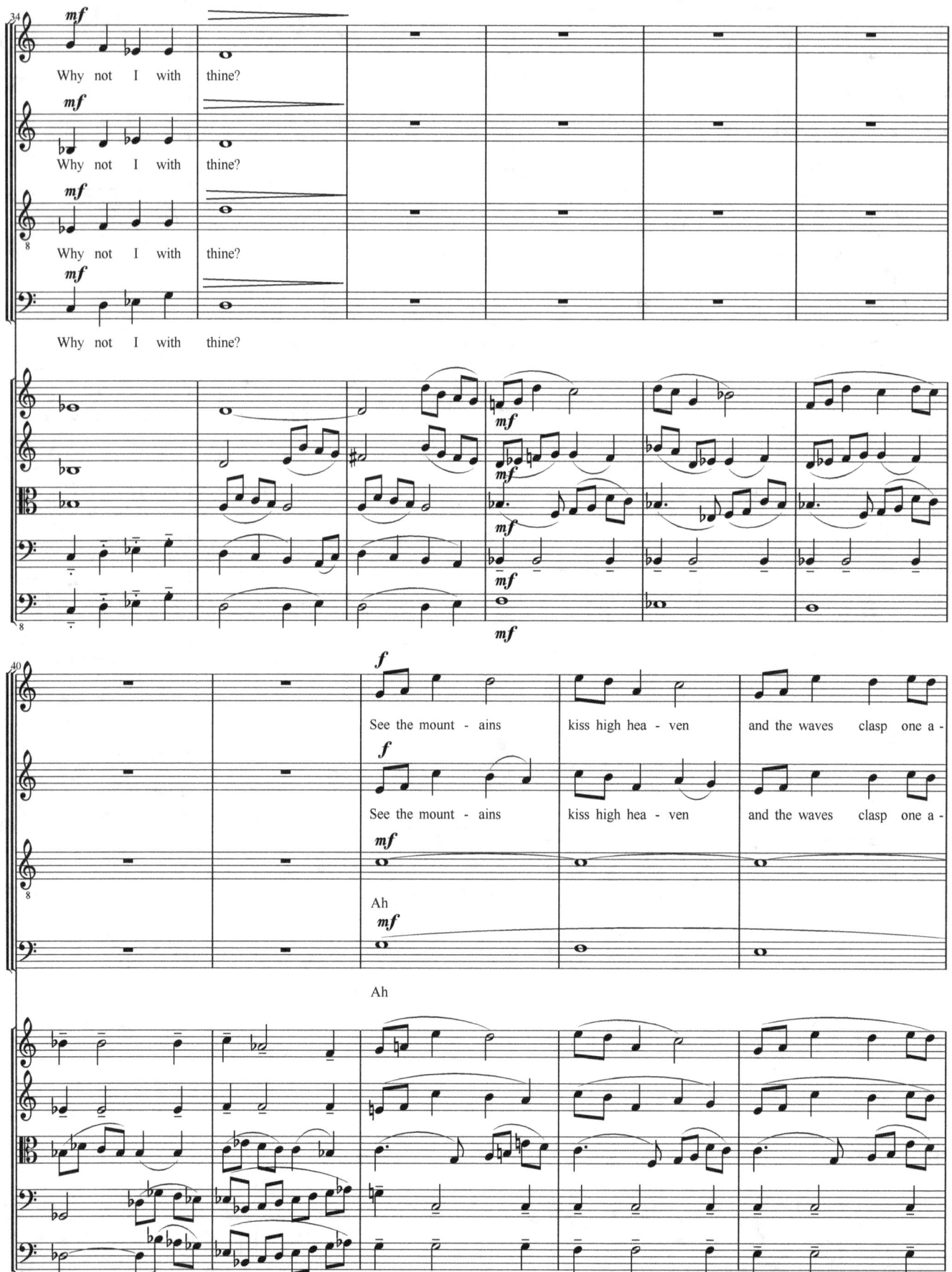

54

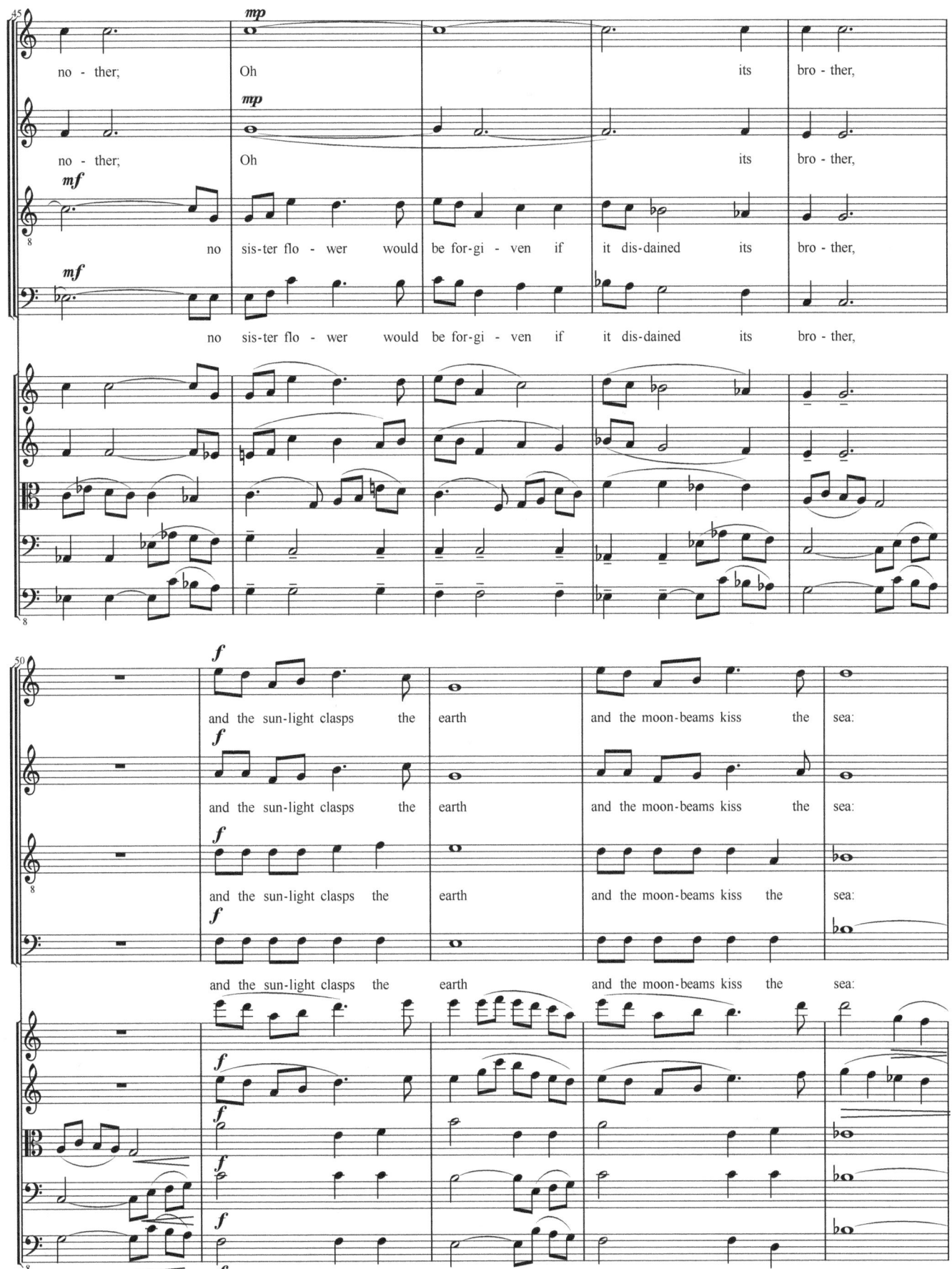

55

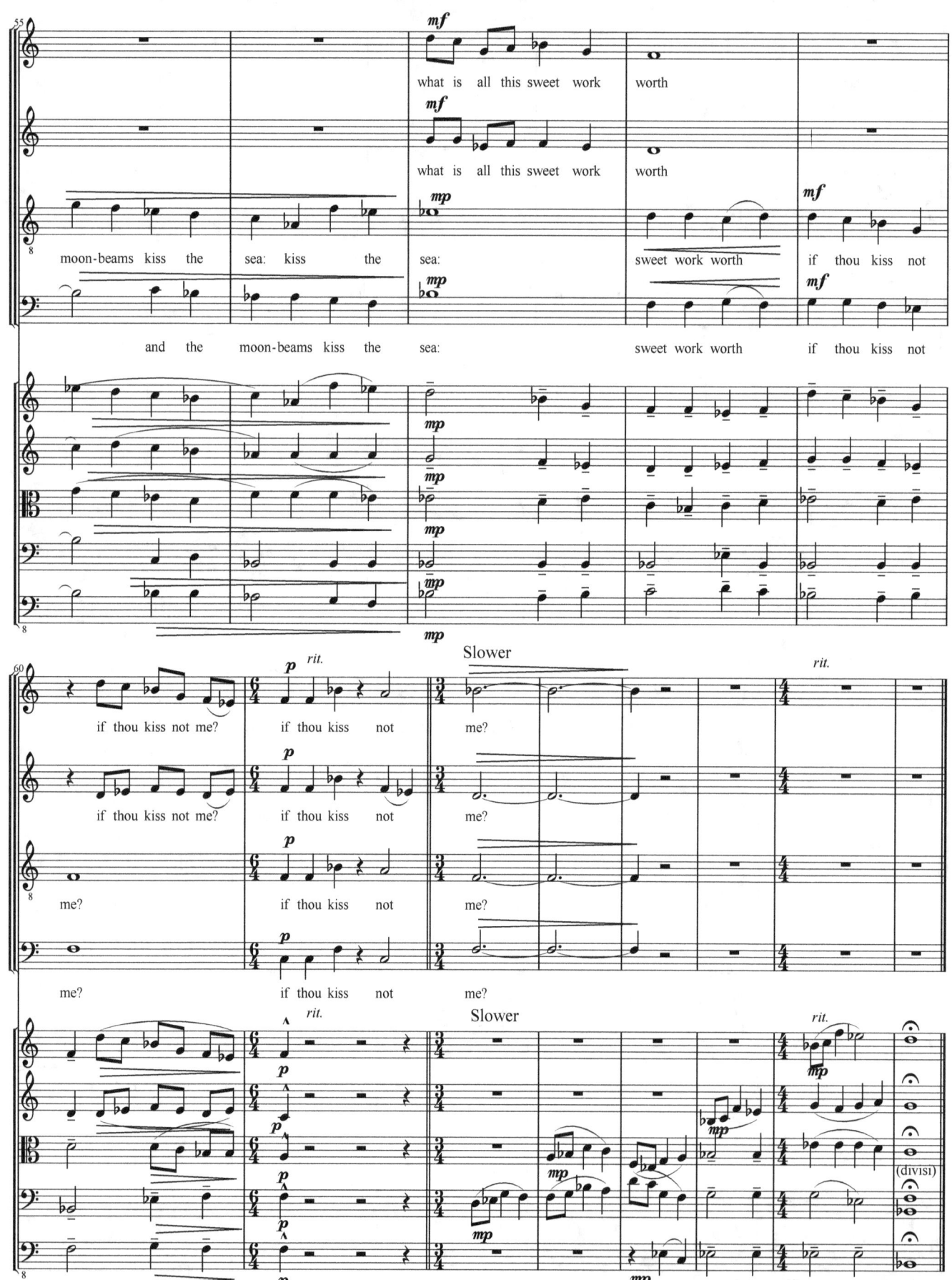

what is all this sweet work worth

what is all this sweet work worth

moon-beams kiss the sea: kiss the sea:

and the moon-beams kiss the sea:

sweet work worth if thou kiss not

sweet work worth if thou kiss not

Slower

if thou kiss not me? if thou kiss not me?

if thou kiss not me? if thou kiss not me?

me? if thou kiss not me?

me? if thou kiss not me?

Slower

(divisi)

56

adapted from
John Greenleaf Whittier

Sound Over All Waters

Ken Langer

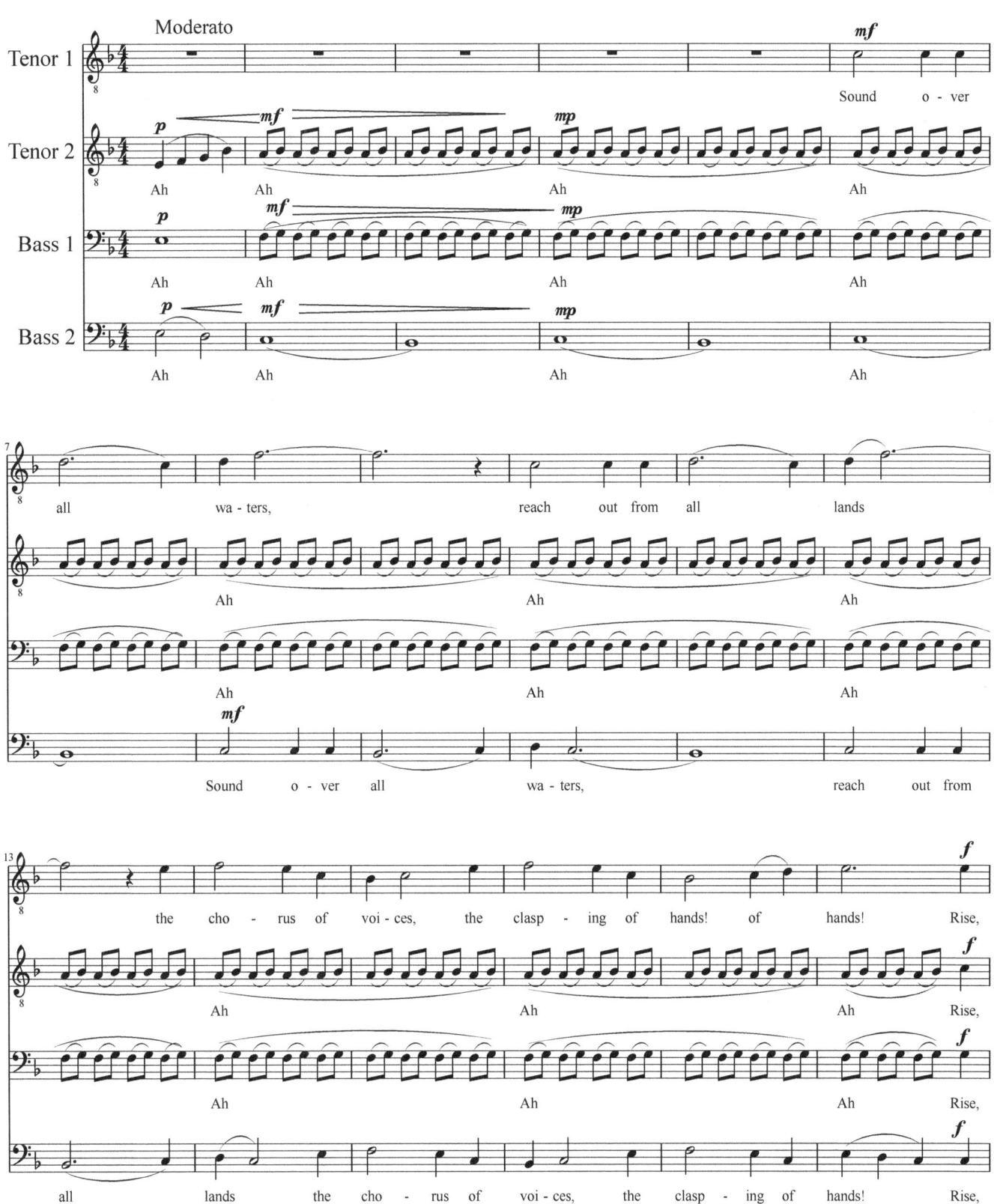

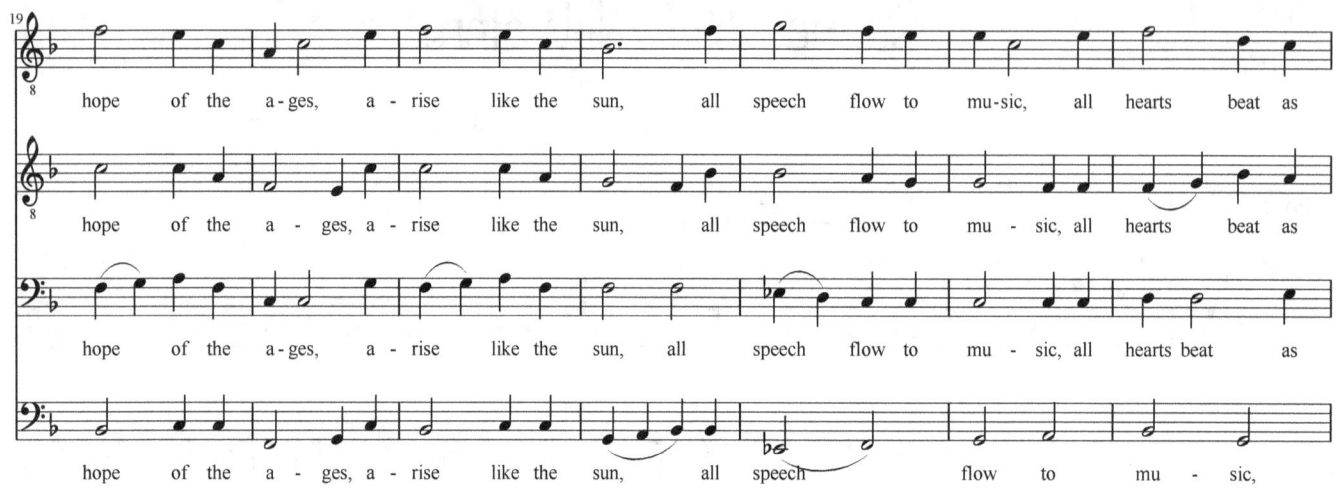

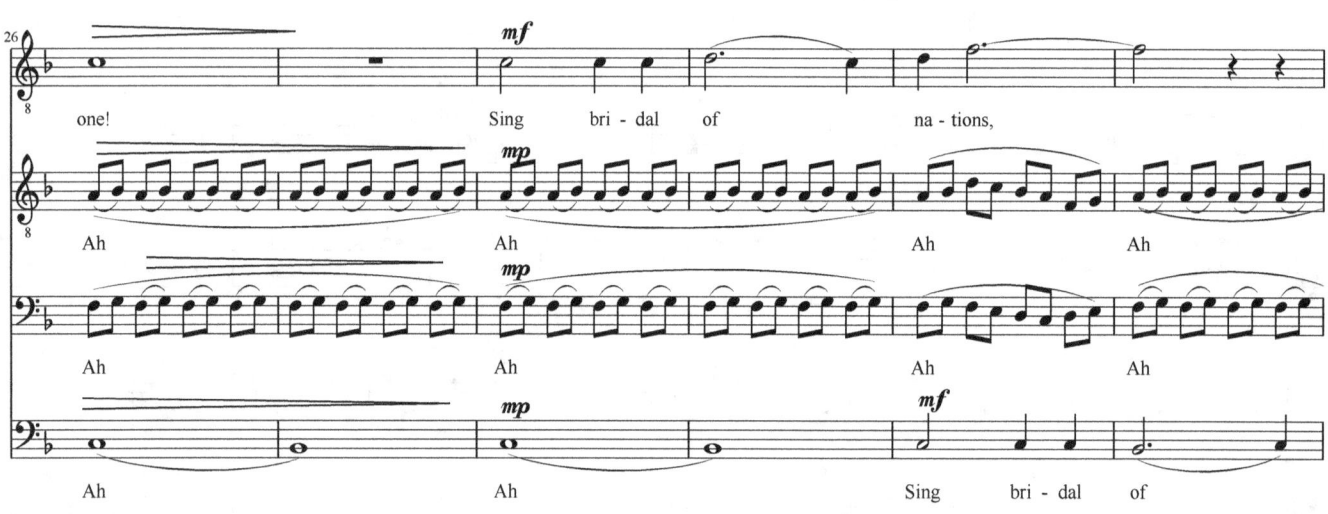

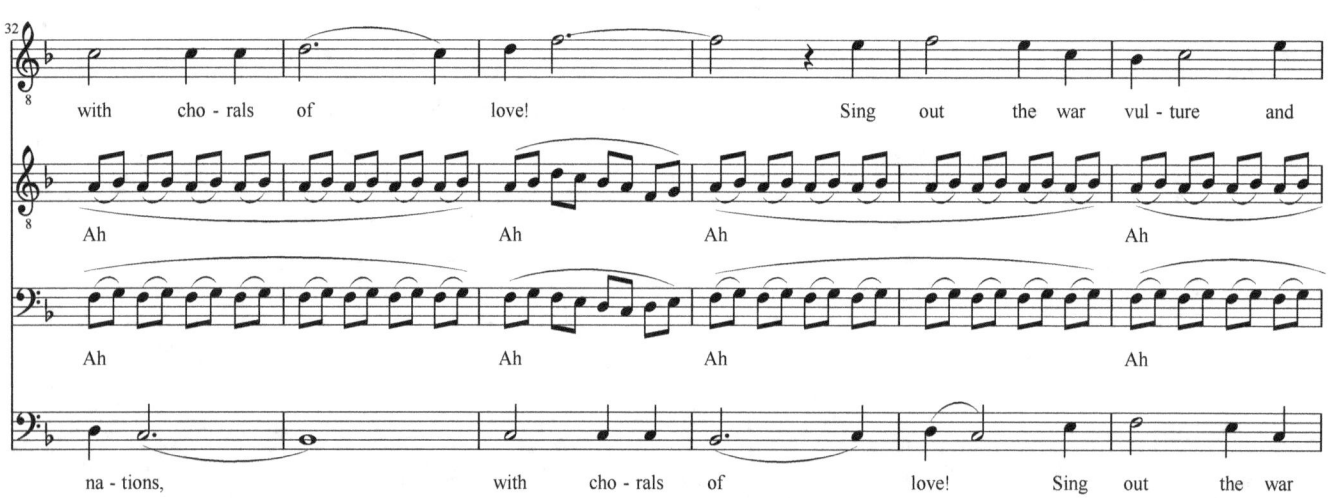

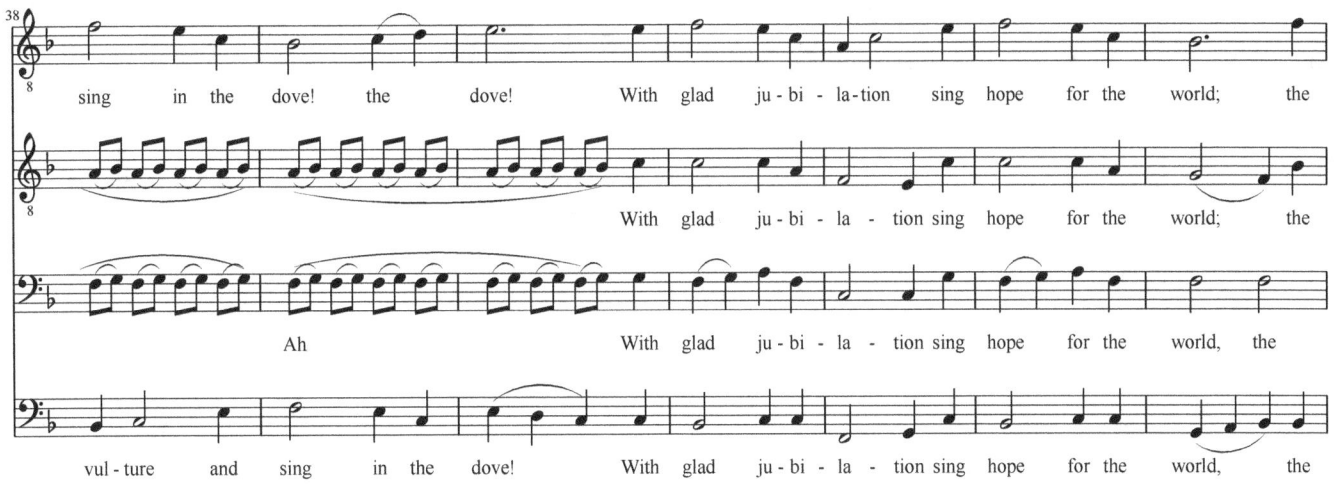

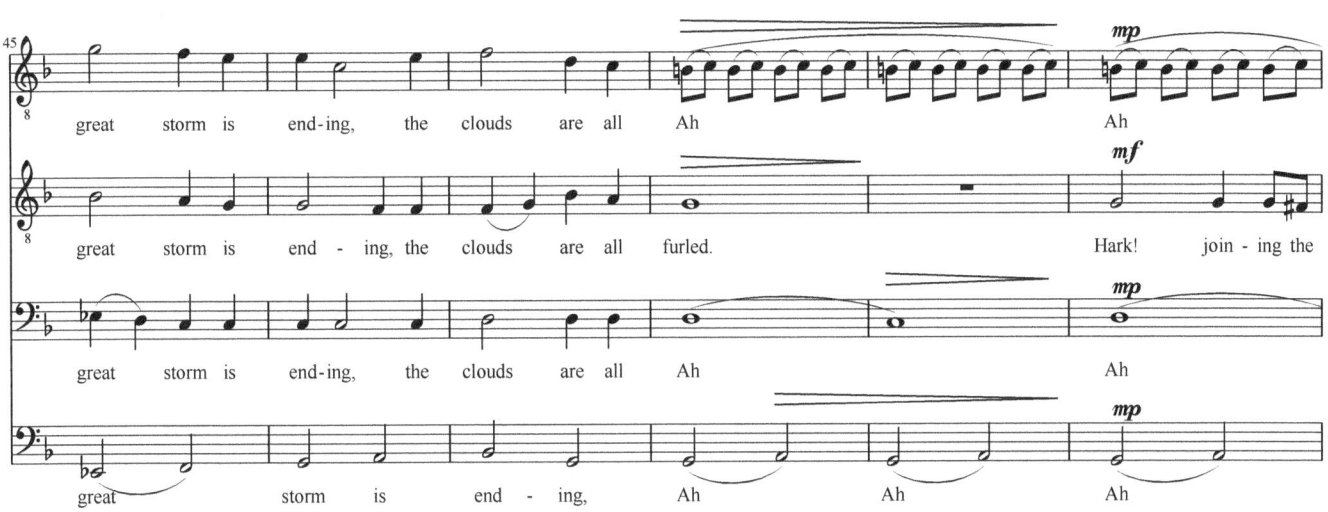

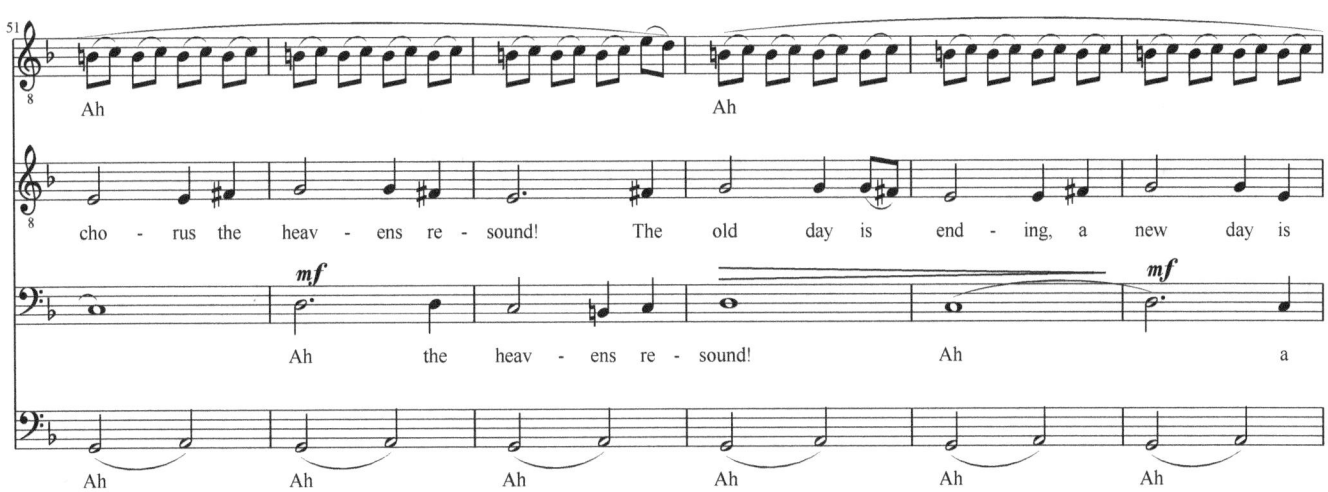

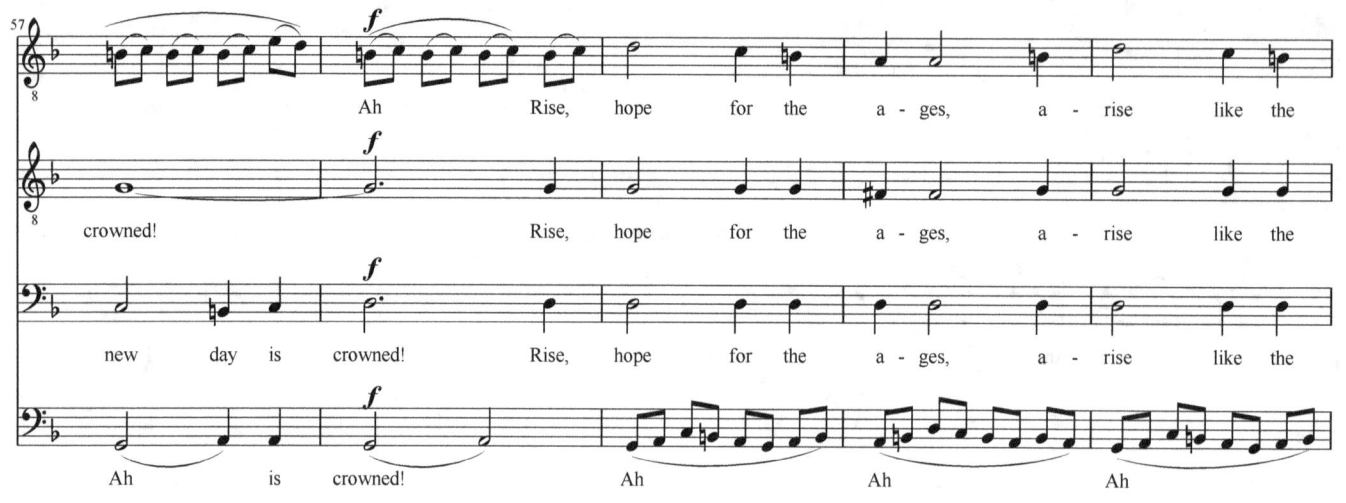

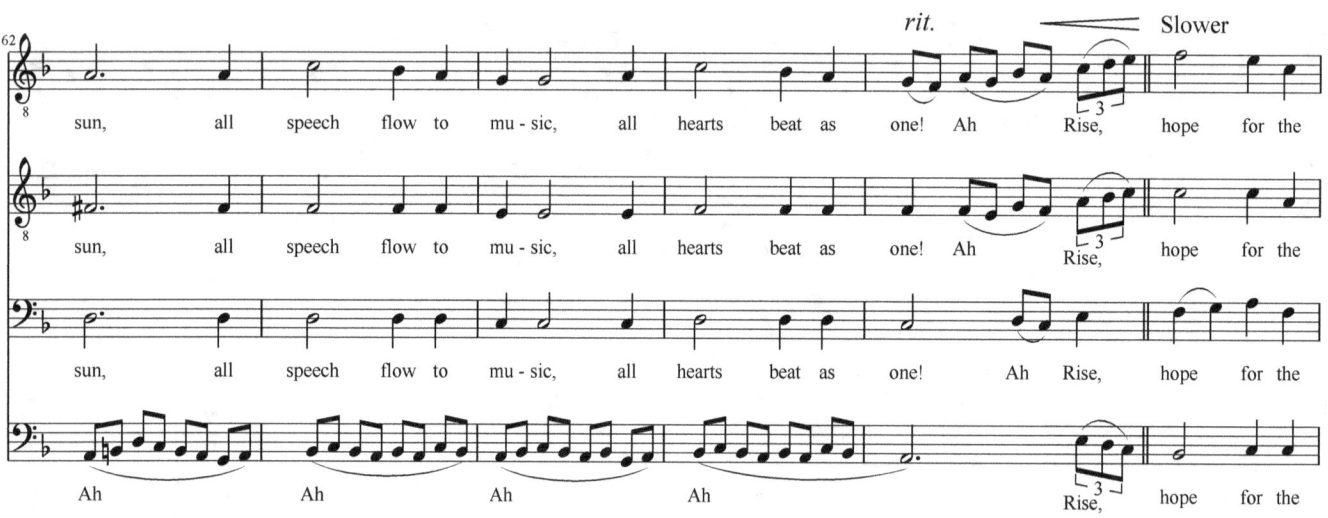

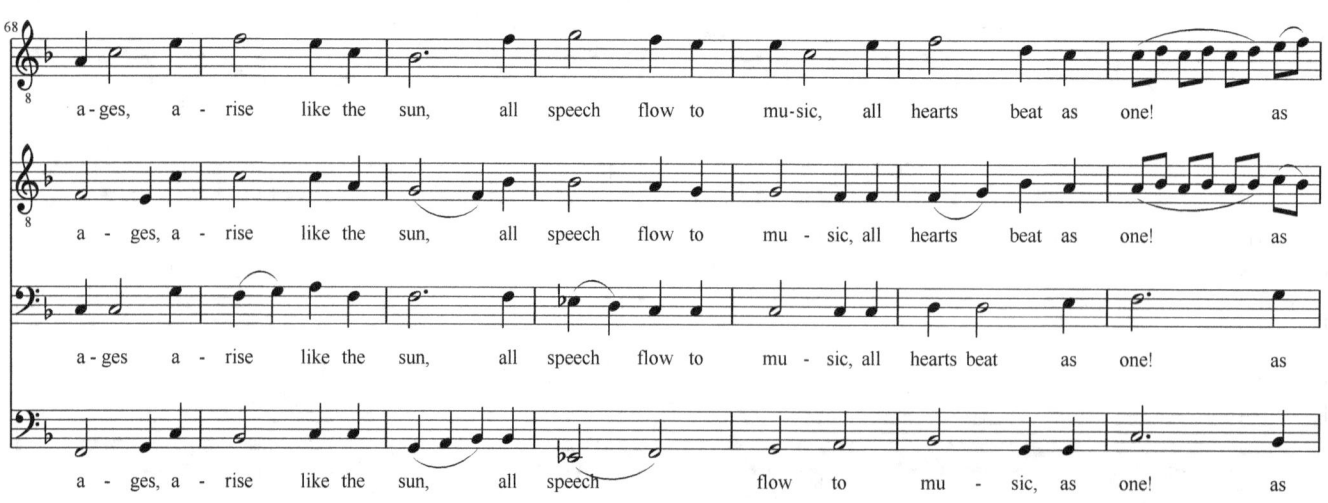

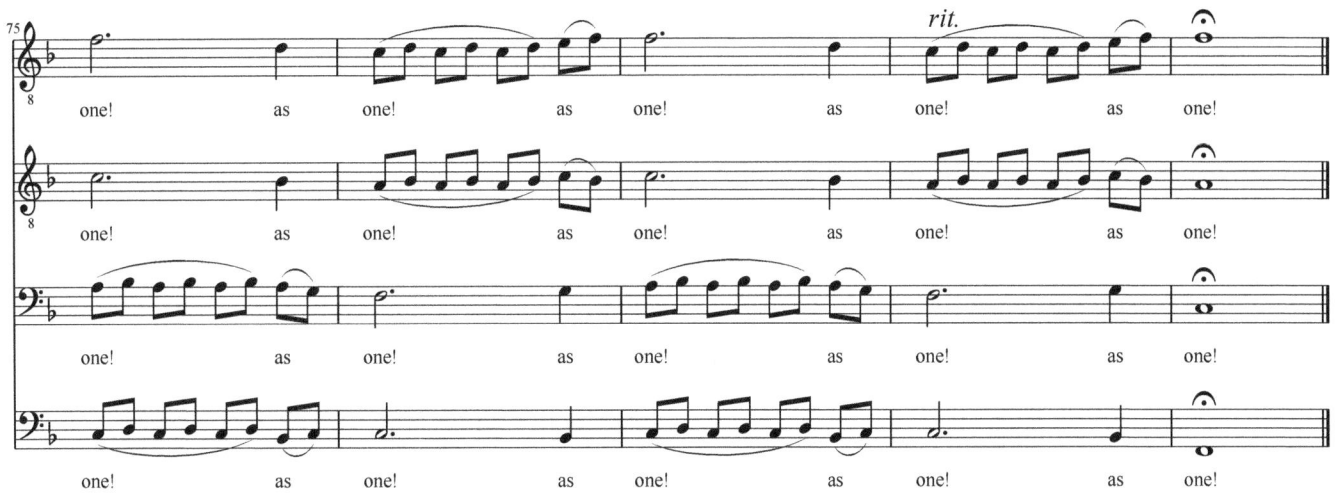

one!   as   one!   as   one!   as   one!   as   one!

one!   as   one!   as   one!   as   one!   as   one!

one!   as   one!   as   one!   as   one!   as   one!

one!   as   one!   as   one!   as   one!   as   one!

The Star Spangled Banner

arr. Ken Langer

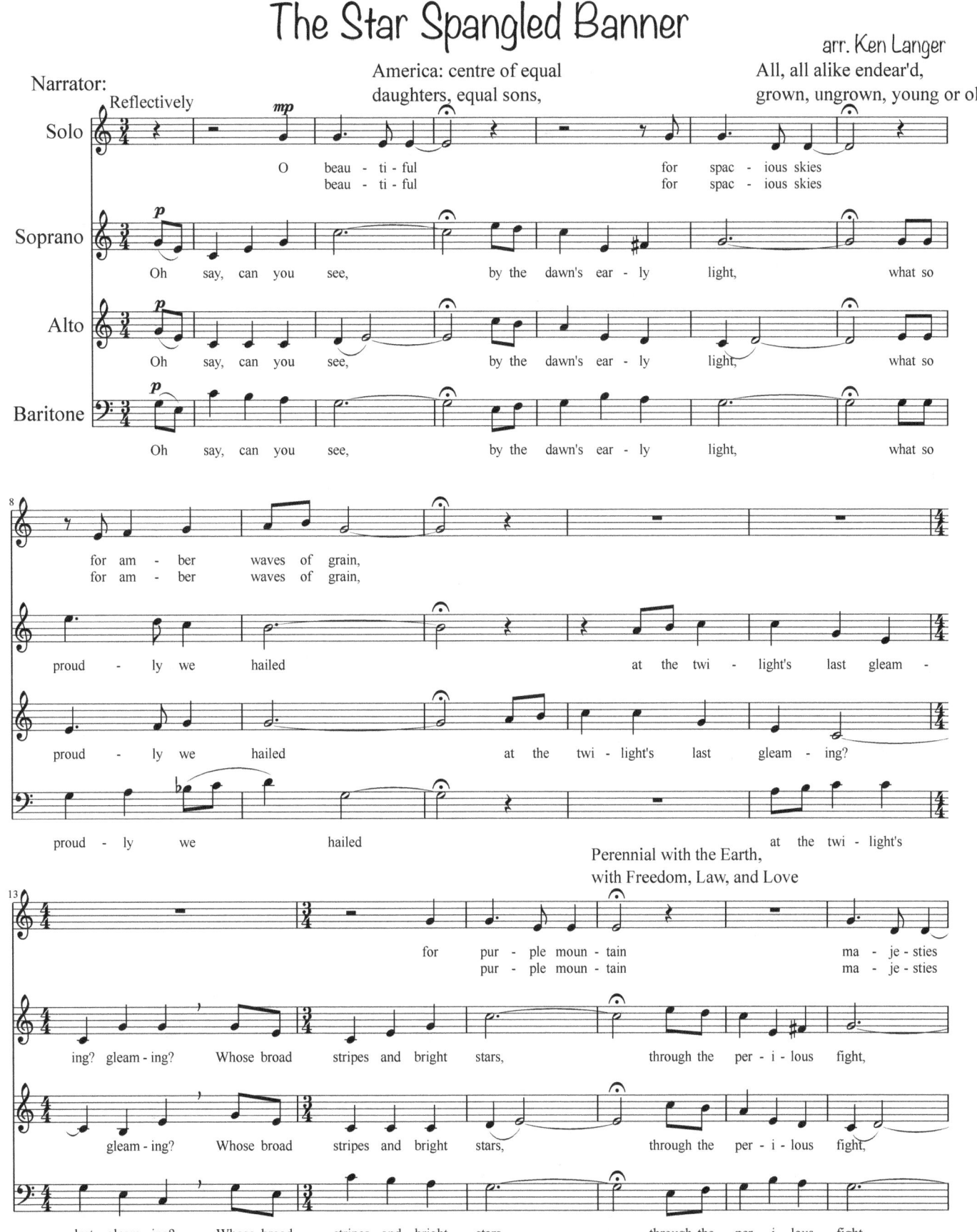

63

A grand, sane, towering, seated Mother   Chair'd in the adamant of time.

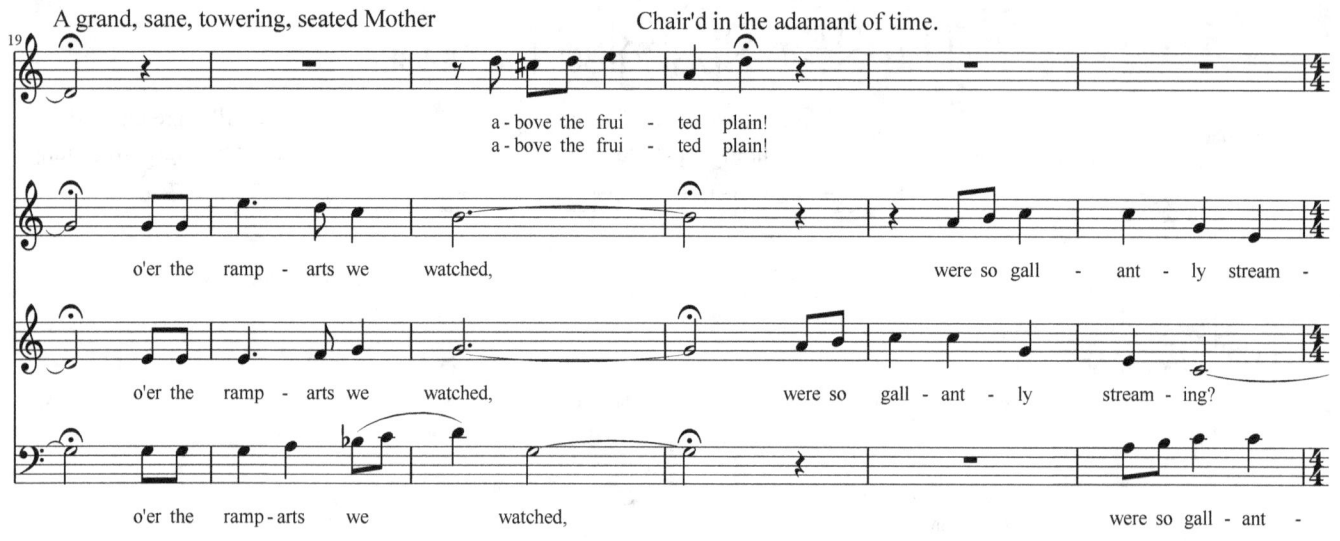

a - bove the frui - ted plain!
a - bove the frui - ted plain!

o'er the ramp - arts we watched,   were so gall - ant - ly stream -

o'er the ramp - arts we watched,   were so gall - ant - ly stream - ing?

o'er the ramp - arts we watched,   were so gall - ant -

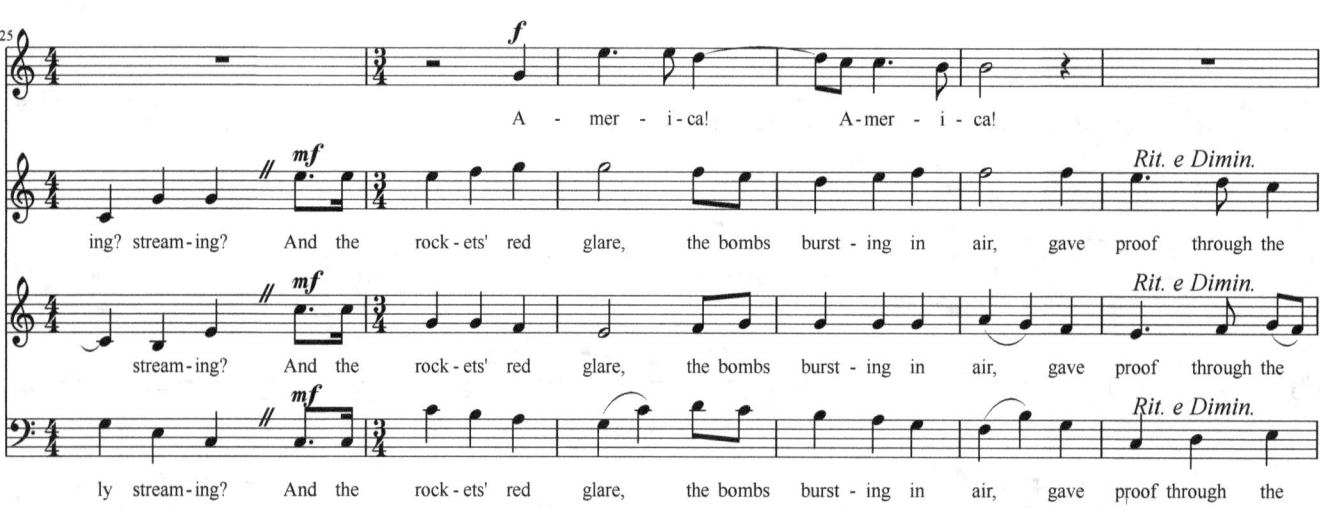

f

A - mer - i - ca!   A - mer - i - ca!

mf   *Rit. e Dimin.*
ing? stream - ing? And the rock - ets' red glare, the bombs burst - ing in air, gave proof through the

mf   *Rit. e Dimin.*
stream - ing? And the rock - ets' red glare, the bombs burst - ing in air, gave proof through the

mf   *Rit. e Dimin.*
ly stream - ing? And the rock - ets' red glare, the bombs burst - ing in air, gave proof through the

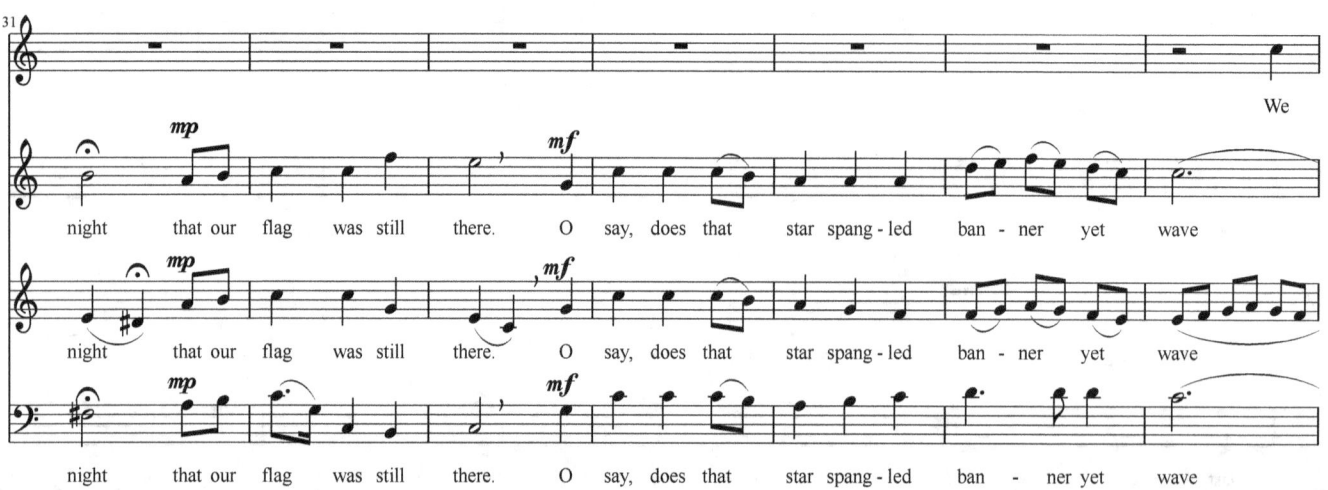

We

mp   *mf*
night that our flag was still there. O say, does that star spang - led ban - ner yet wave

mp   *mf*
night that our flag was still there. O say, does that star spang - led ban - ner yet wave

mp   *mf*
night that our flag was still there. O say, does that star spang - led ban - ner yet wave

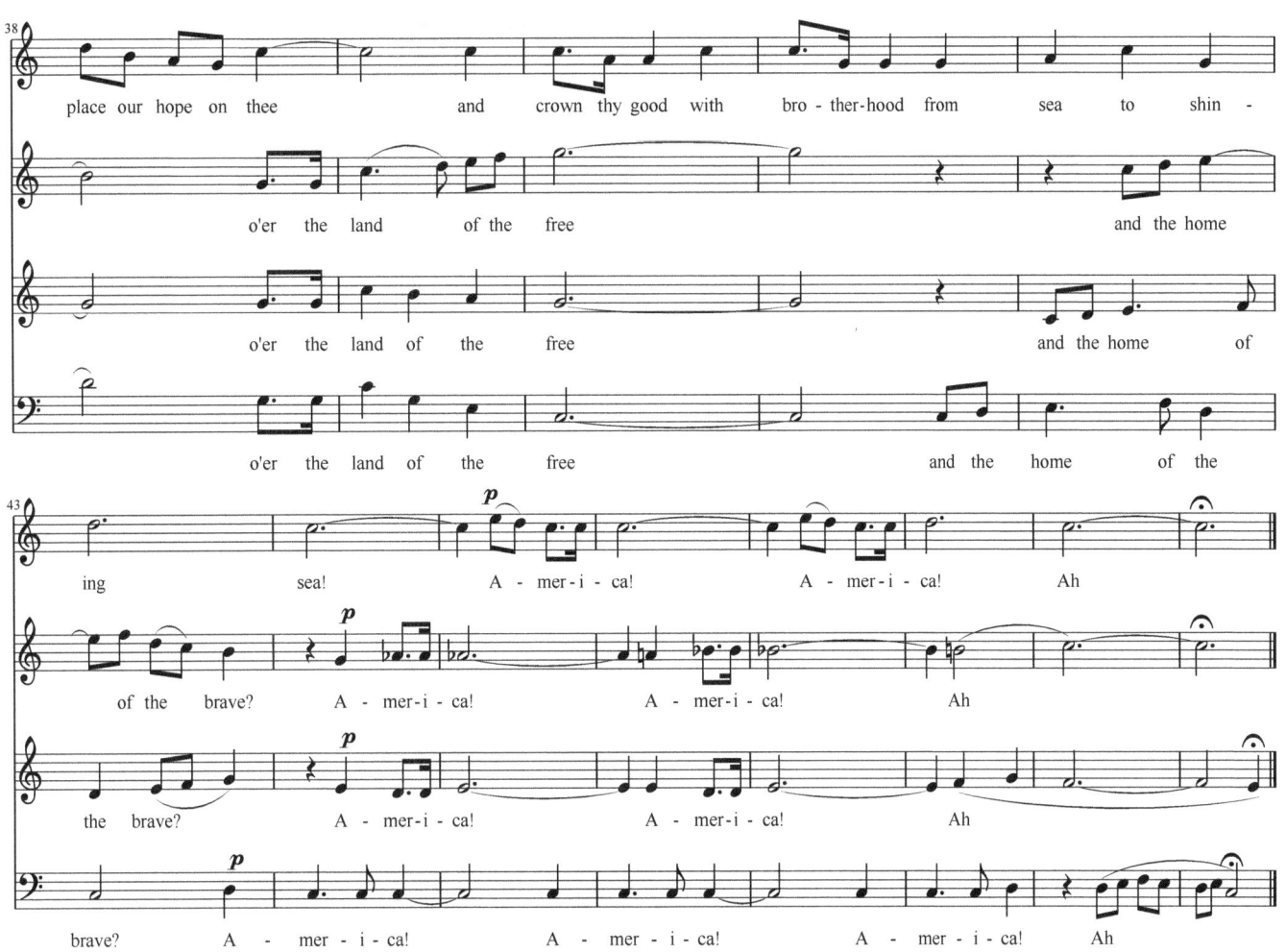

"The Star Spangled Banner" was written by Francis Scott Key
"America The Beautiful" was written by Katherine Lee Bates
The poem "America" was written by Walt Whitman

There's A Way

Ken Langer

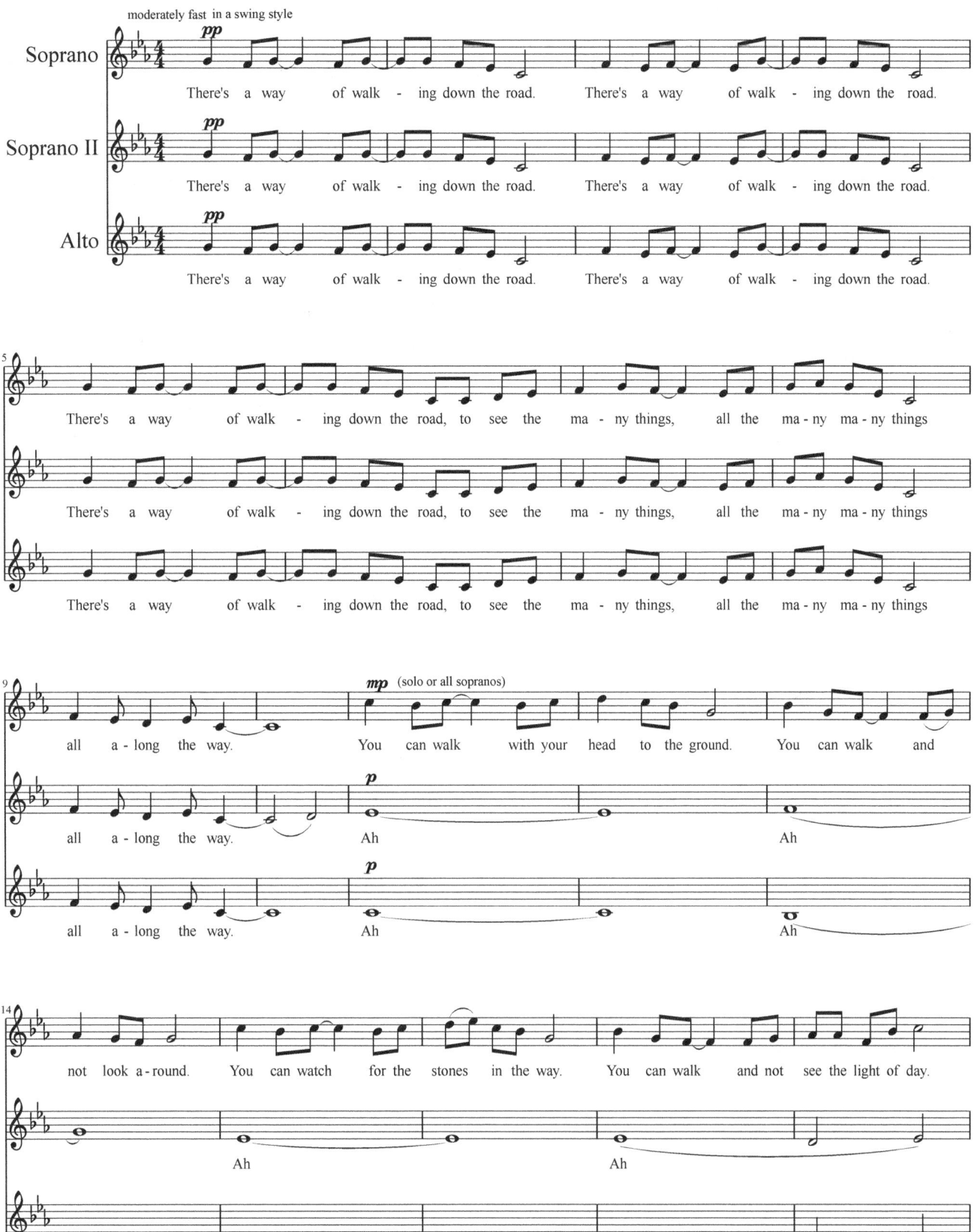

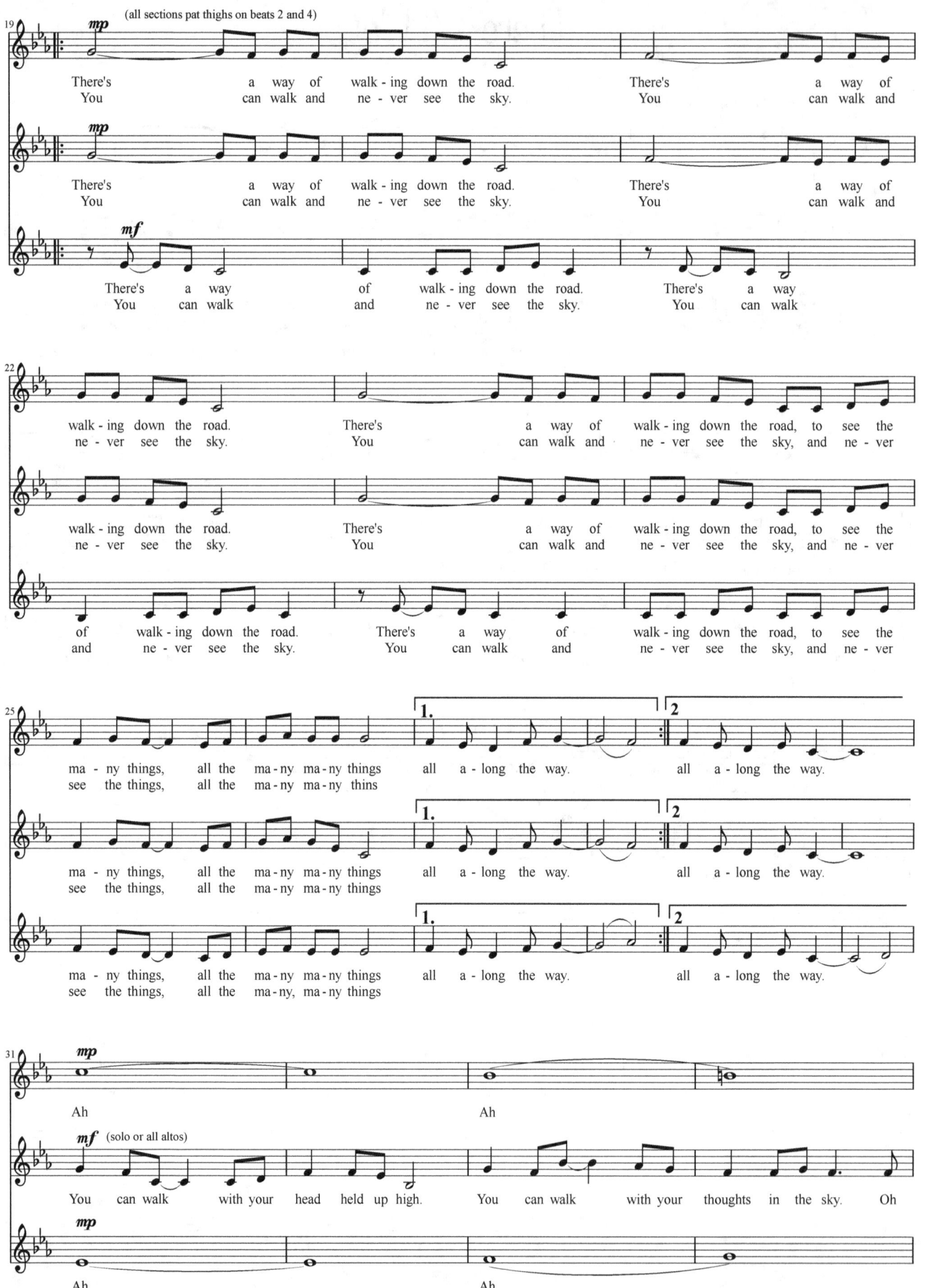

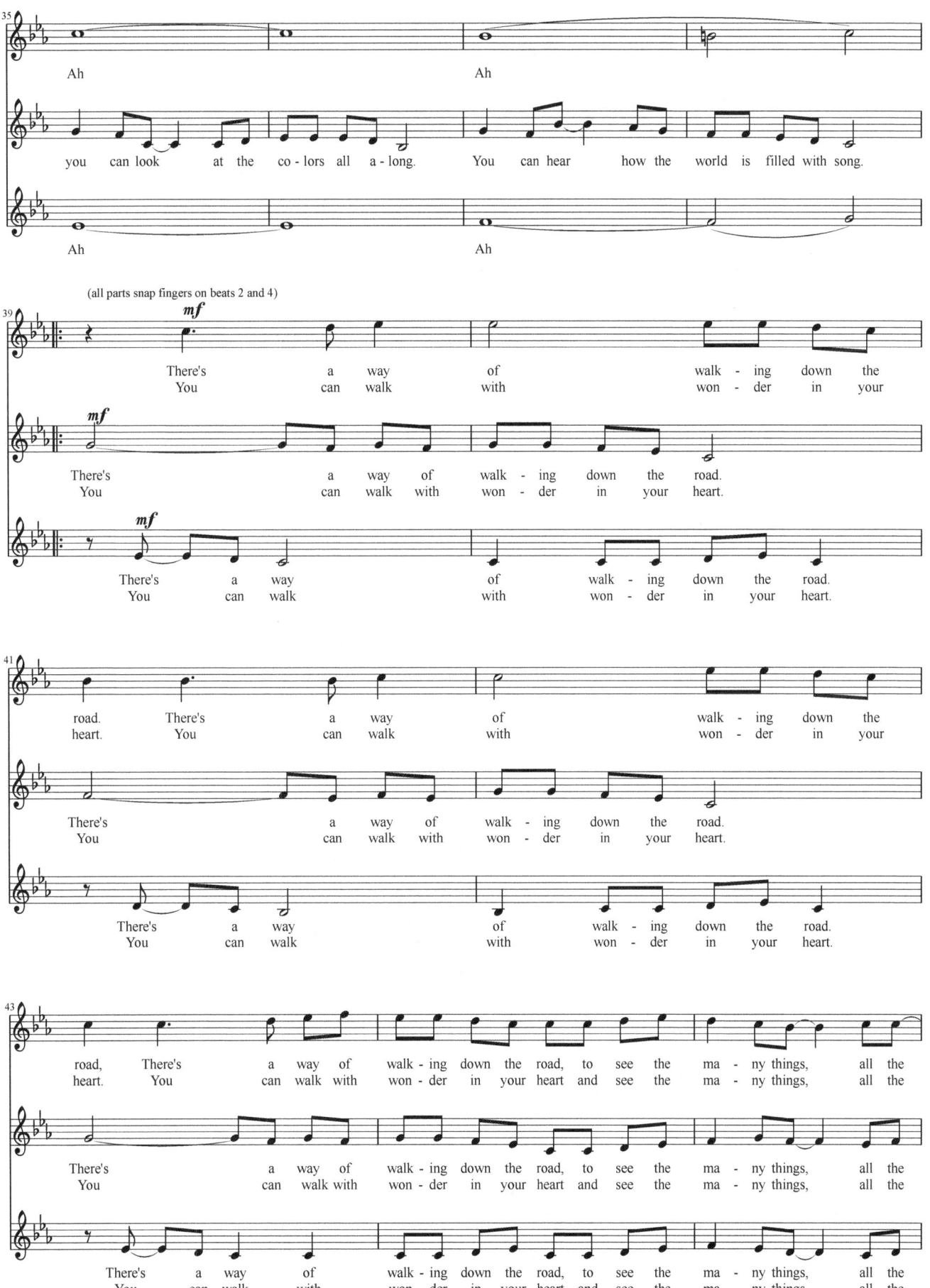

(all parts snap fingers on beats 2 and 4)

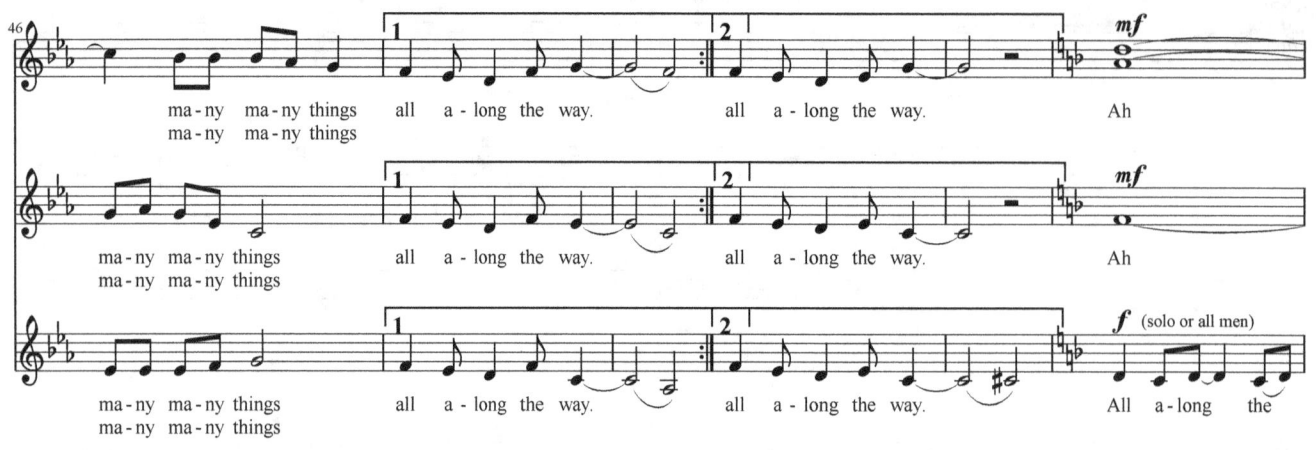

many many things all a-long the way. all a-long the way. Ah
many many things

many many things all a-long the way. all a-long the way. Ah
many many things

many many things all a-long the way. all a-long the way. All a-long the
many many things

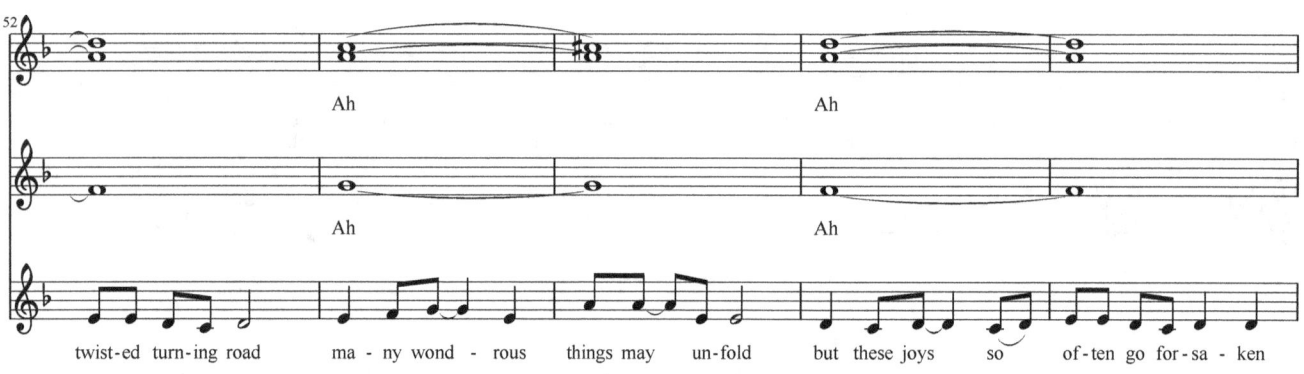

Ah Ah

Ah Ah

twist-ed turn-ing road ma-ny wond-rous things may un-fold but these joys so of-ten go for-sa-ken

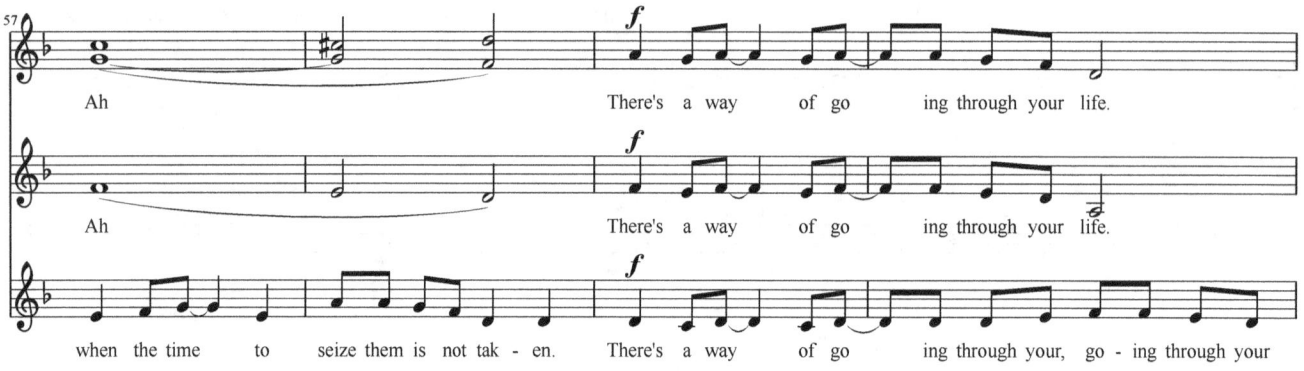

Ah There's a way of go ing through your life.

Ah There's a way of go ing through your life.

when the time to seize them is not tak-en. There's a way of go ing through your, go-ing through your

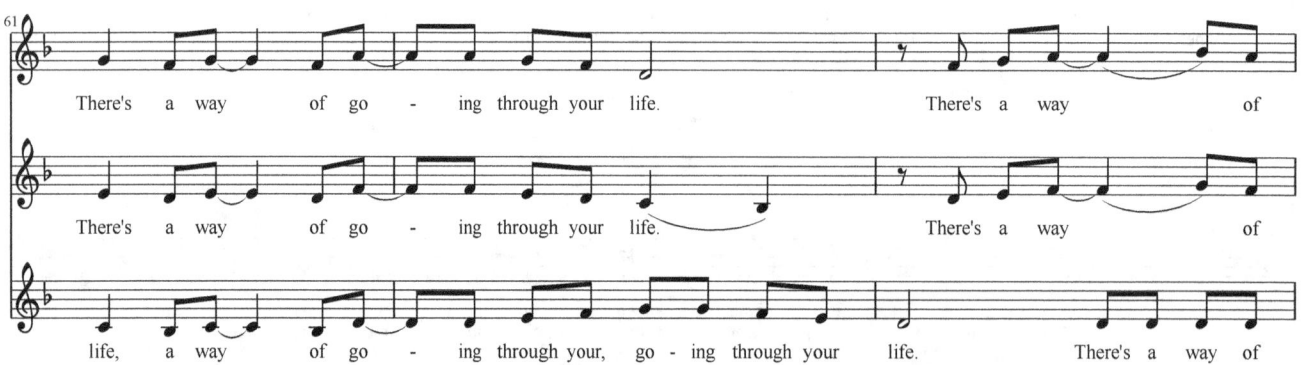

There's a way of go - ing through your life. There's a way of

There's a way of go - ing through your life. There's a way of

life, a way of go - ing through your, go-ing through your life. There's a way of

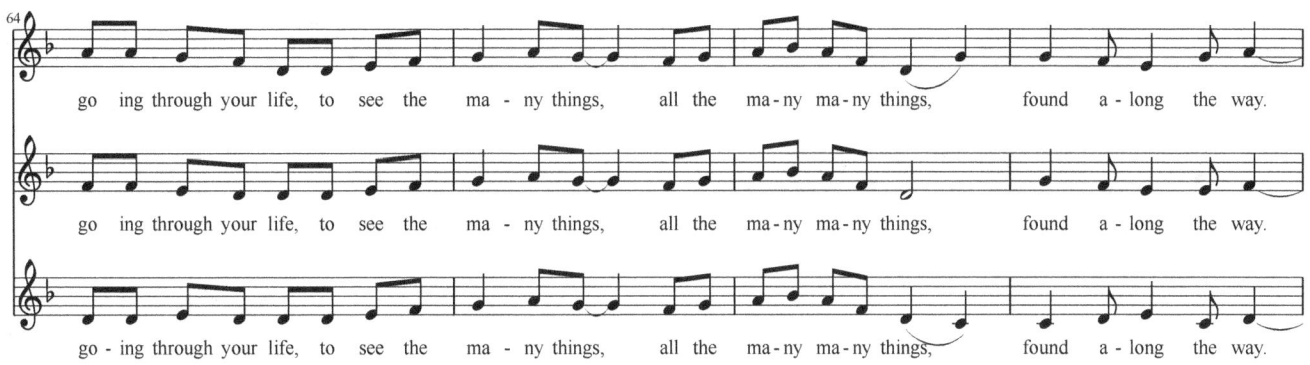

go - ing through your life, to see the ma - ny things, all the ma - ny ma - ny things, found a - long the way.

go - ing through your life, to see the ma - ny things, all the ma - ny ma - ny things, found a - long the way.

go - ing through your life, to see the ma - ny things, all the ma - ny ma - ny things, found a - long the way.

(all parts clap hands on beats 2 and 4)

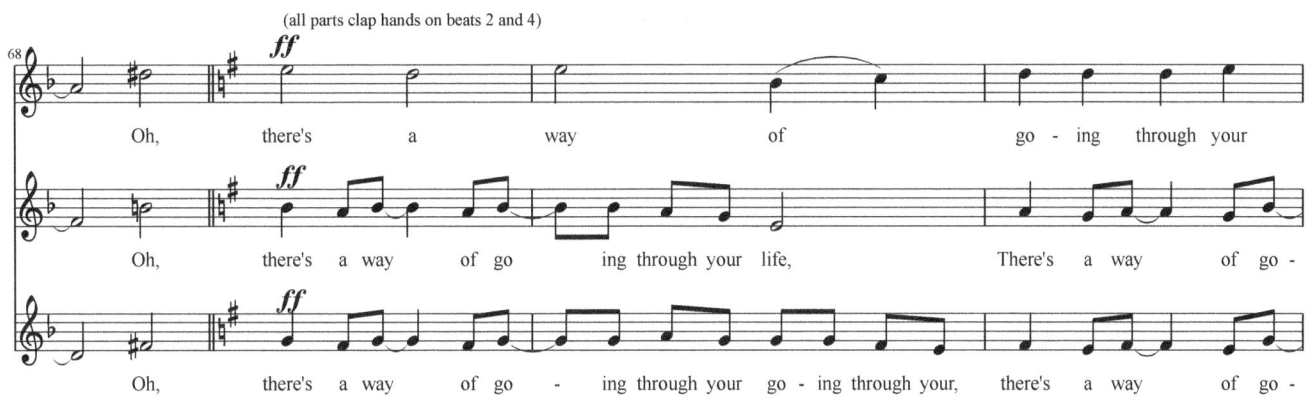

ff

Oh, there's a way of go - ing through your

ff

Oh, there's a way of go ing through your life, There's a way of go -

ff

Oh, there's a way of go - ing through your go - ing through your, there's a way of go -

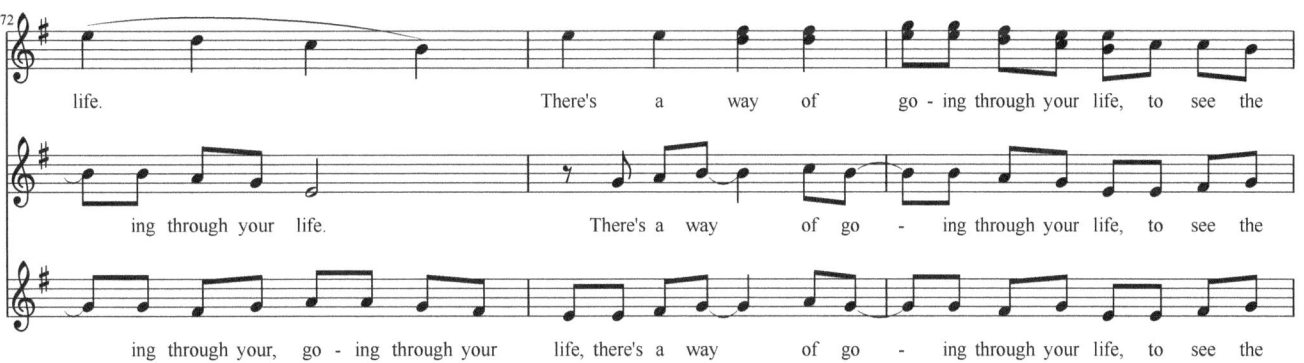

life. There's a way of go - ing through your life, to see the

ing through your life. There's a way of go - ing through your life, to see the

ing through your, go - ing through your life, there's a way of go - ing through your life, to see the

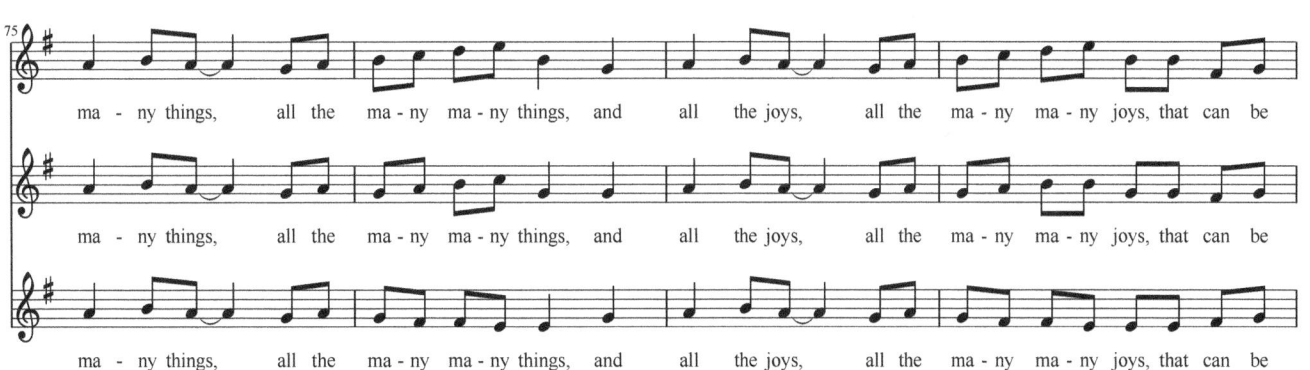

ma - ny things, all the ma - ny ma - ny things, and all the joys, all the ma - ny ma - ny joys, that can be

ma - ny things, all the ma - ny ma - ny things, and all the joys, all the ma - ny ma - ny joys, that can be

ma - ny things, all the ma - ny ma - ny things, and all the joys, all the ma - ny ma - ny joys, that can be

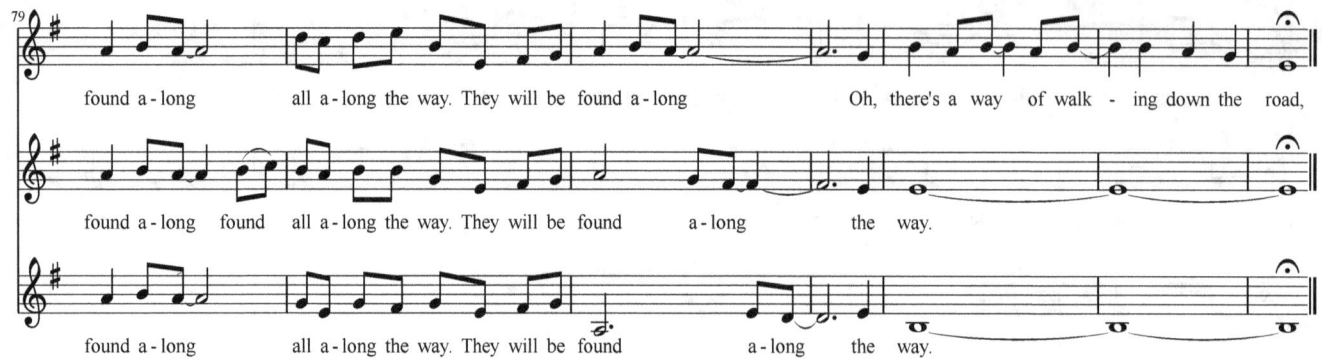

found a - long   all a - long the way. They will be found a - long   Oh, there's a way   of walk - ing down the road,

found a - long   found   all a - long the way. They will be found   a - long   the way.

found a - long   all a - long the way. They will be found   a - long   the way.

Three Prayers
I Am That Great and Fiery Force

Hildegard of Bingen

Ken Langer

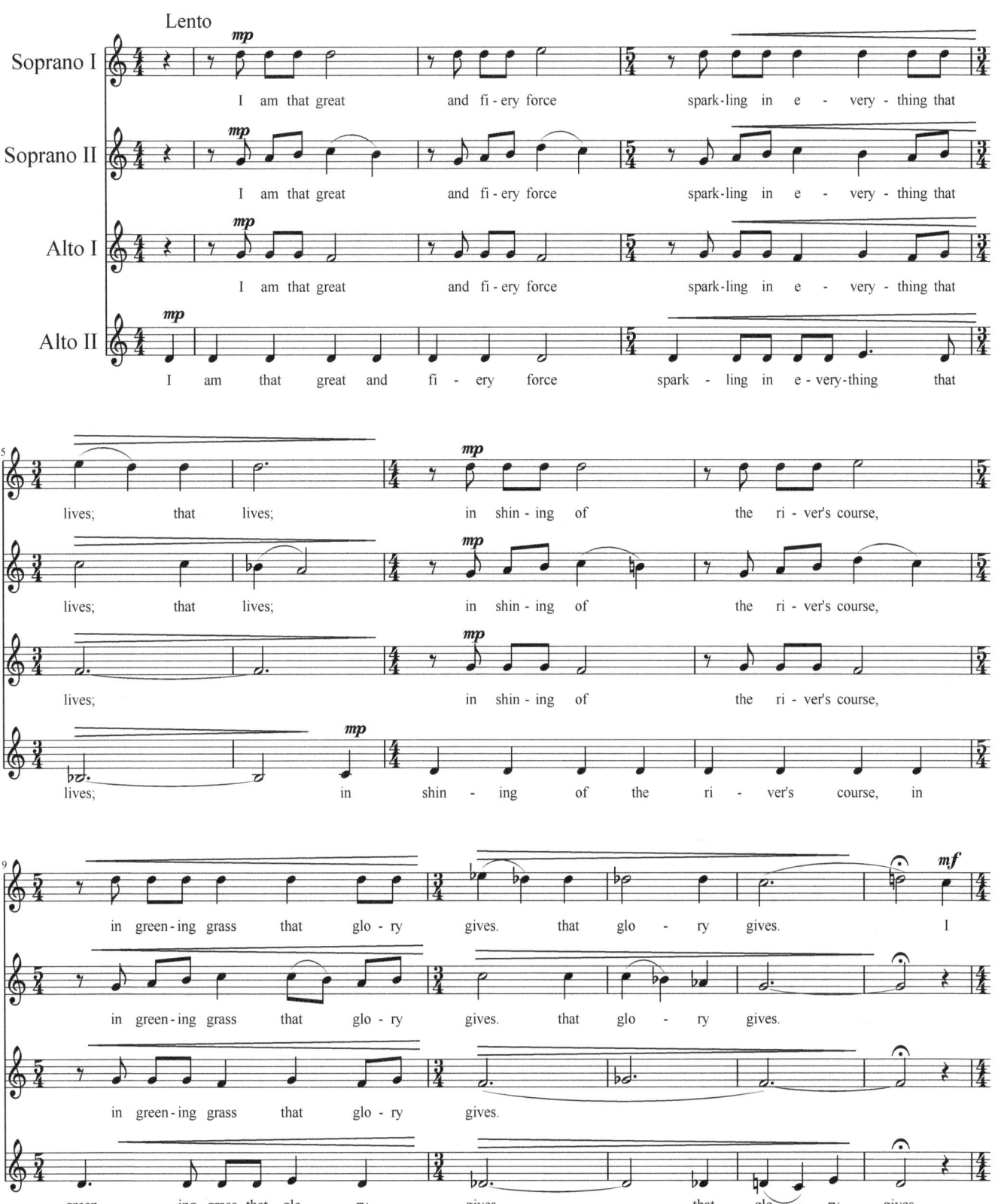

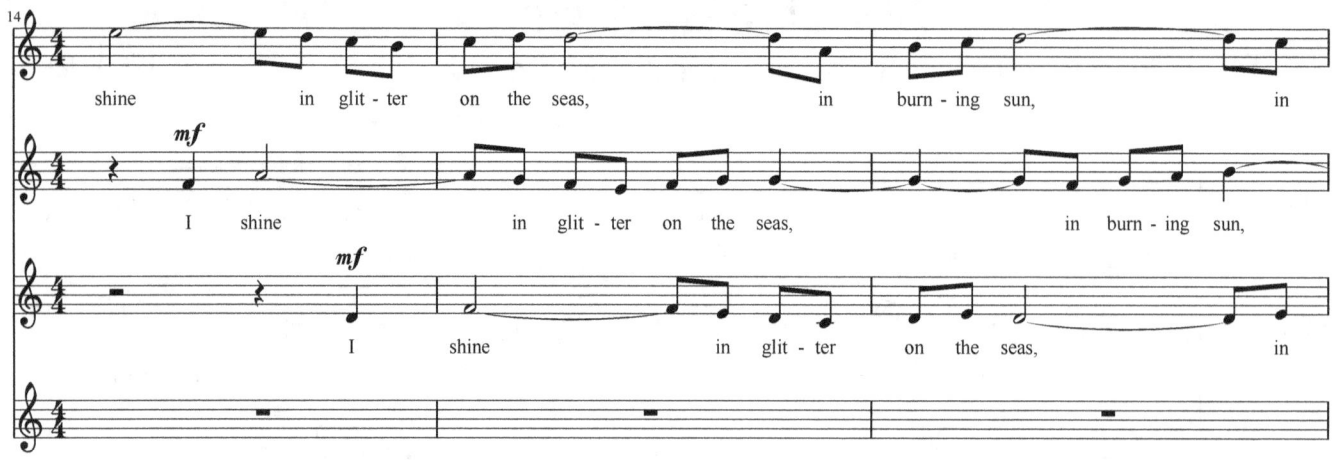

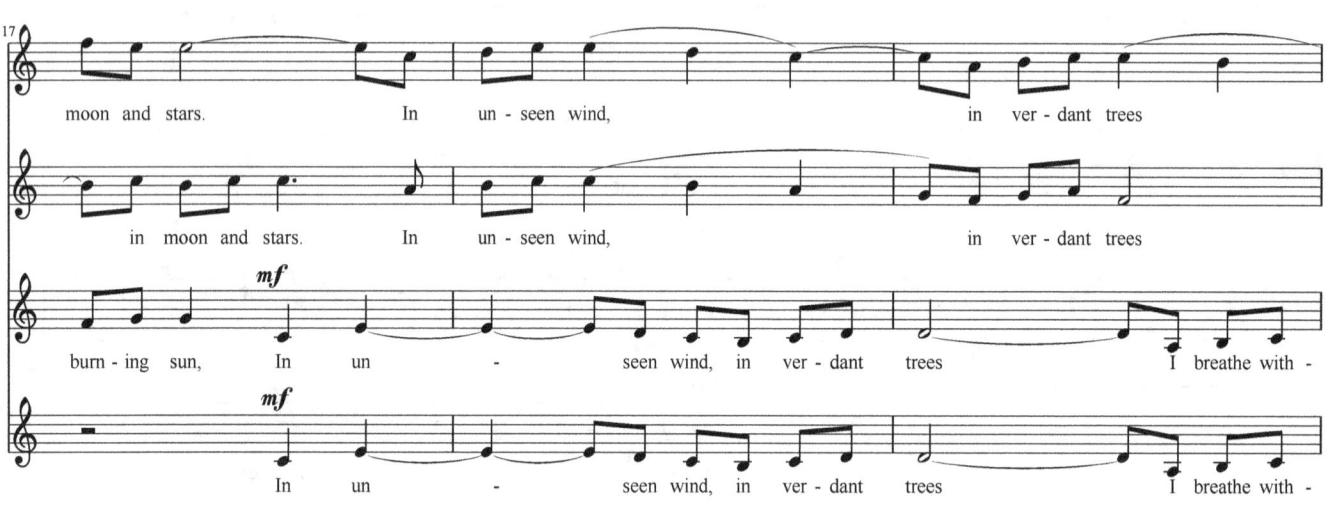

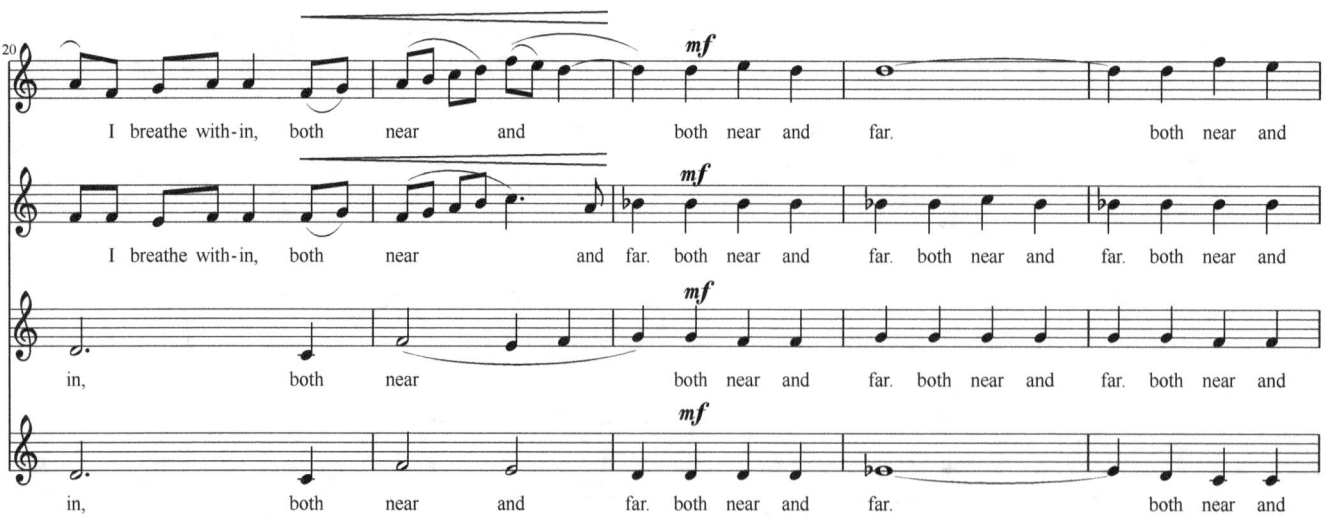

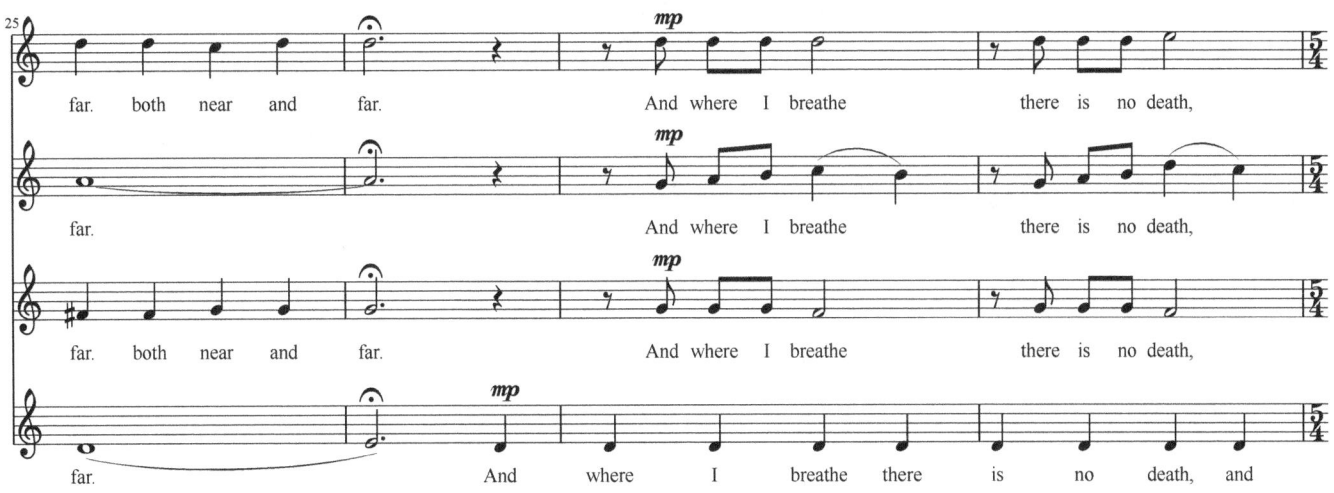

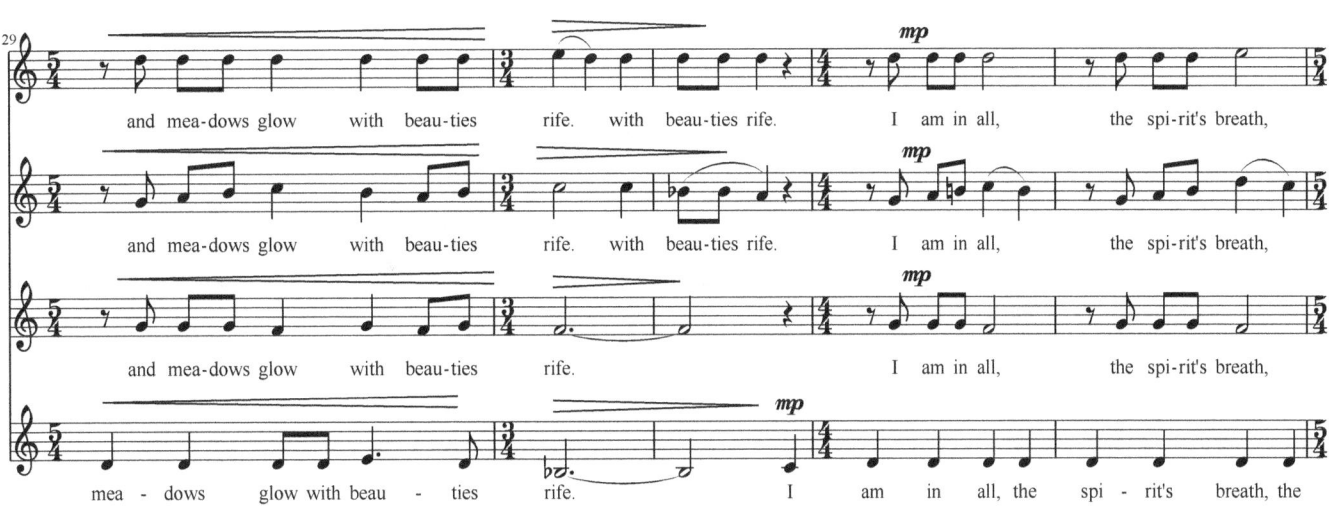

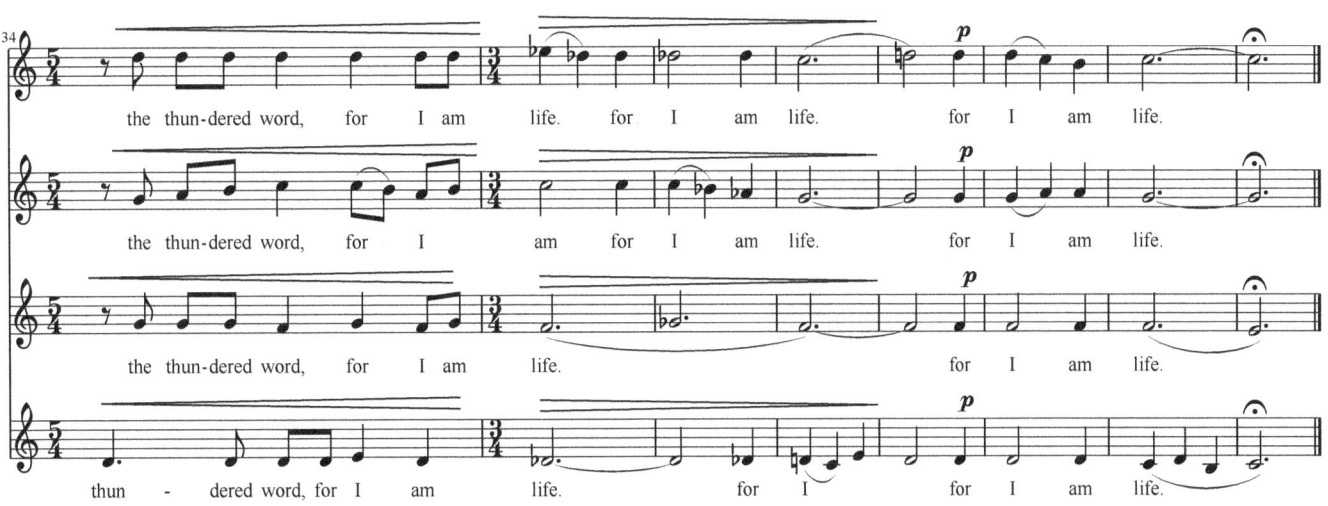

Three Prayers
Holy Spirit

Hildegard of Bingen

Ken Langer

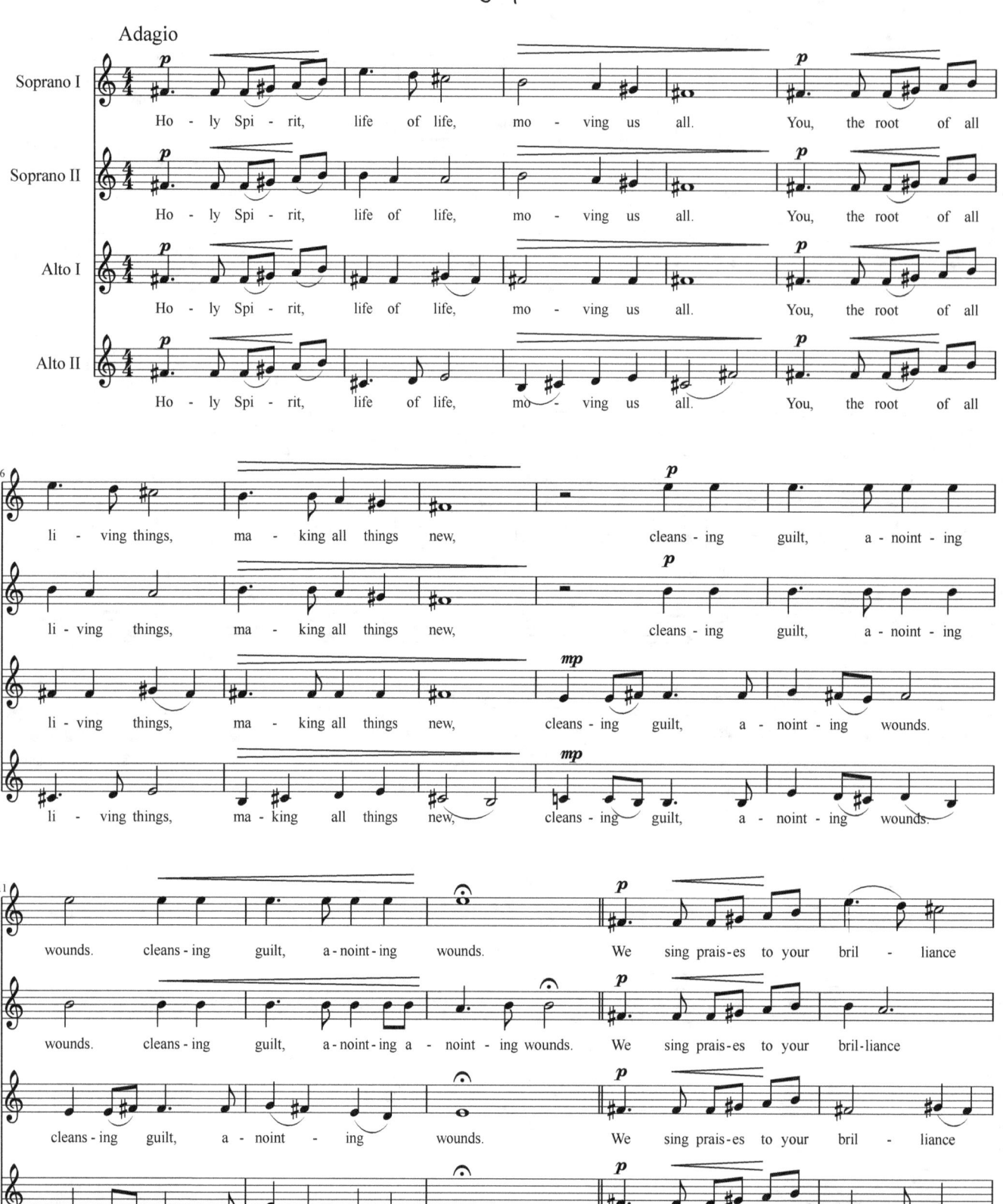

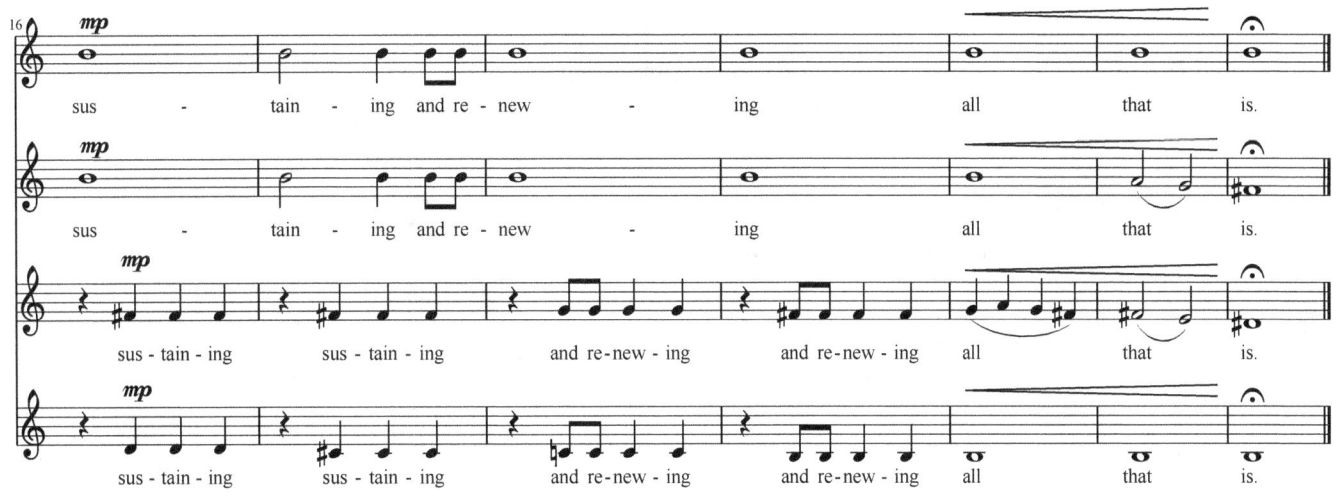

sus - tain - ing and re - new - ing all that is.

sus - tain - ing and re - new - ing all that is.

sus - tain - ing sus - tain - ing and re - new - ing and re - new - ing all that is.

sus - tain - ing sus - tain - ing and re - new - ing and re - new - ing all that is.

77

Three Prayers
O Most Noble Power

Hildegard of Bingen

Ken Langer

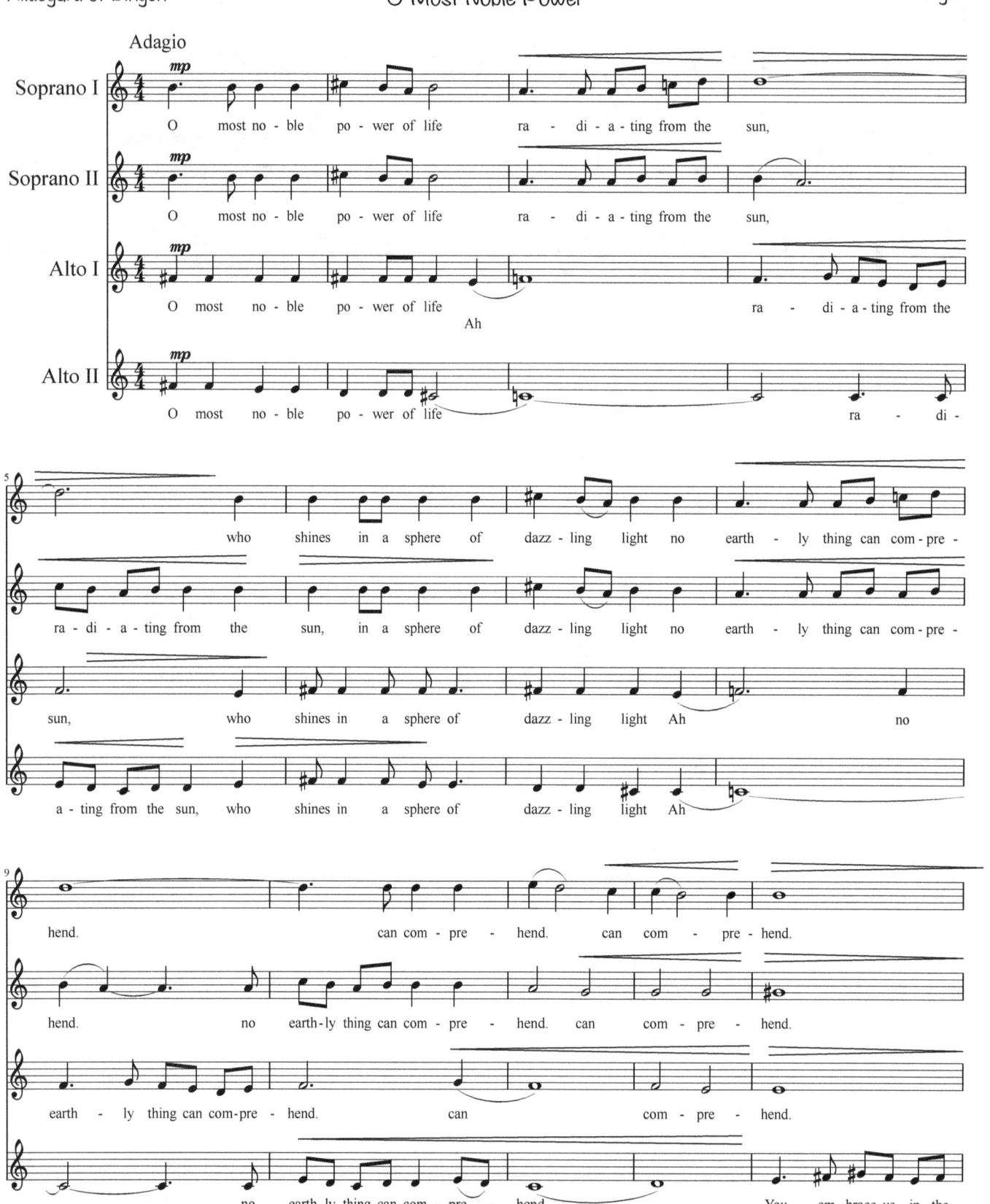

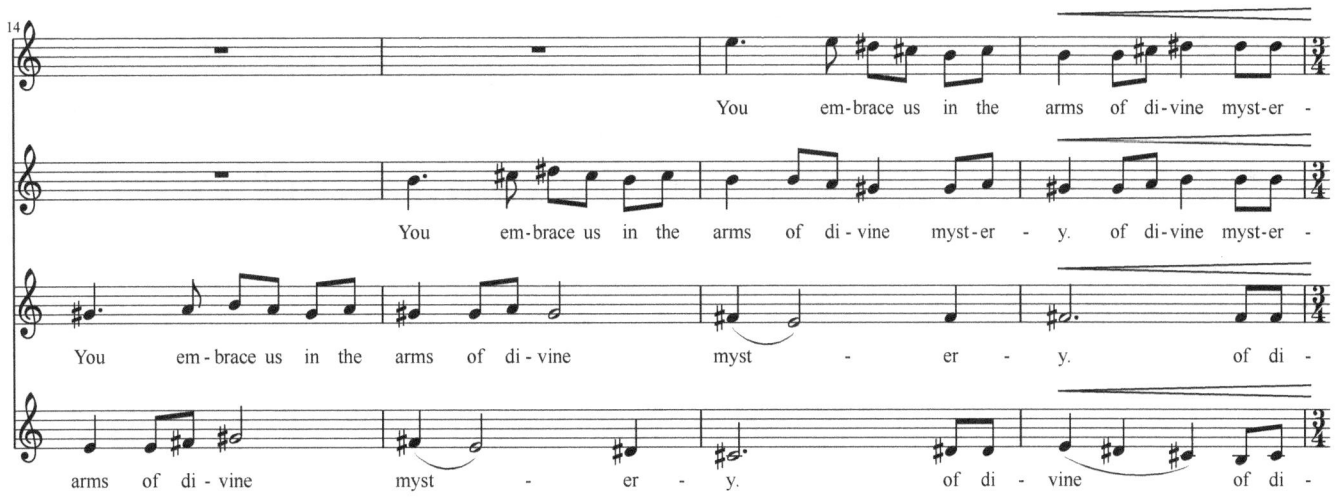

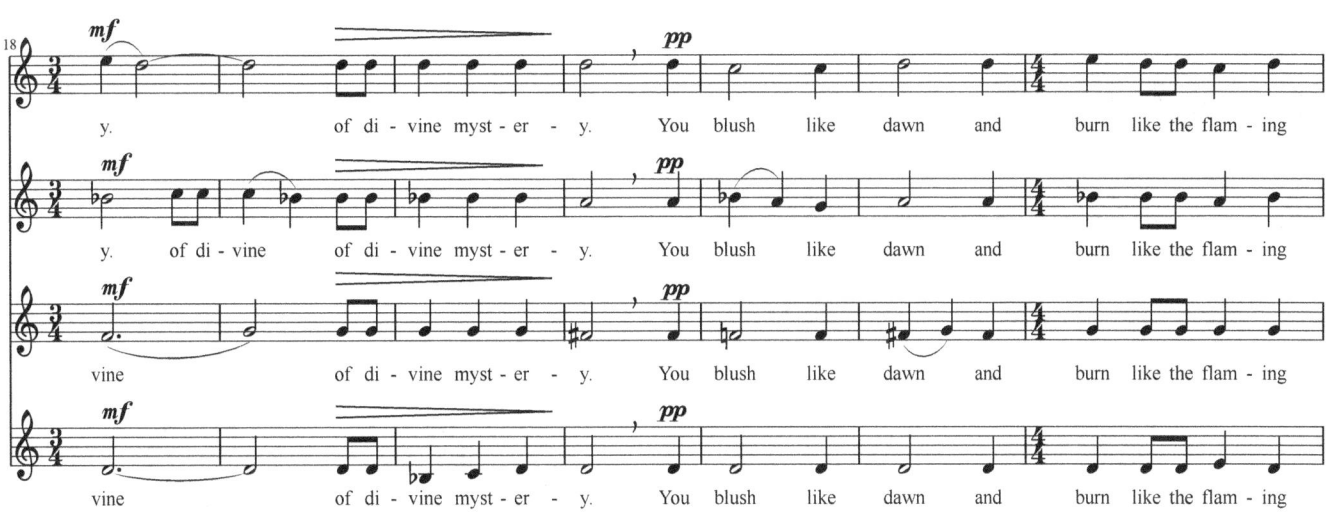

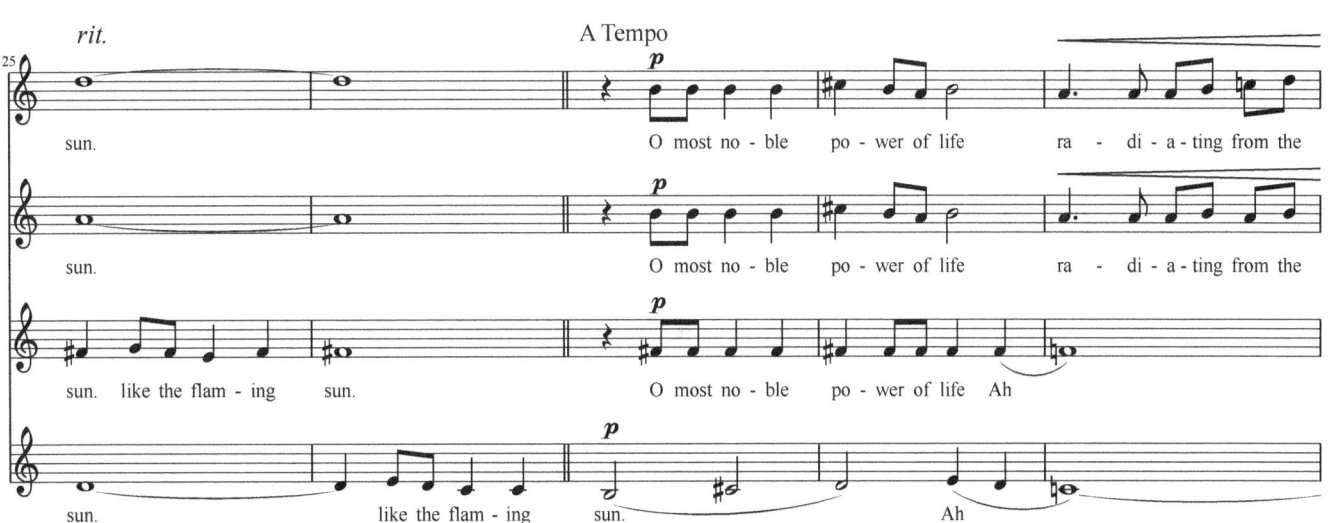

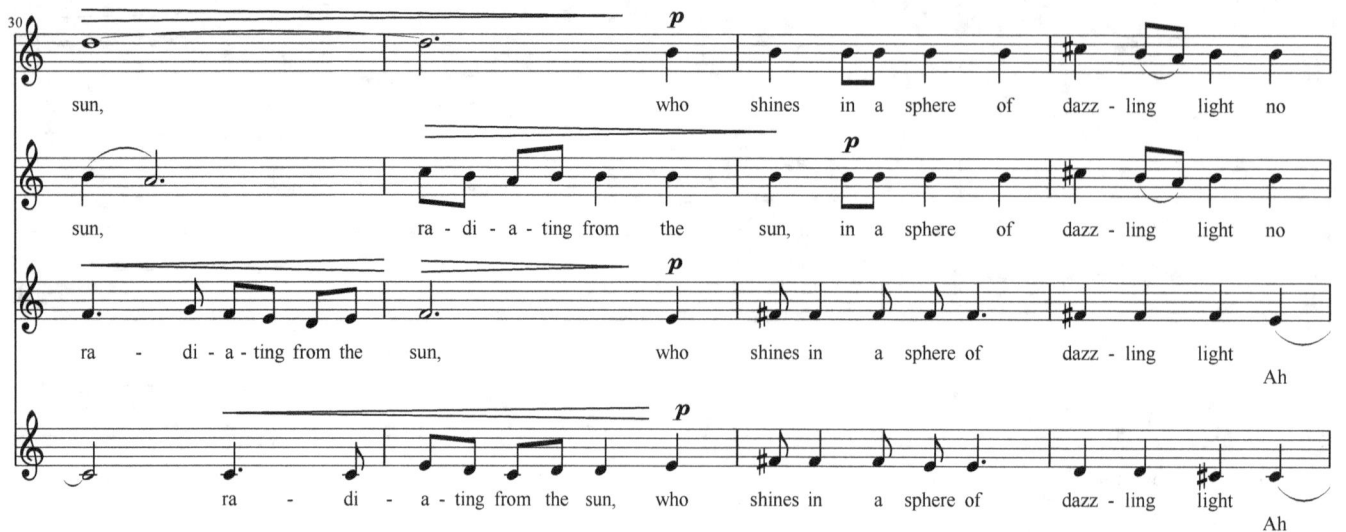

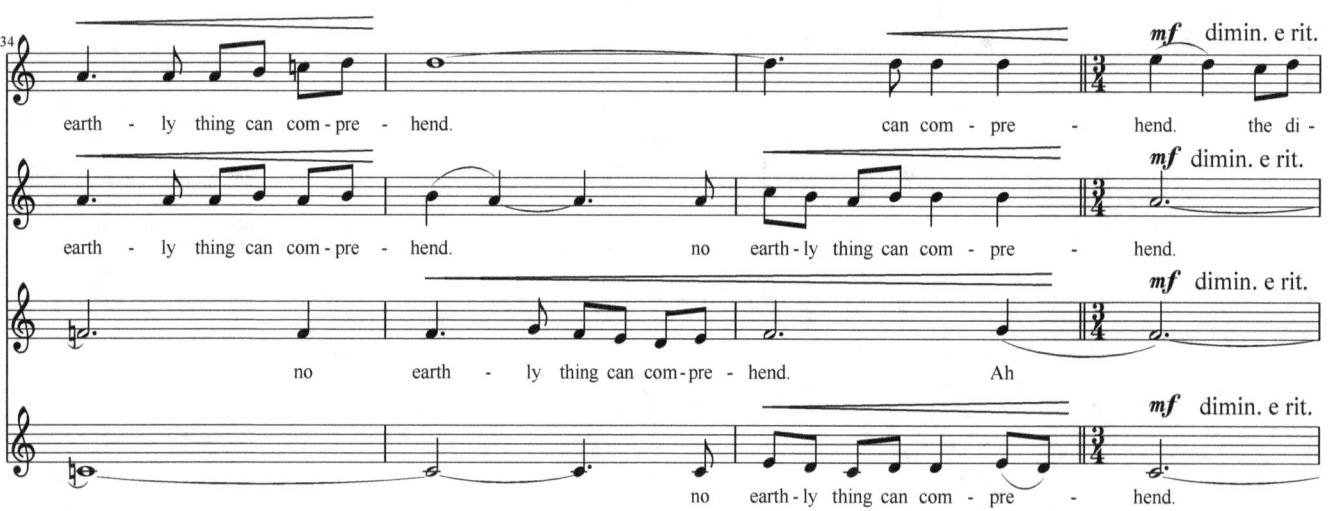

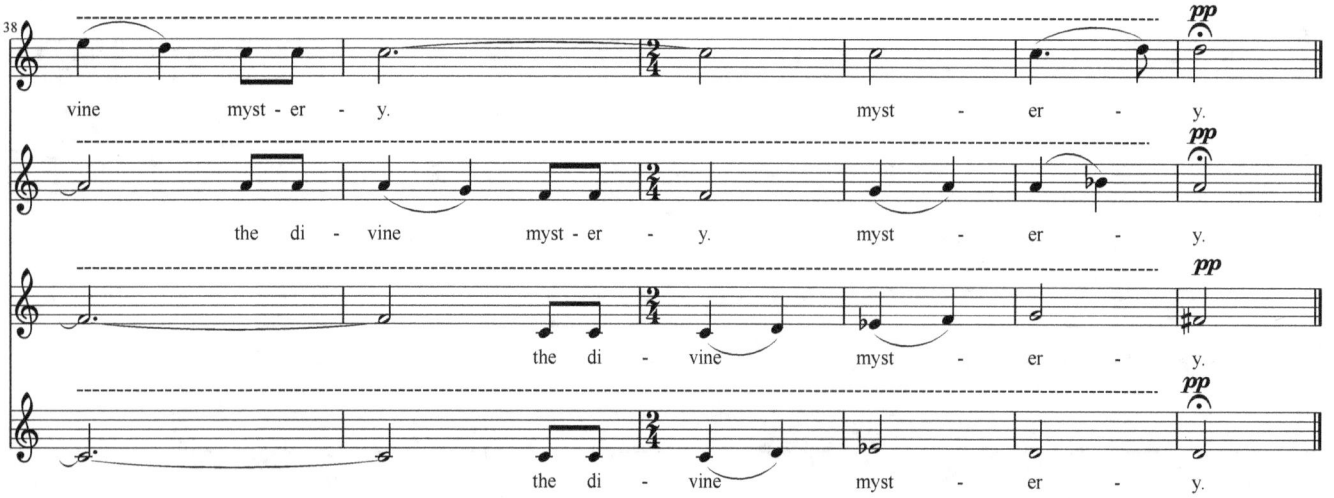

The Vapor and the Dusk

text by Walt Whitman

music by Ken Langer

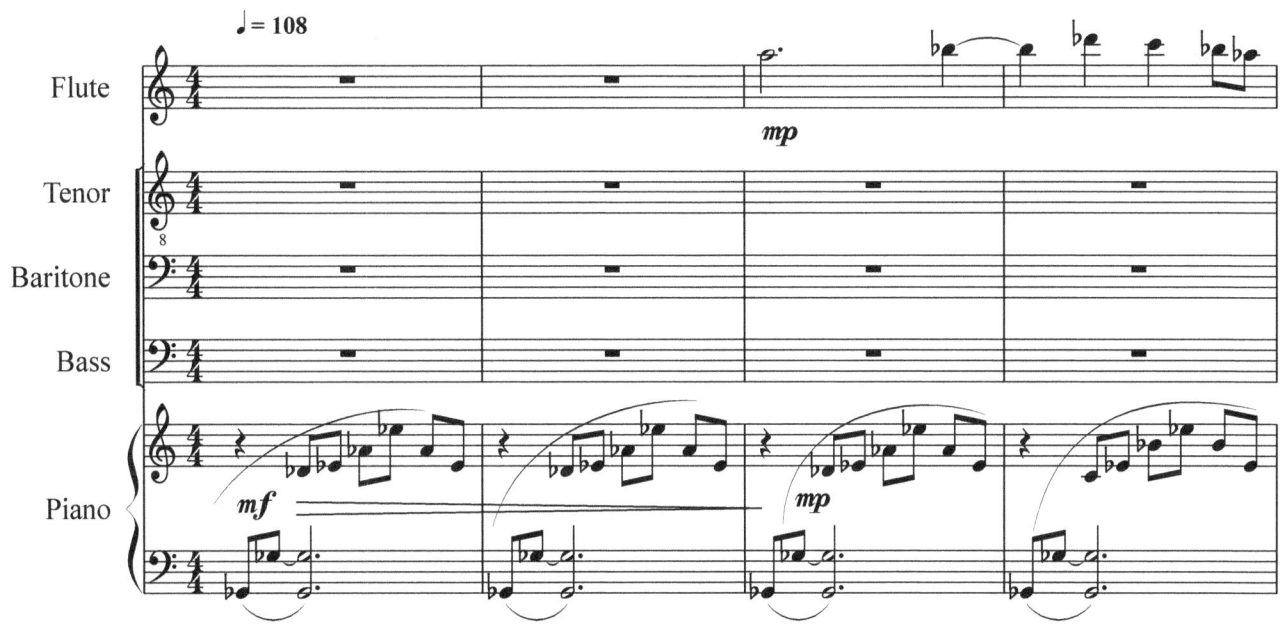

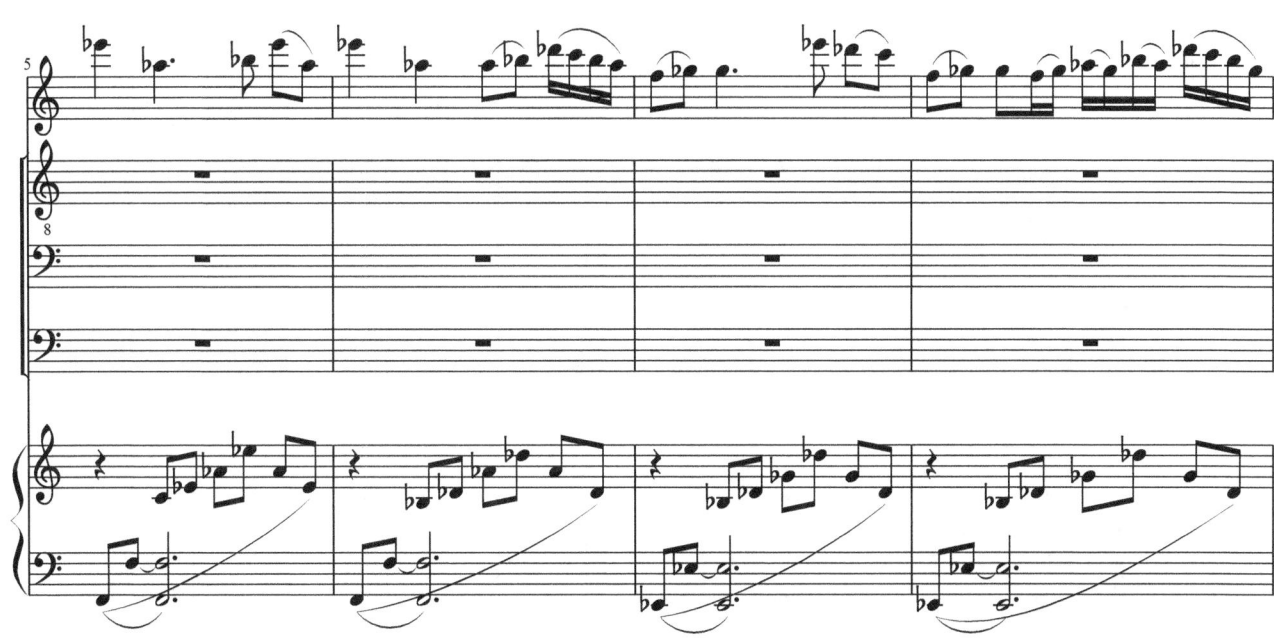

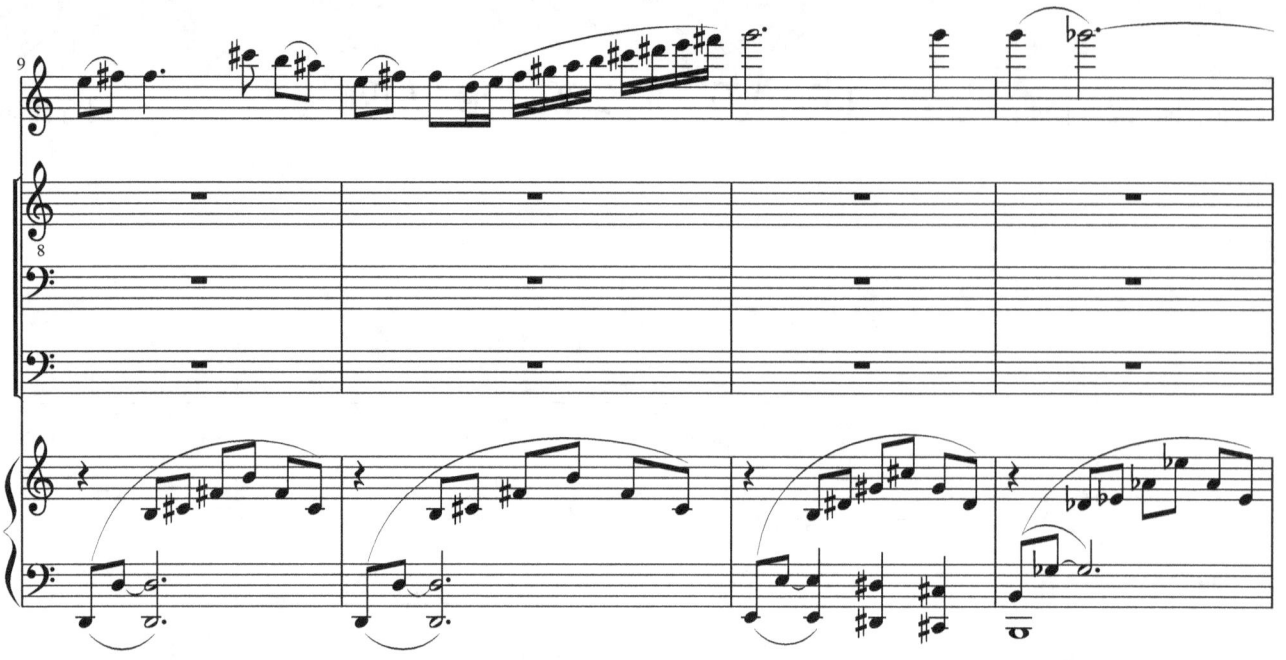

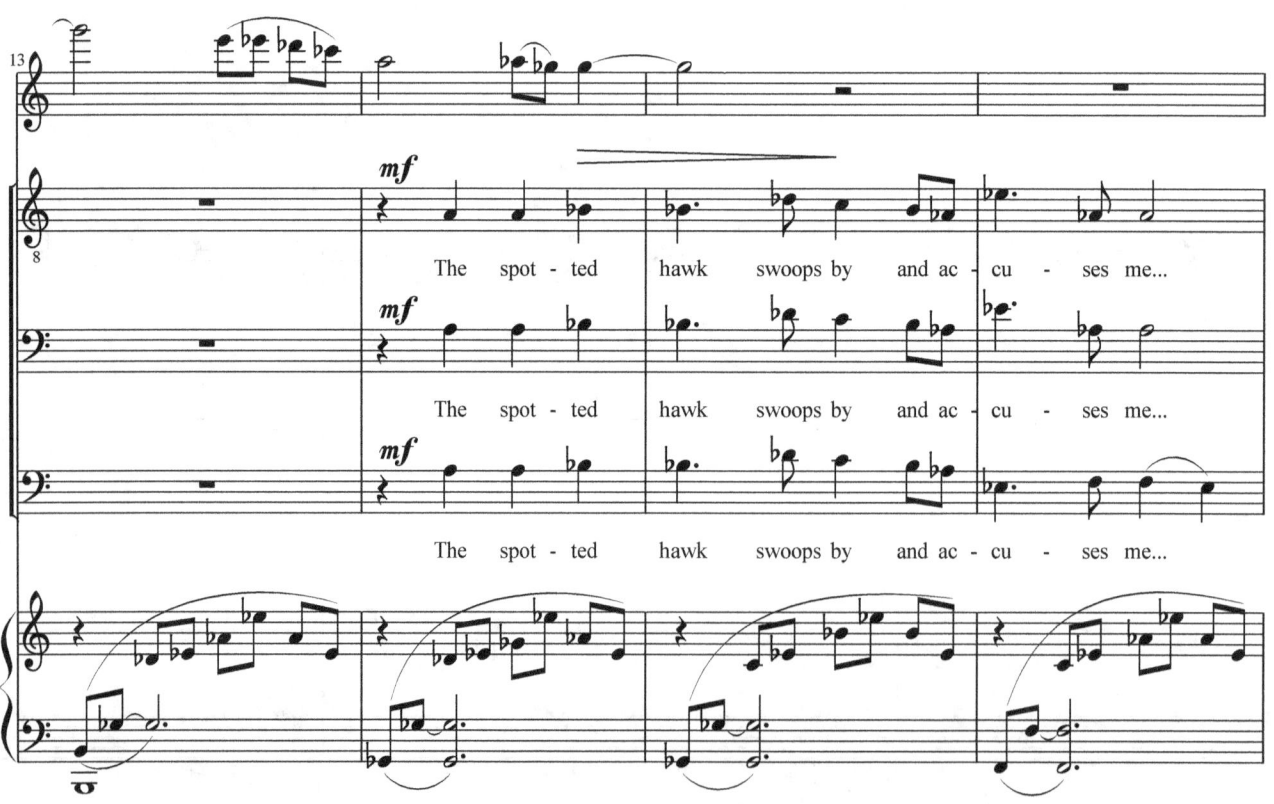

The spot - ted hawk swoops by and ac - cu - ses me...

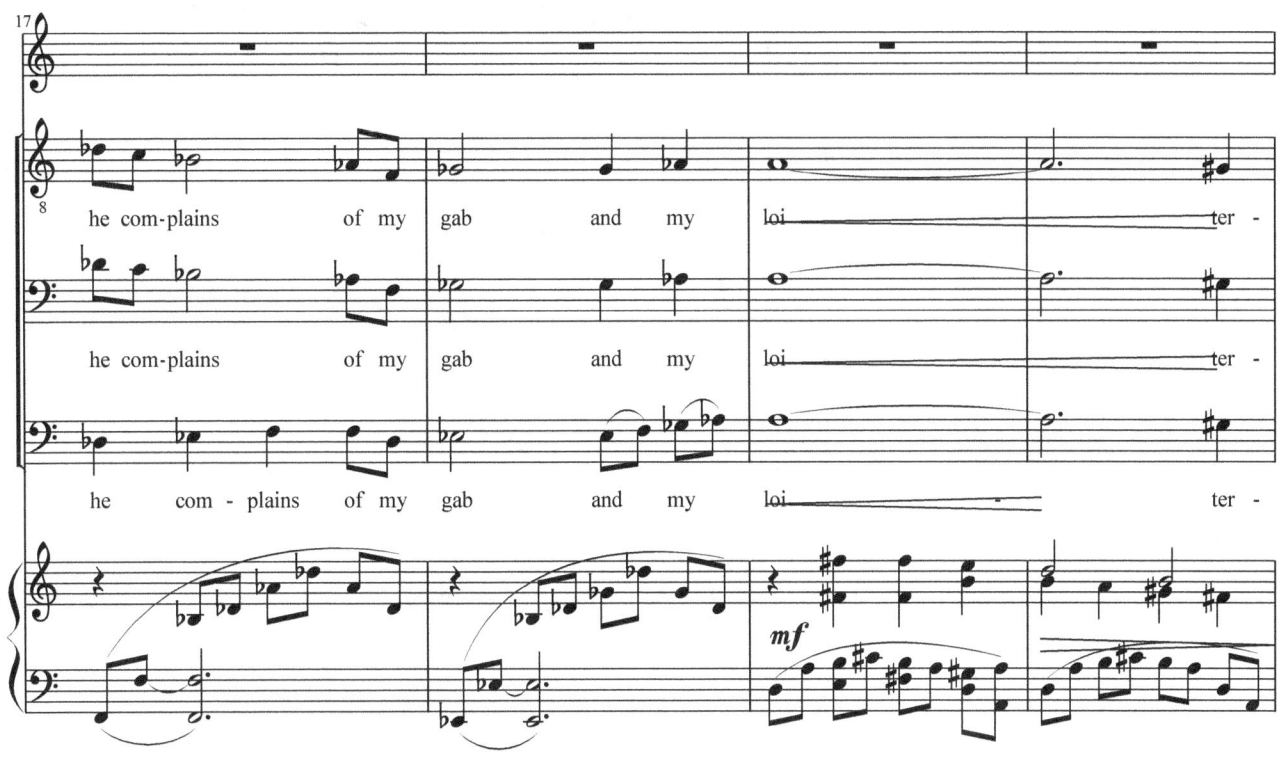

he com-plains of my gab and my loi ____ ter -
he com-plains of my gab and my loi ____ ter -
he com-plains of my gab and my loi ____ ter -

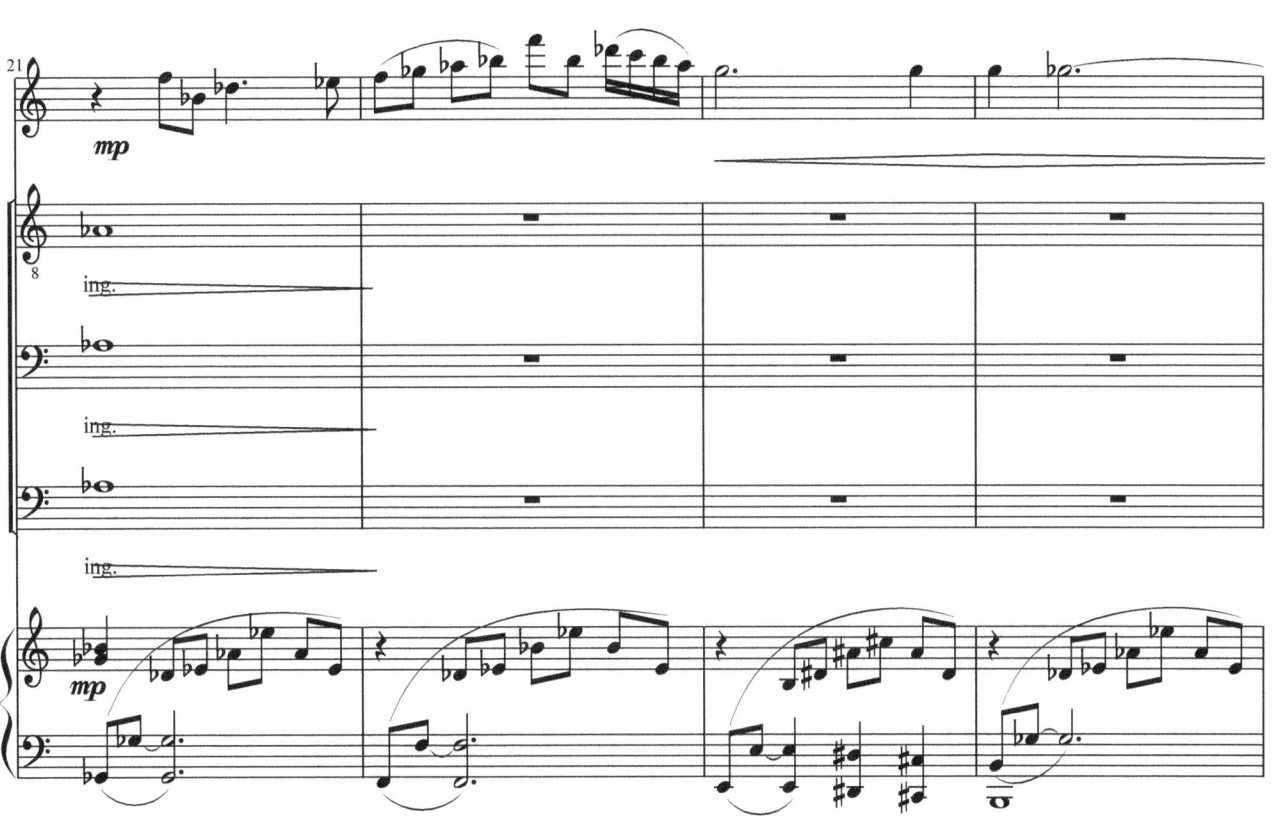

ing.
ing.
ing.

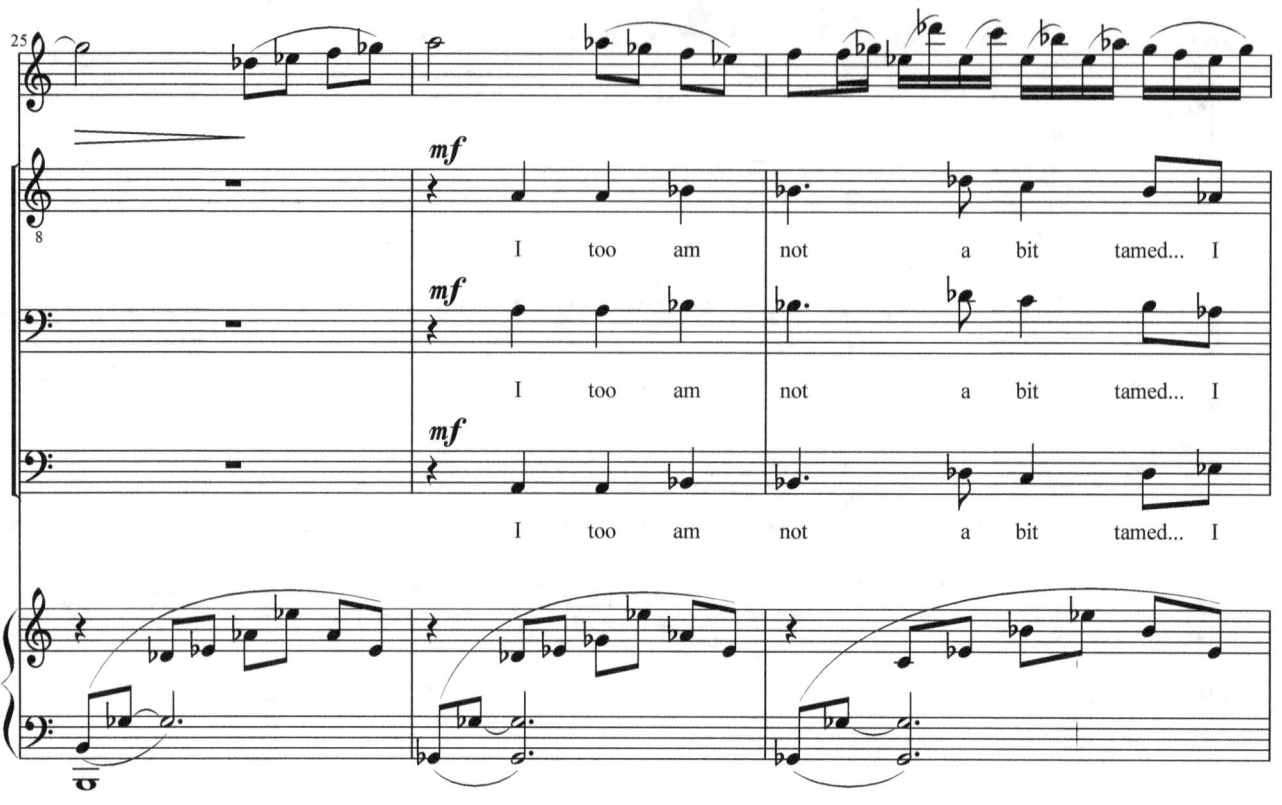

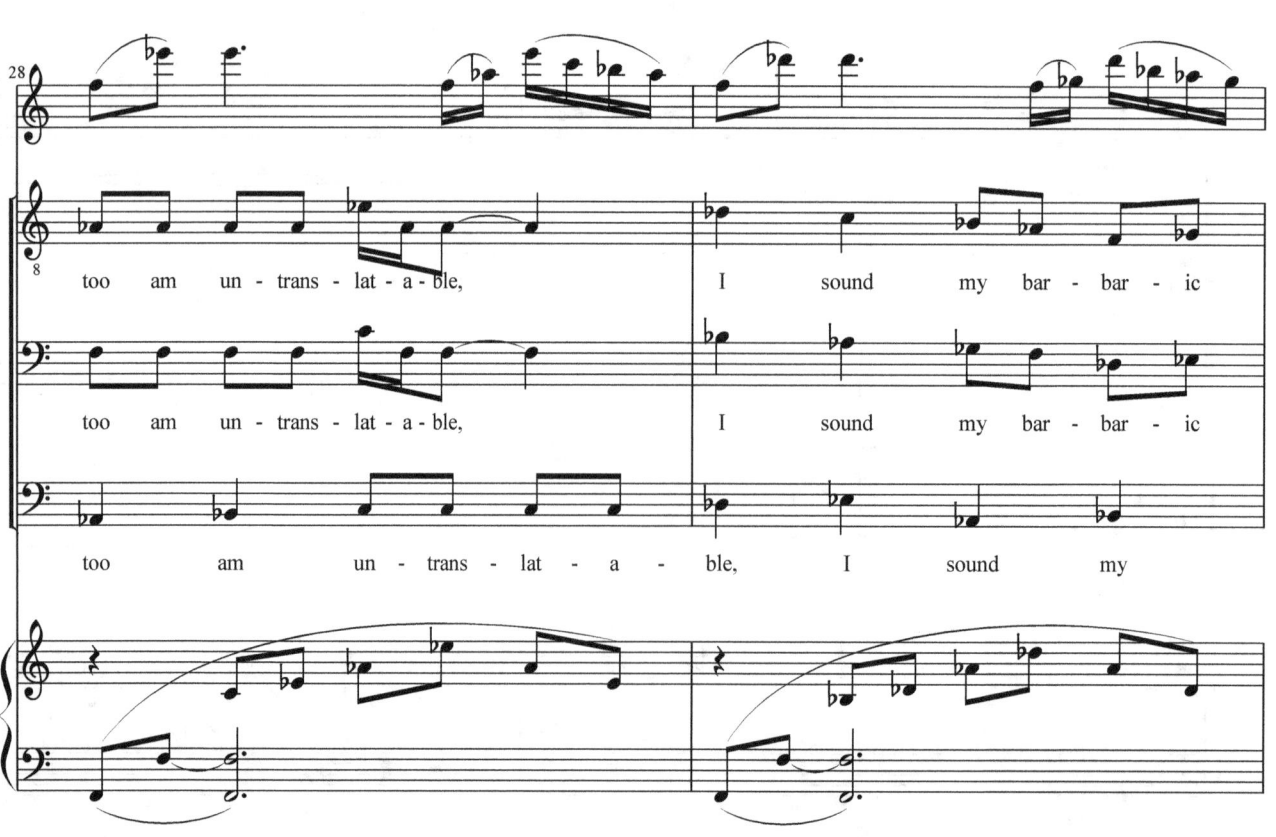

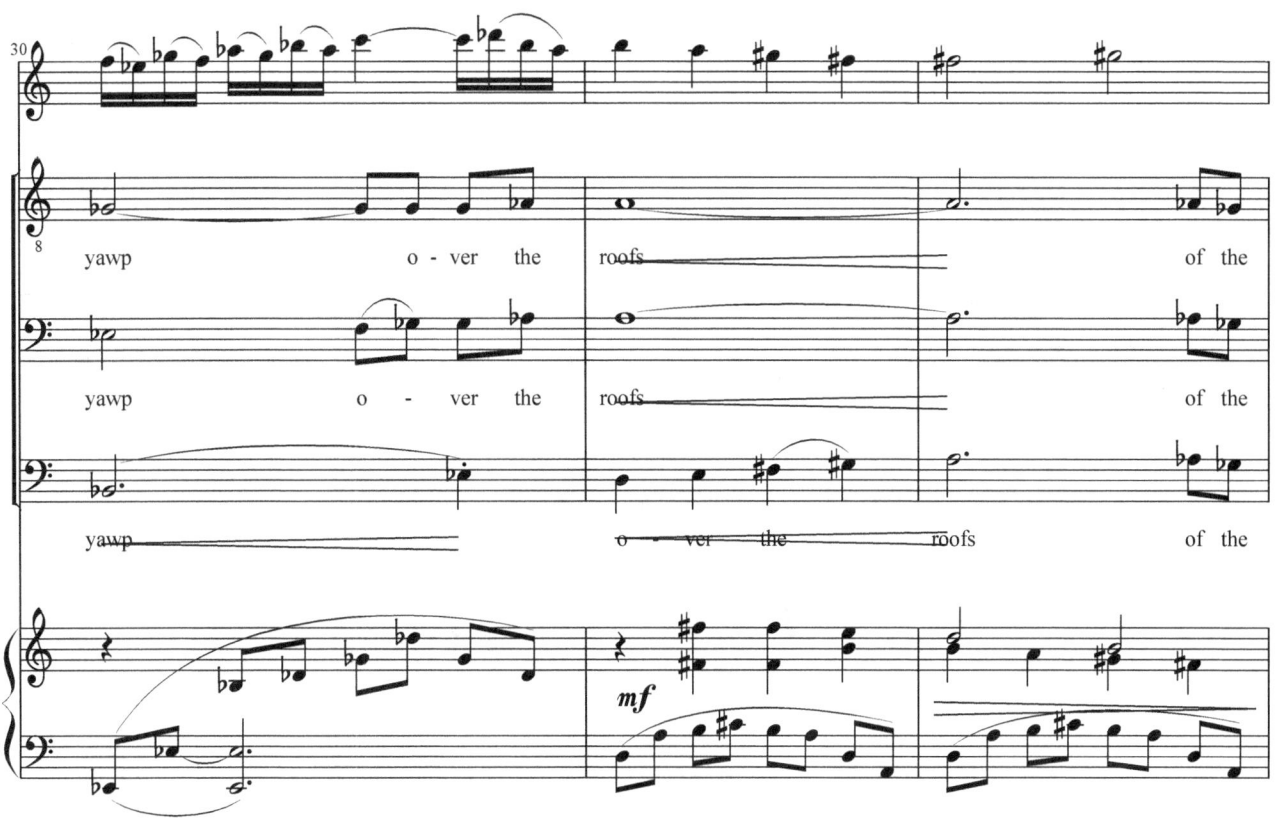

yawp _____ o - ver the roofs _____ of the

yawp _____ o - ver the roofs _____ of the

yawp _____ o - ver the _____ roofs _____ of the

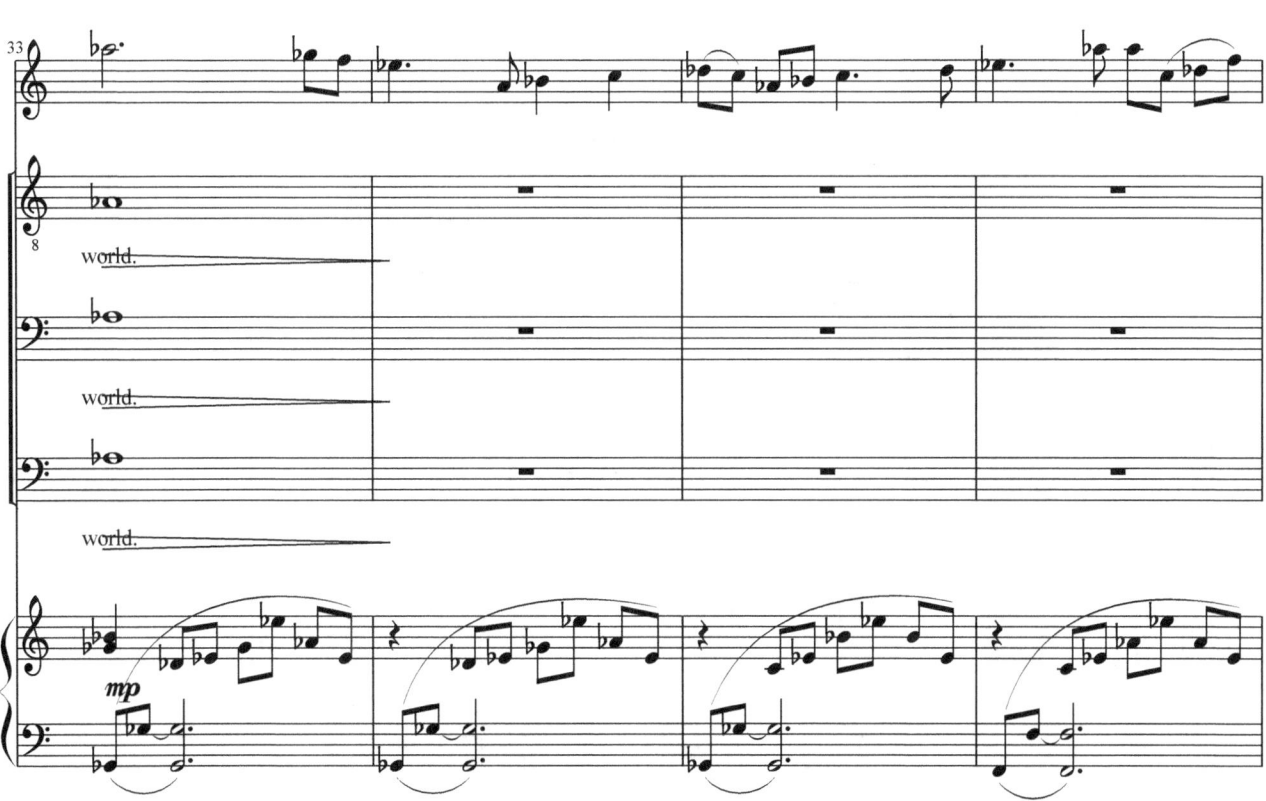

world.

world.

world.

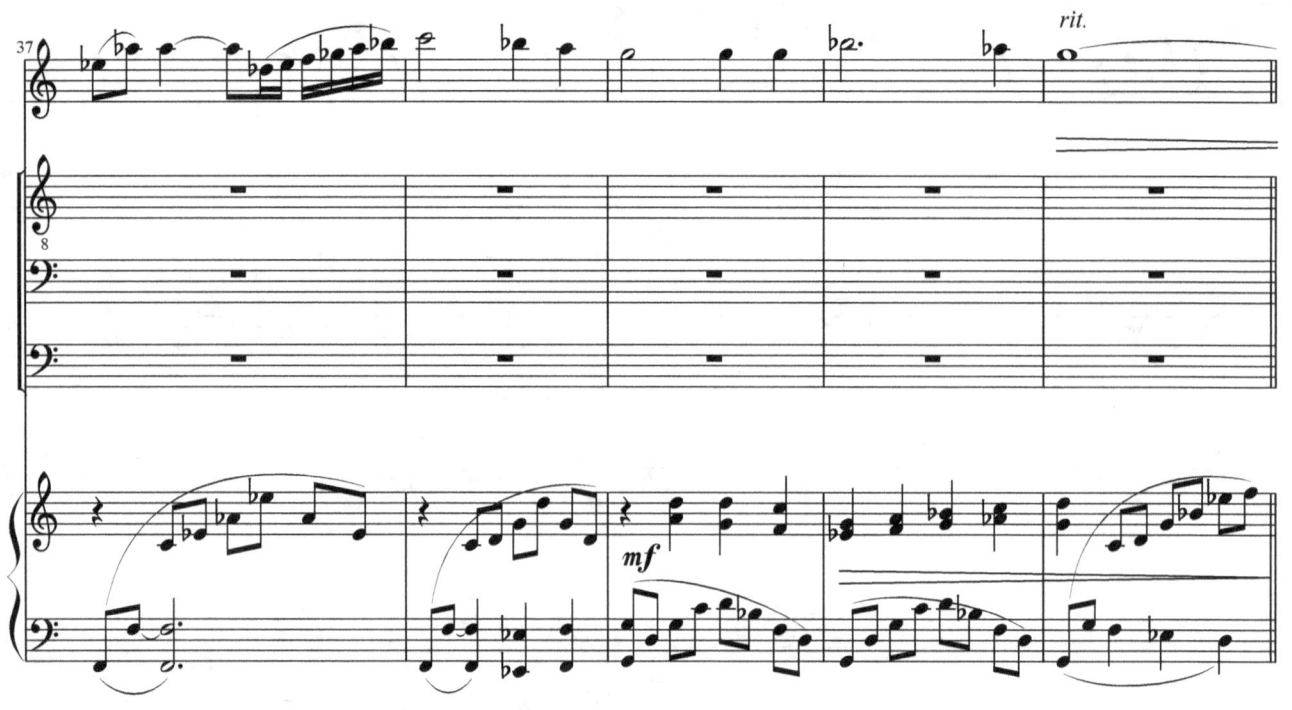

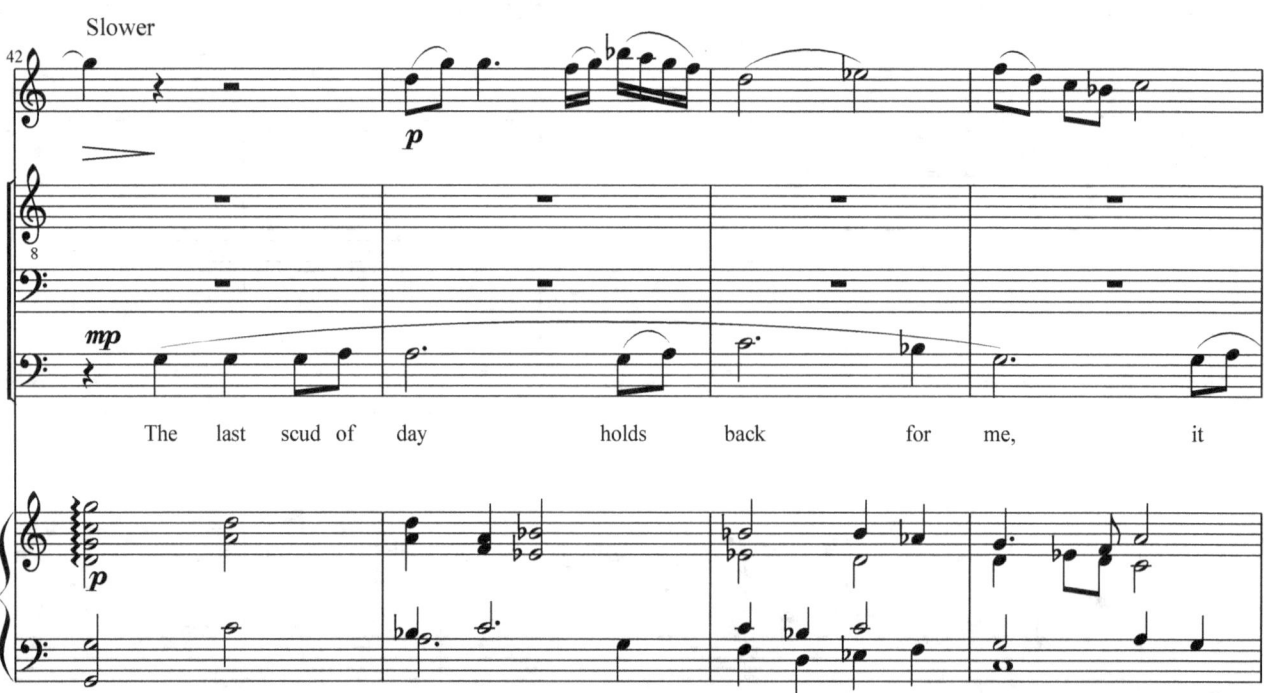

The last scud of day holds back for me, it

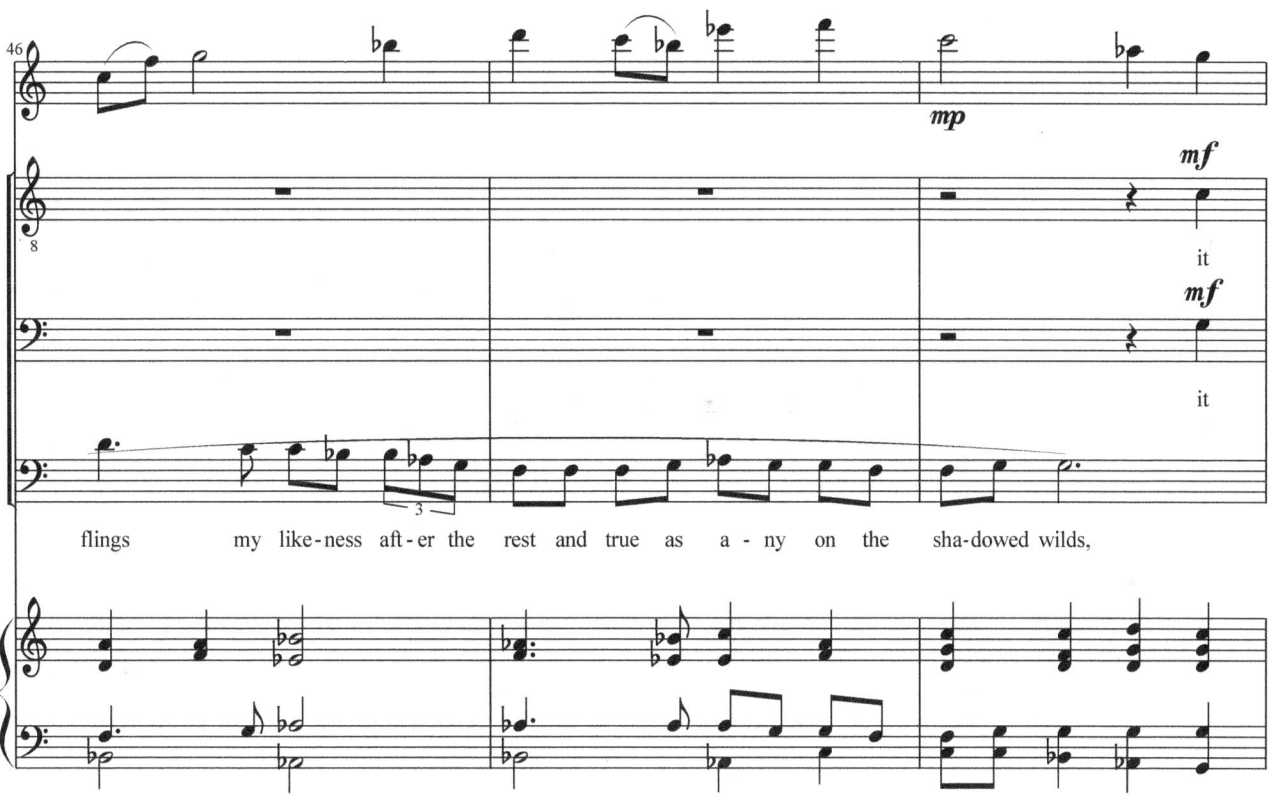

flings my like-ness aft-er the rest and true as a - ny on the sha-dowed wilds,

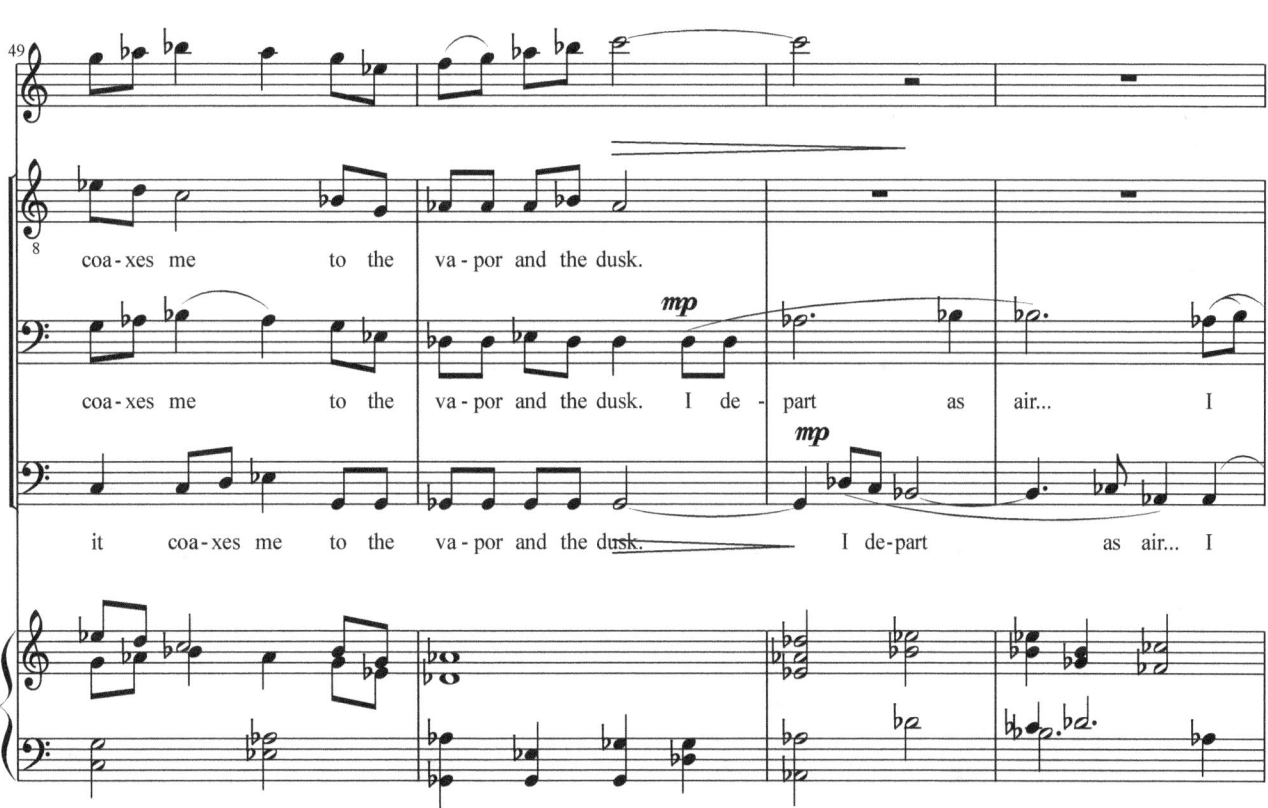

coa-xes me to the va-por and the dusk.

coa-xes me to the va-por and the dusk. I de-part as air... I

it coa-xes me to the va-por and the dusk. I de-part as air... I

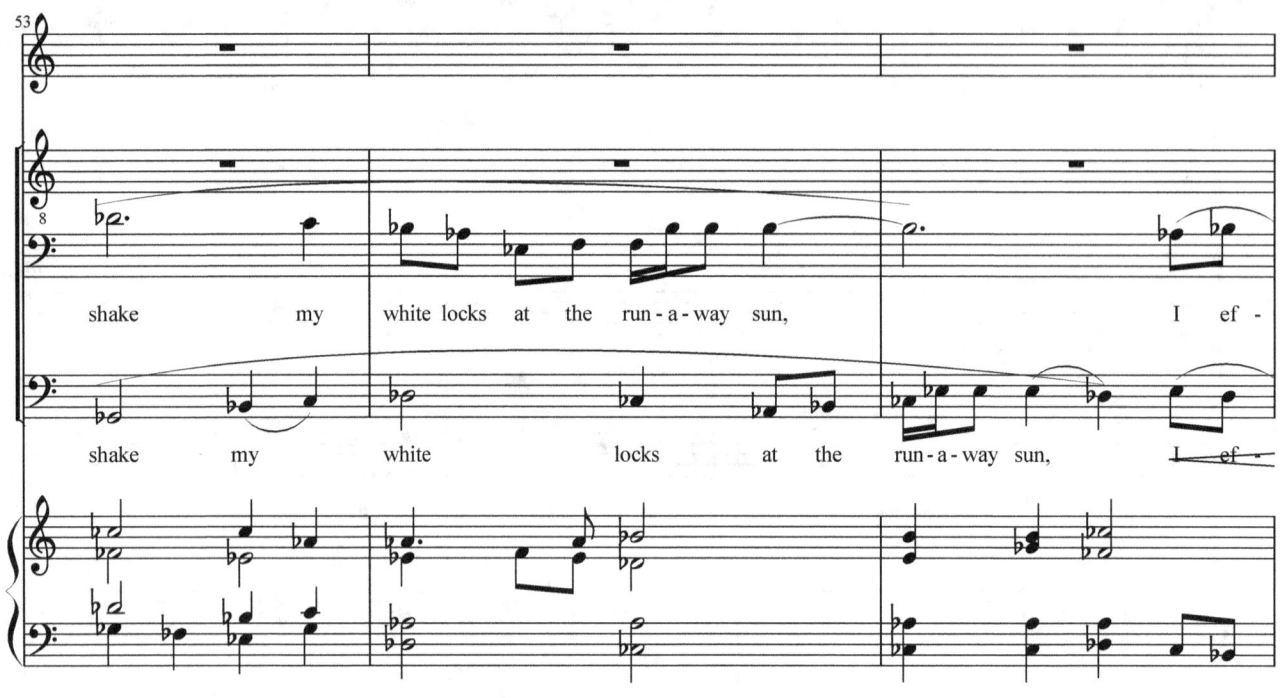

shake my white locks at the run-a-way sun,   I ef -

shake my white locks at the run-a-way sun,   I ef -

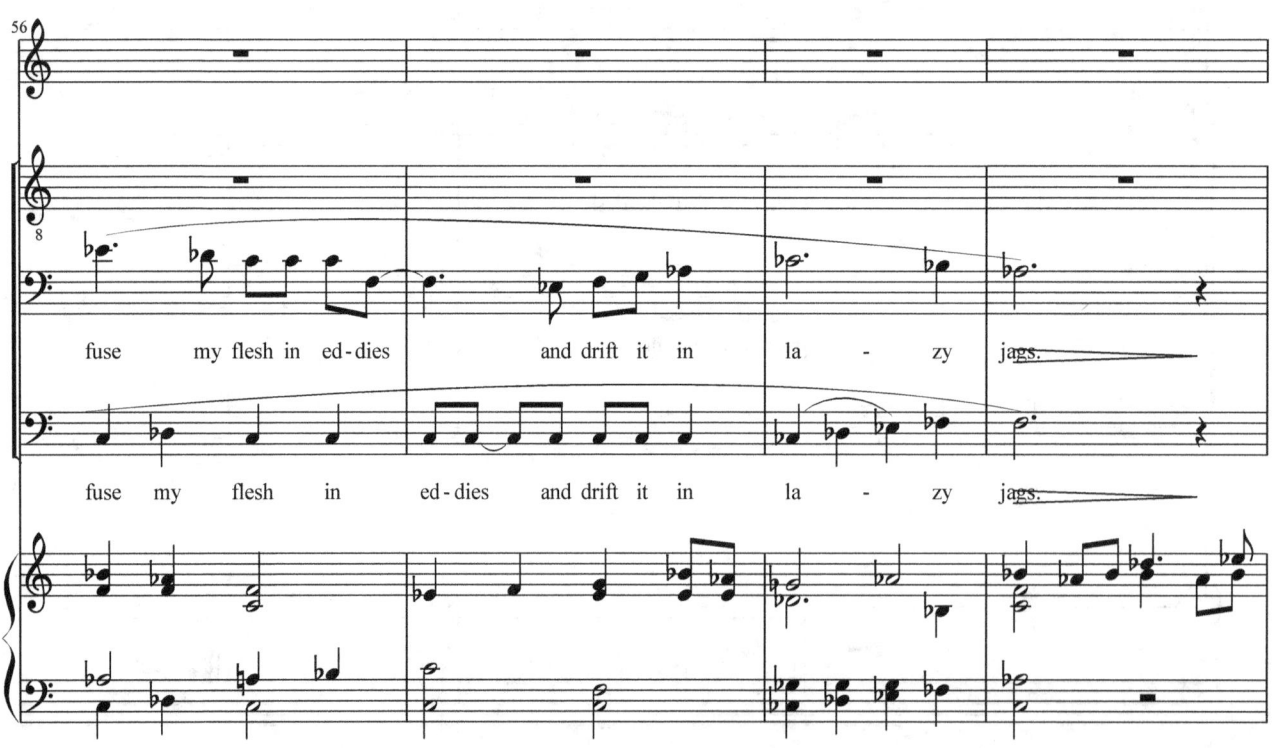

fuse my flesh in ed-dies   and drift it in   la   -   zy   jags.

fuse my flesh in ed-dies and drift it in   la   -   zy   jags.

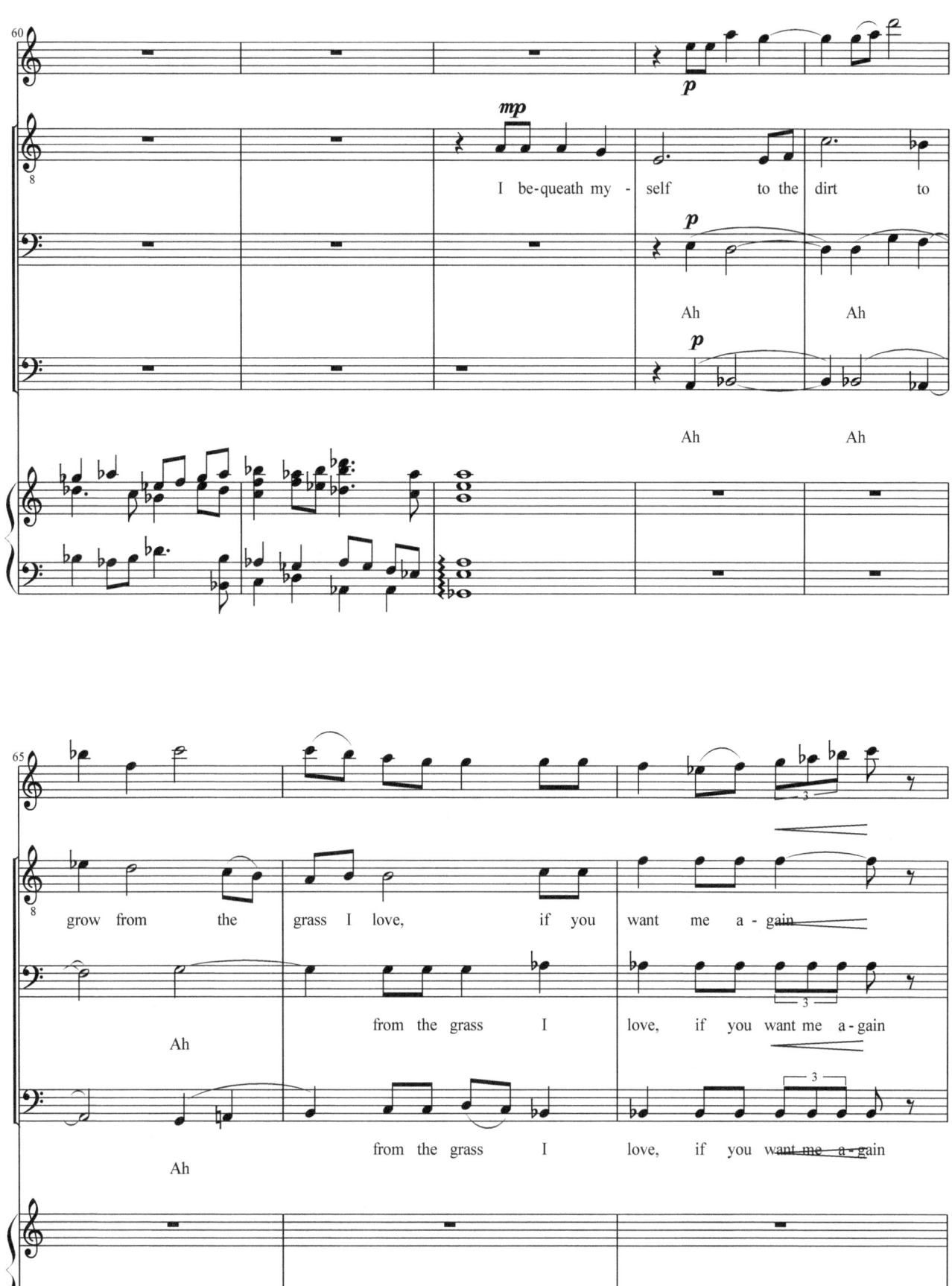

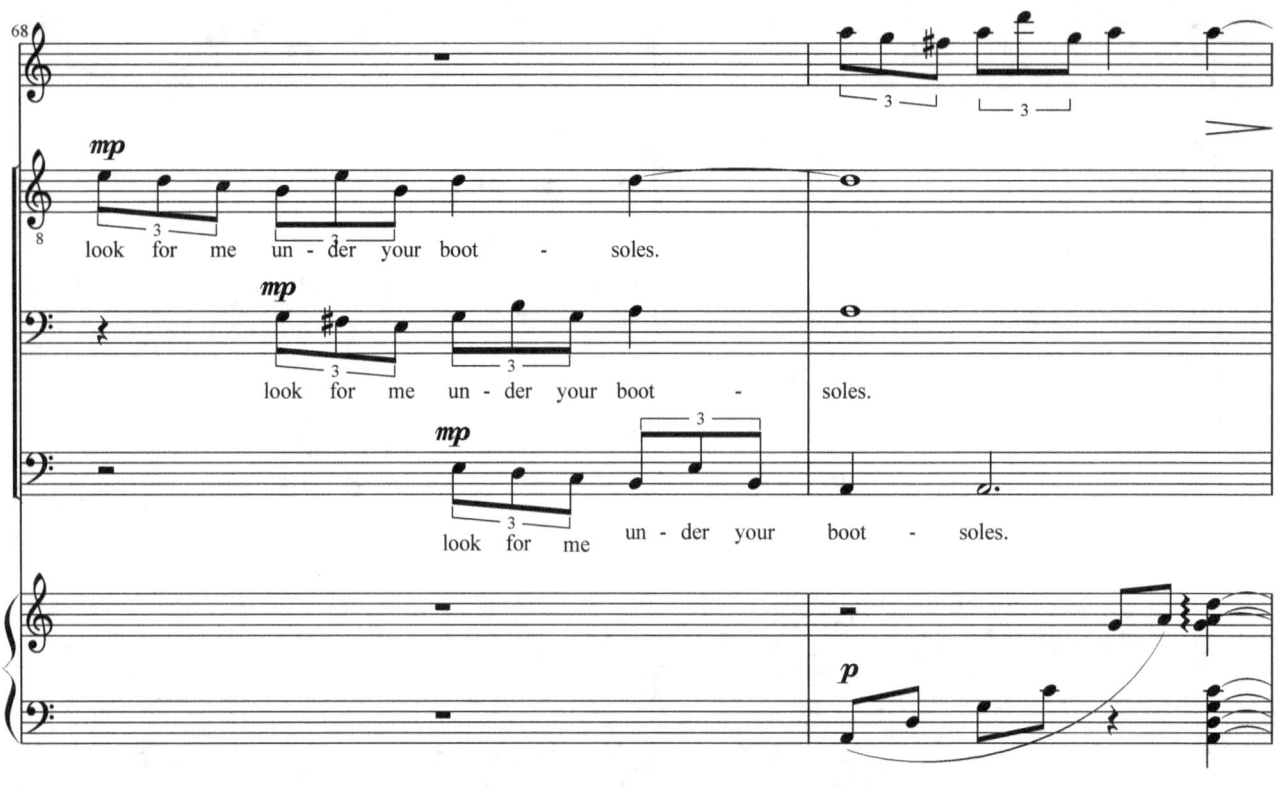

look for me un - der your boot - soles.

look for me un - der your boot - soles.

look for me un - der your boot - soles.

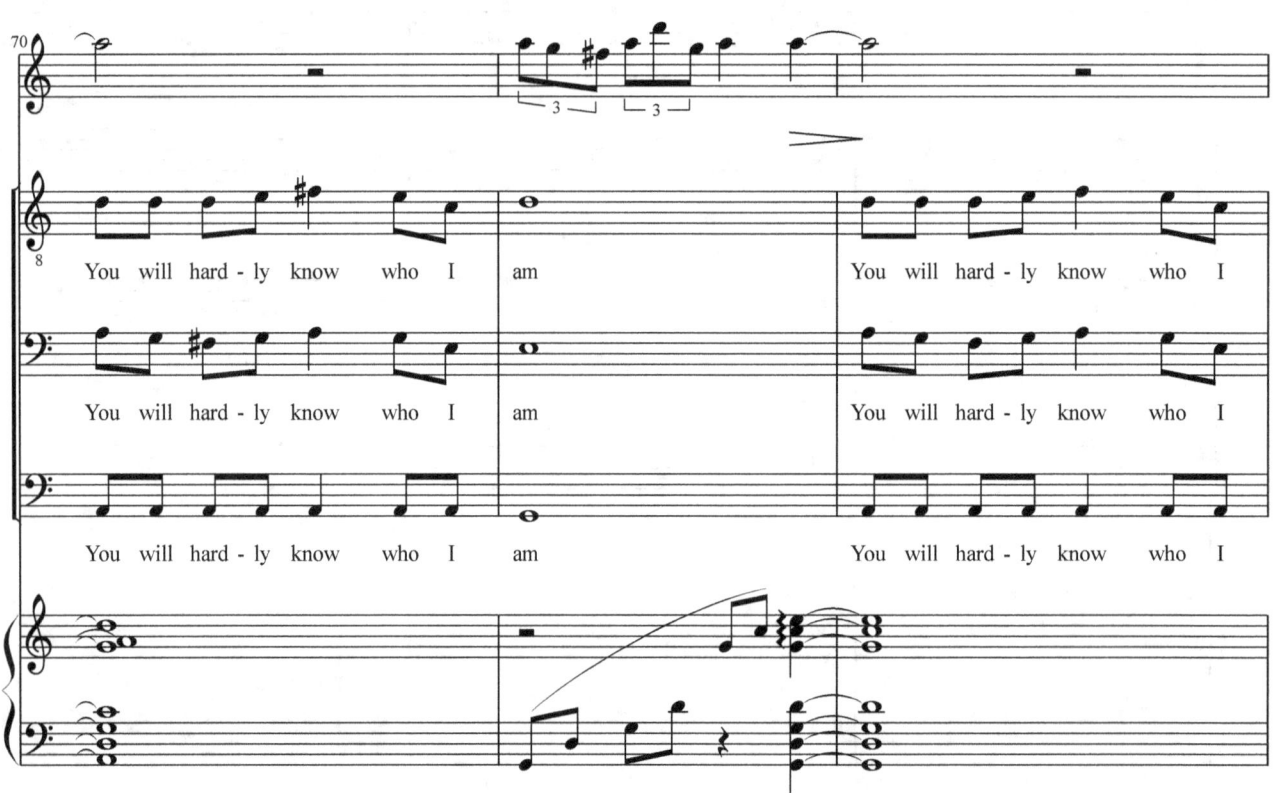

You will hard - ly know who I am

You will hard - ly know who I am

You will hard - ly know who I am

You will hard - ly know who I

You will hard - ly know who I

You will hard - ly know who I

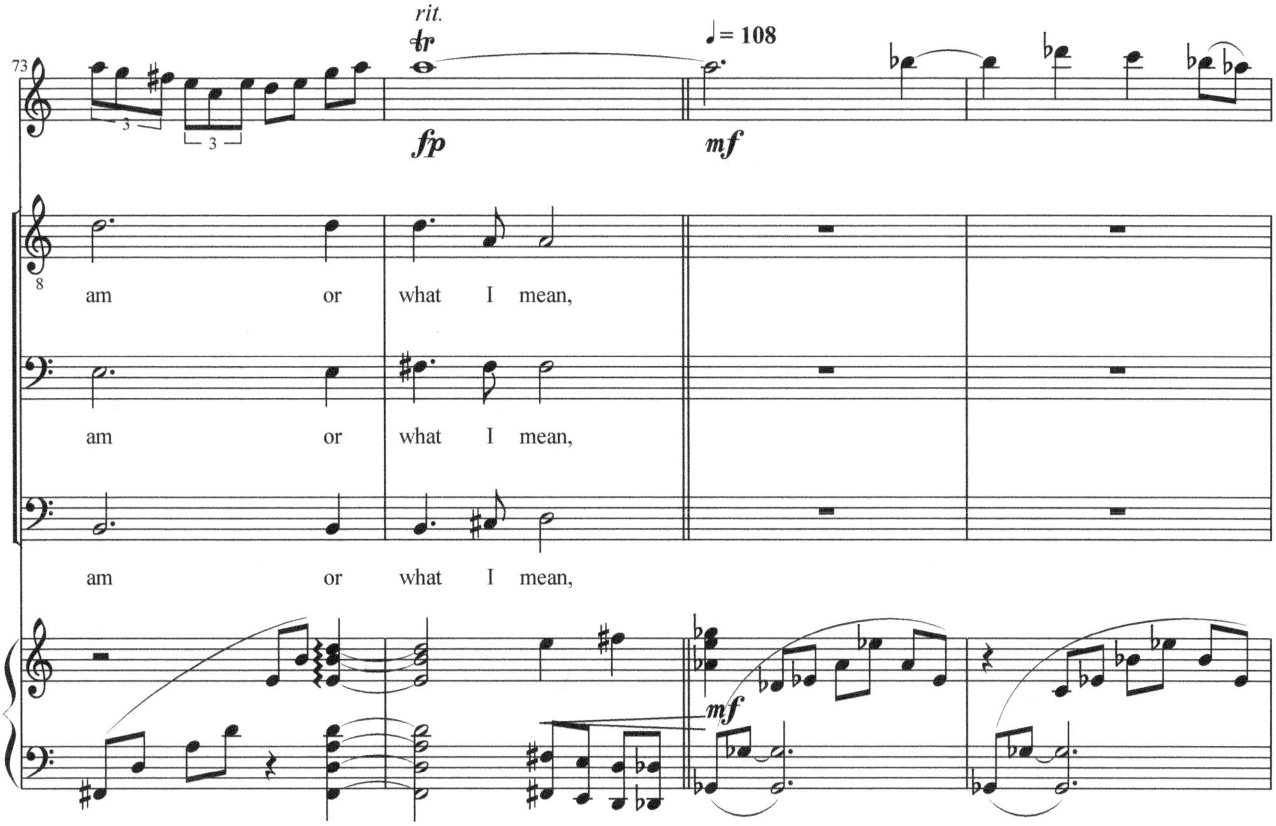

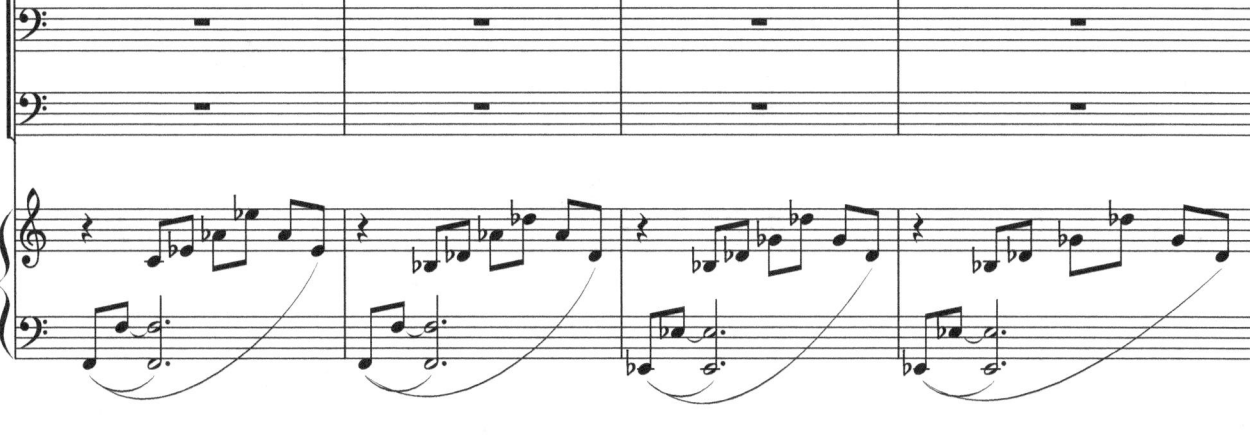

am or what I mean,

am or what I mean,

am or what I mean,

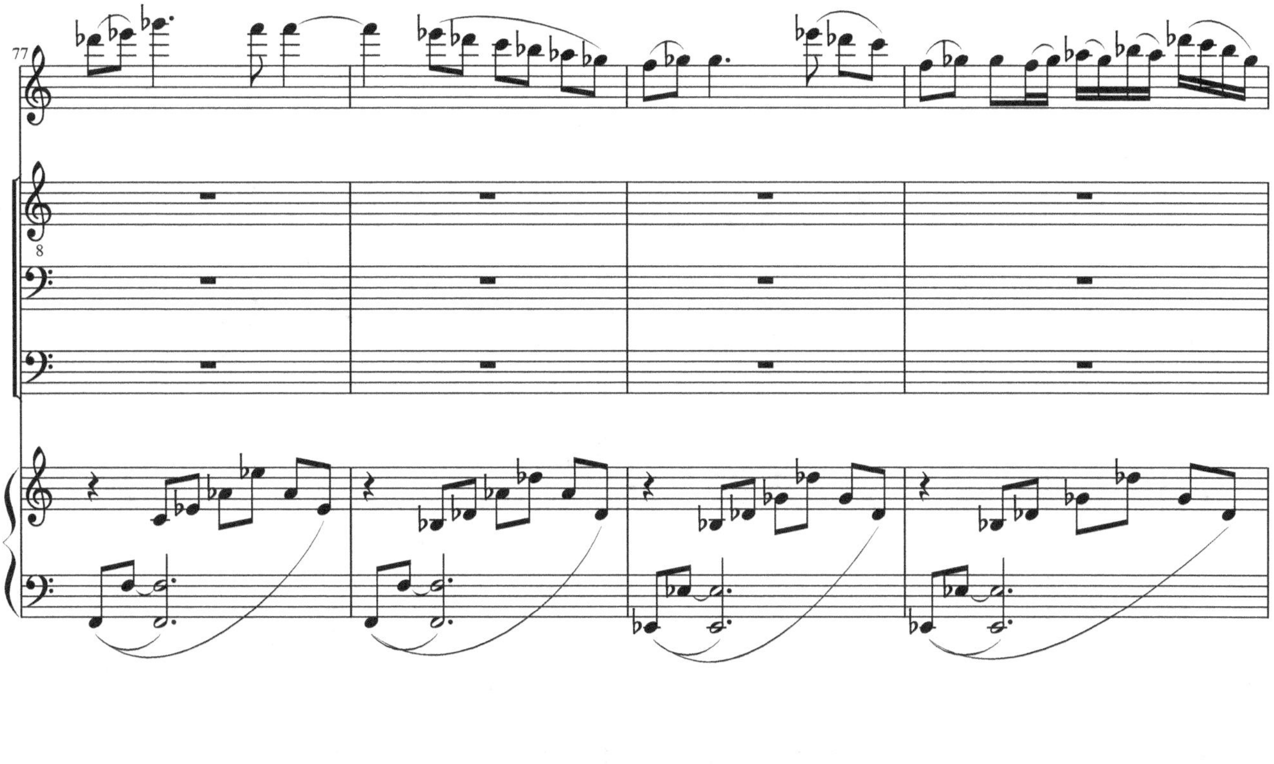

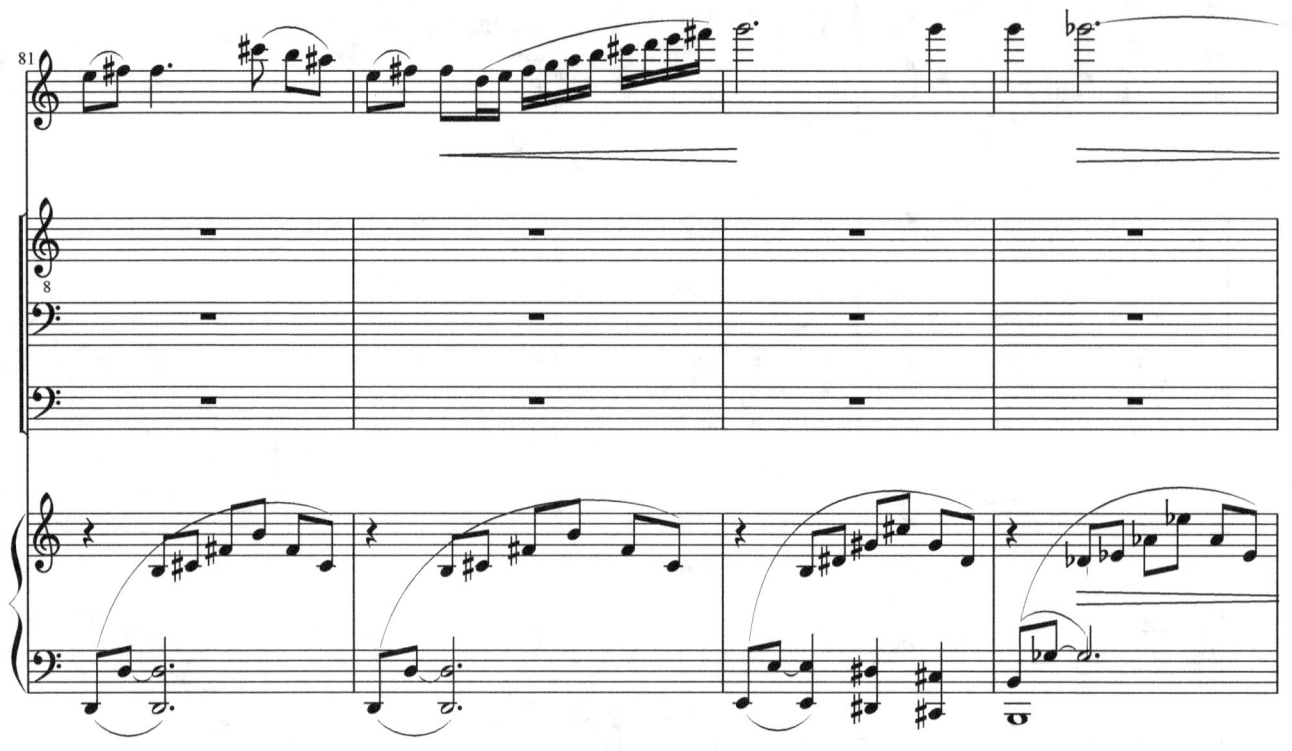

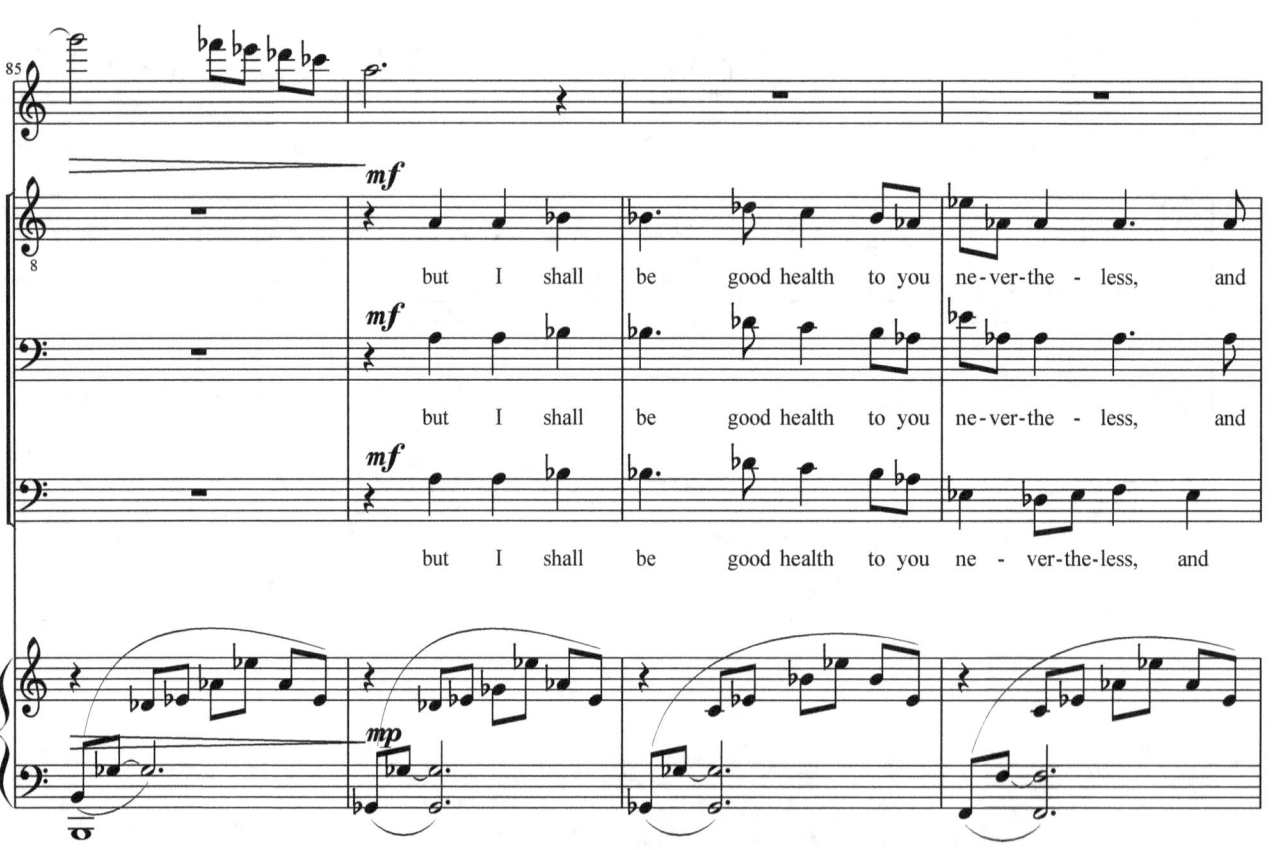

but I shall be good health to you ne-ver-the - less, and

but I shall be good health to you ne-ver-the - less, and

but I shall be good health to you ne - ver-the - less, and

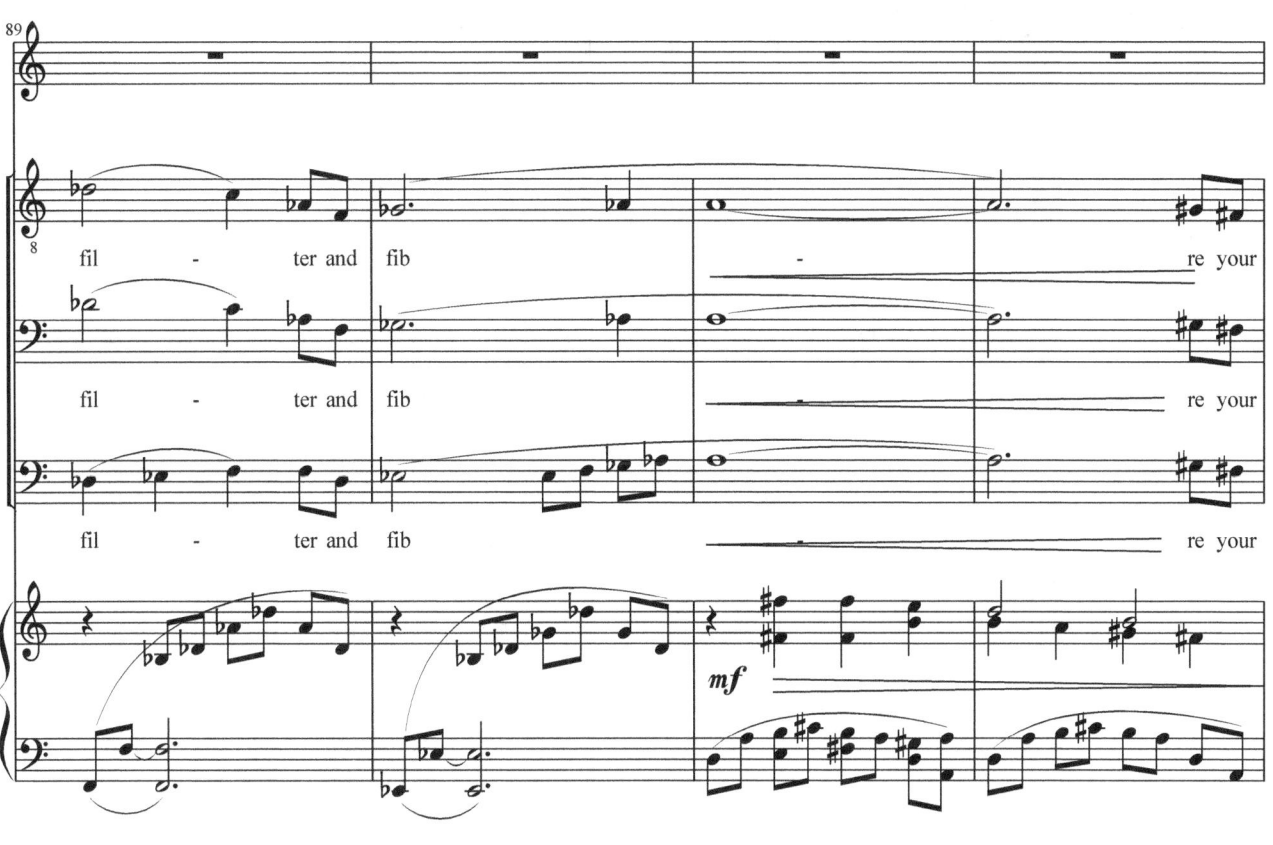

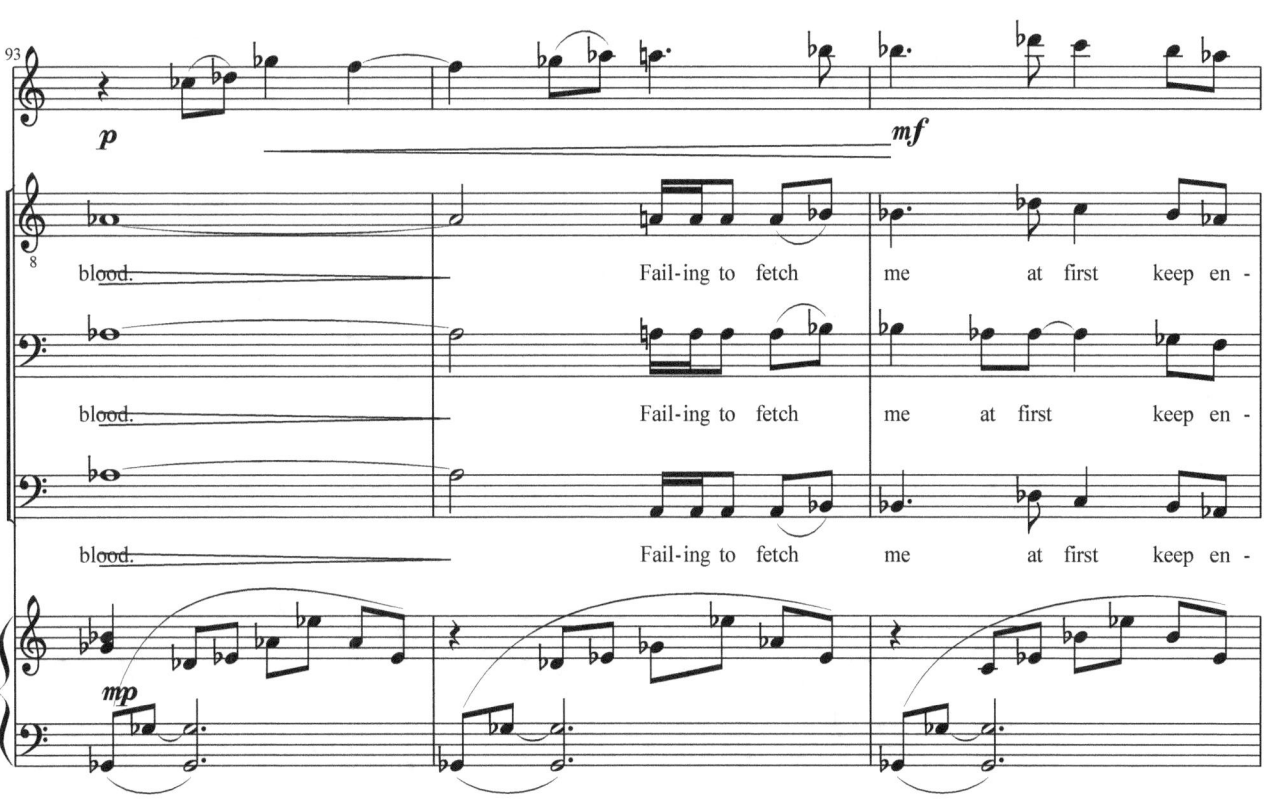

89

fil - ter and fib - re your
fil - ter and fib re your
fil - ter and fib - re your

mf

93

p mf

blood.
blood.
blood.

Fail-ing to fetch me at first keep en -
Fail-ing to fetch me at first keep en -
Fail-ing to fetch me at first keep en -

mp

93

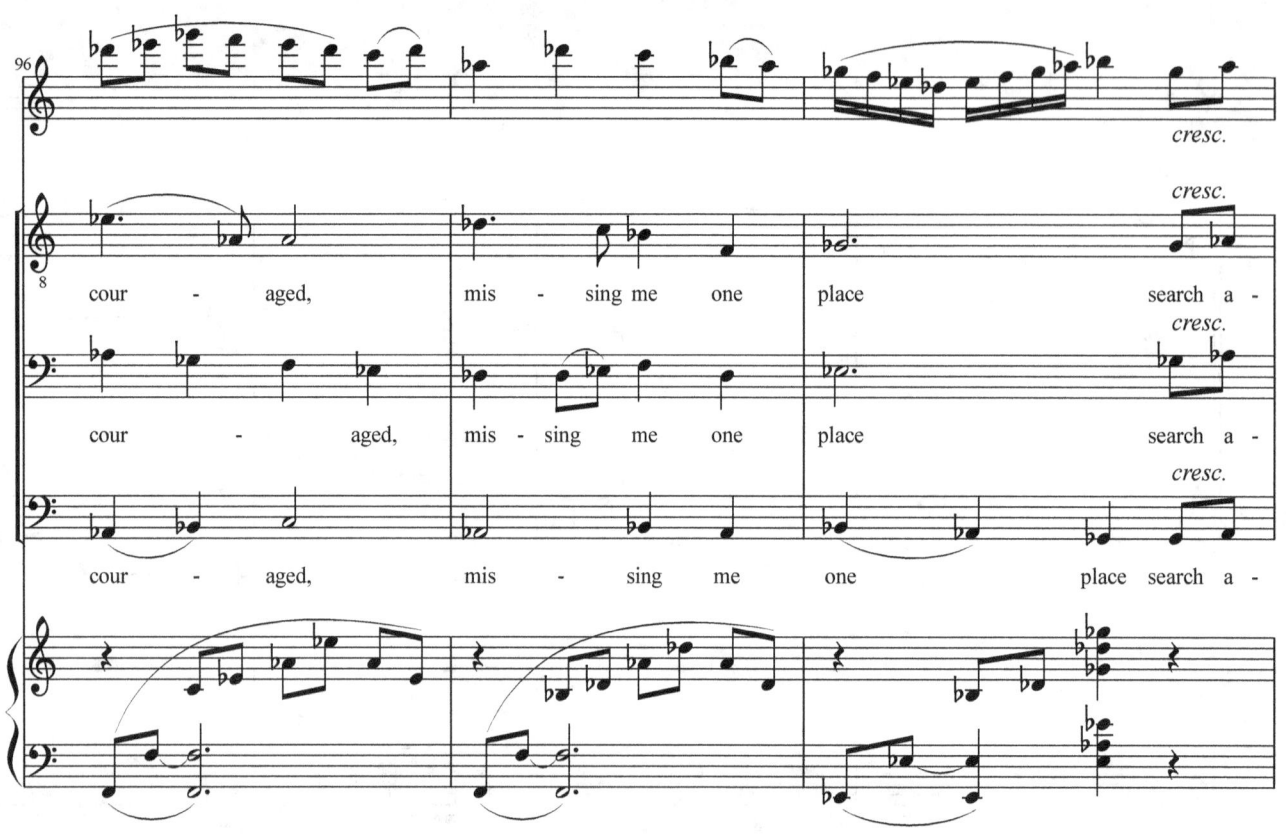

cour - aged, mis - sing me one place search a -

cour - aged, mis - sing me one place search a -

cour - aged, mis - sing me one place search a -

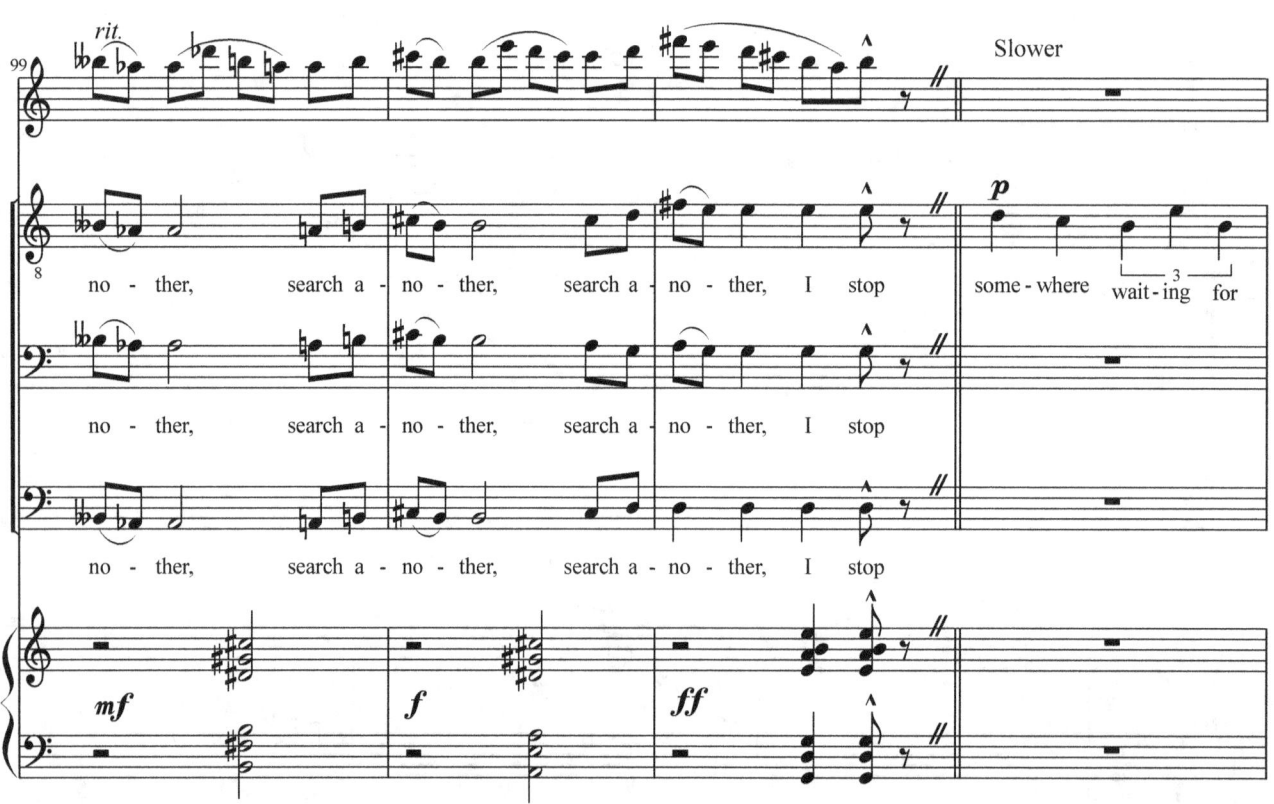

no - ther, search a - no - ther, search a - no - ther, I stop some - where wait-ing for

no - ther, search a - no - ther, search a - no - ther, I stop

no - ther, search a - no - ther, search a - no - ther, I stop

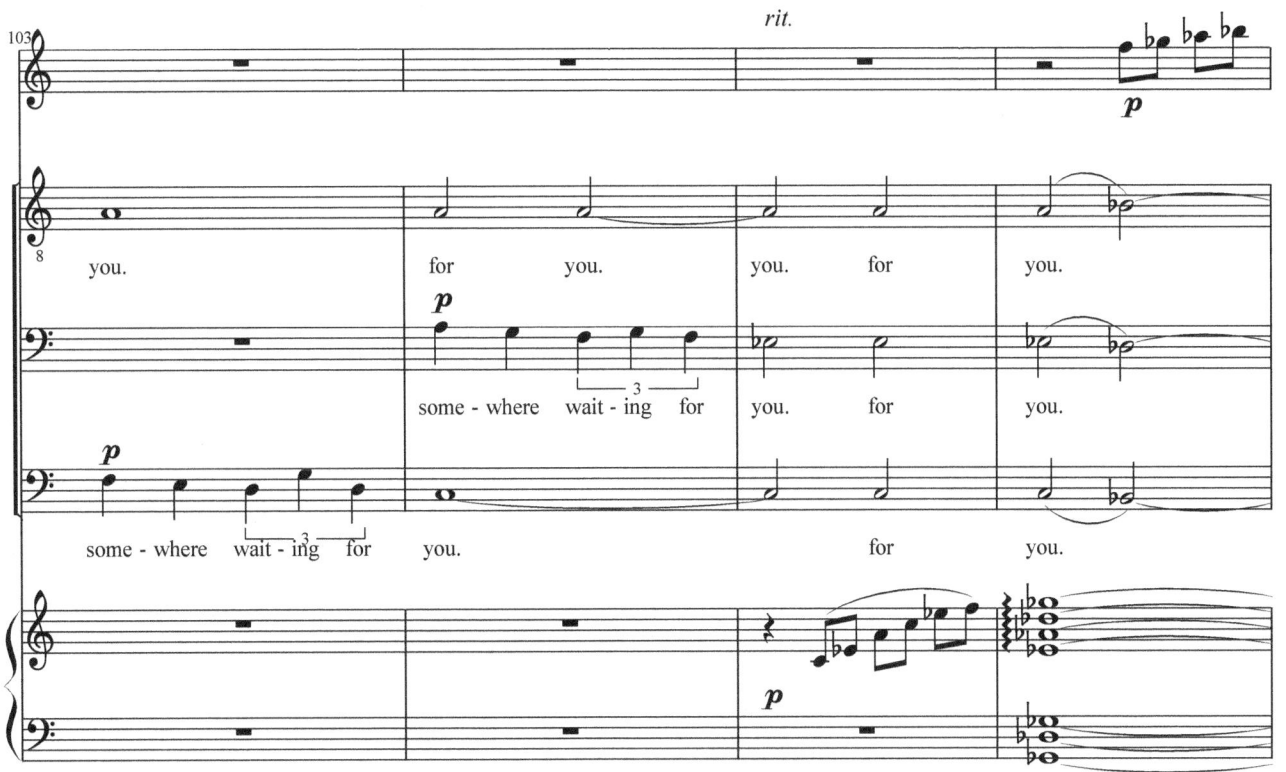

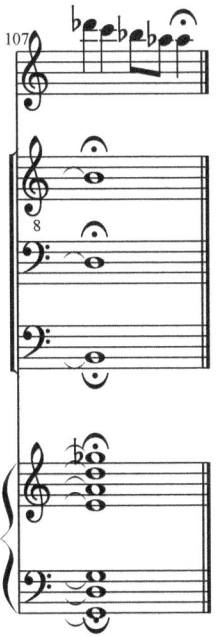

We Welcome You

Ken Langer

Slow Swing

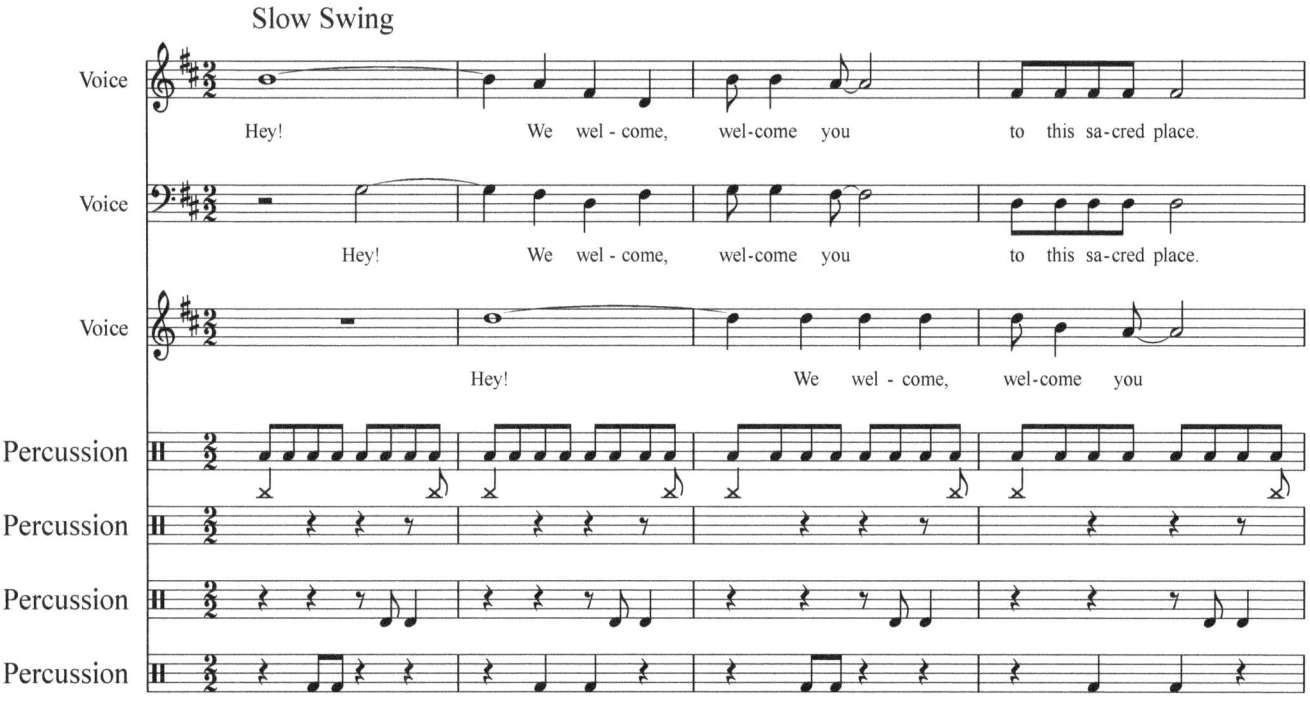

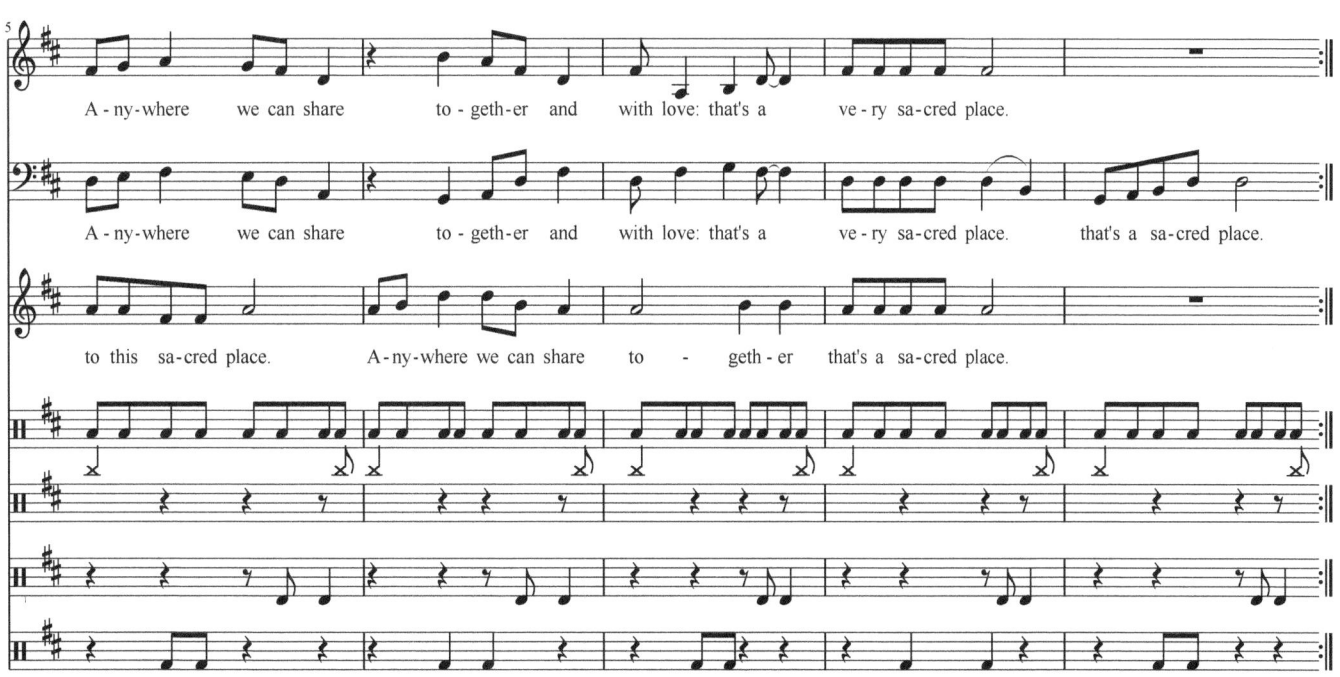

Wayfarin' Stranger

arr. Ken Langer

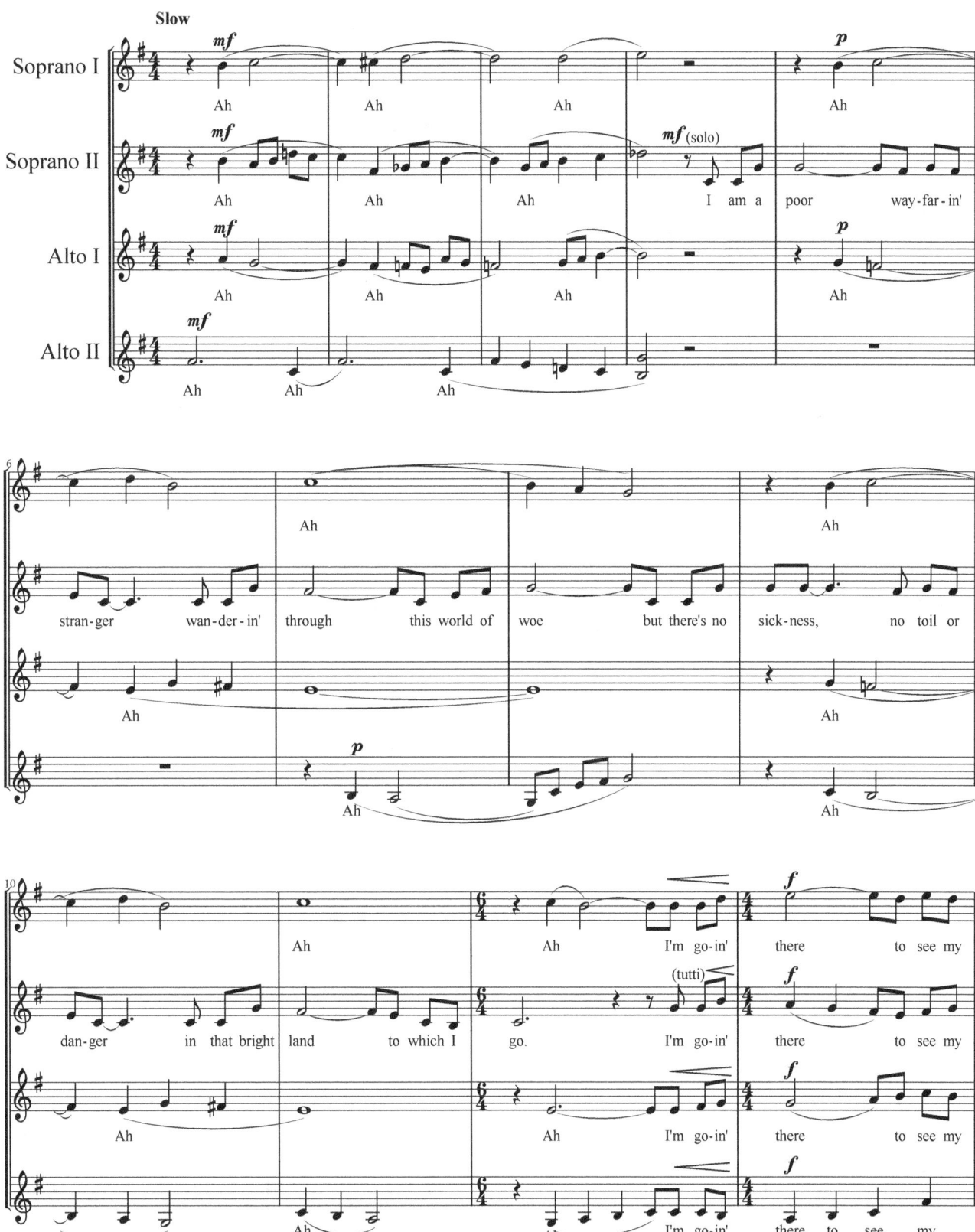

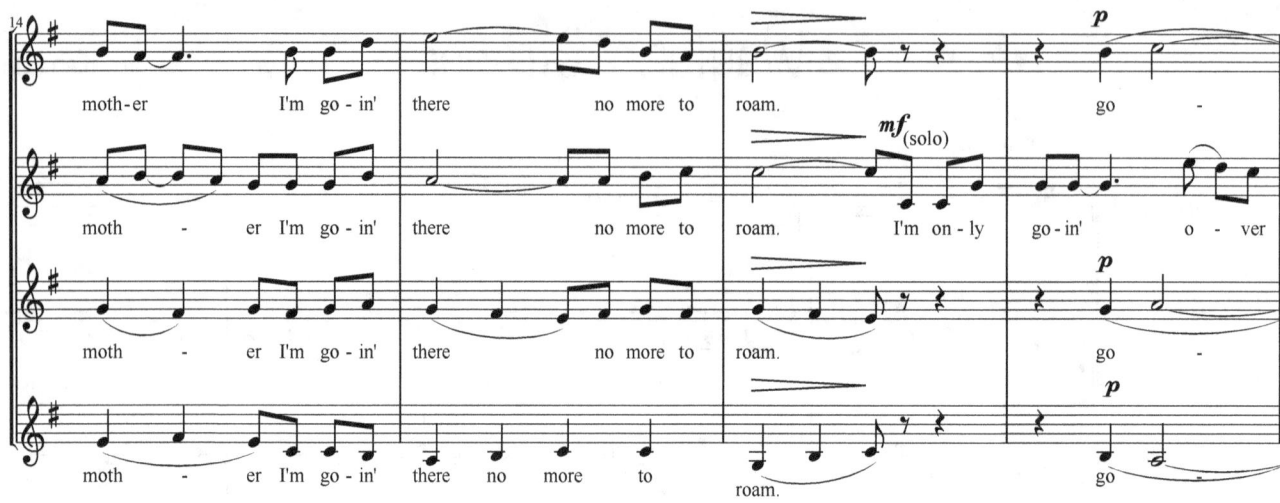

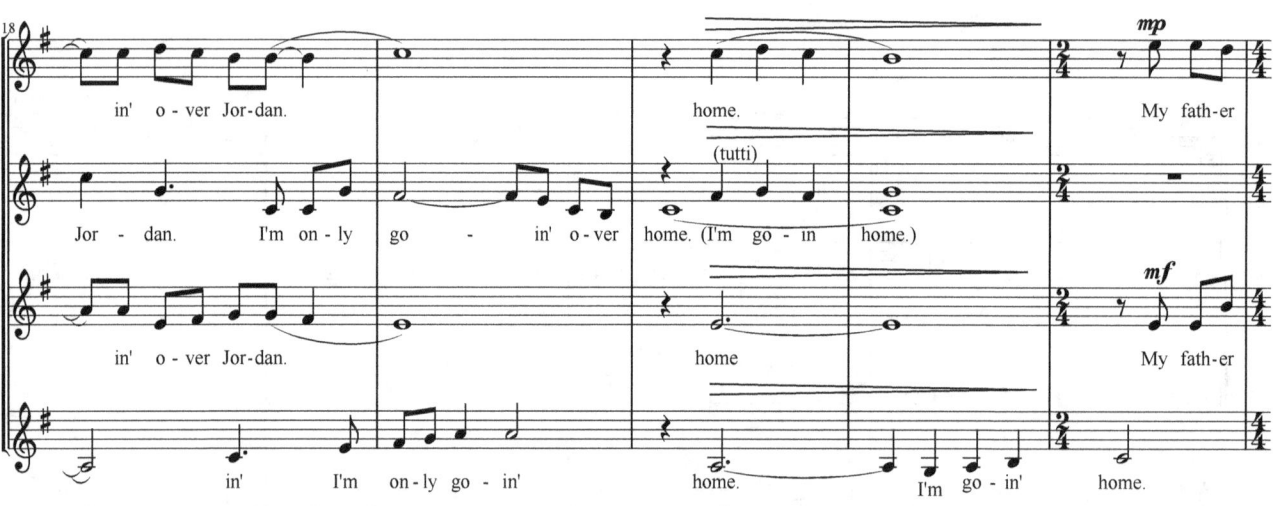

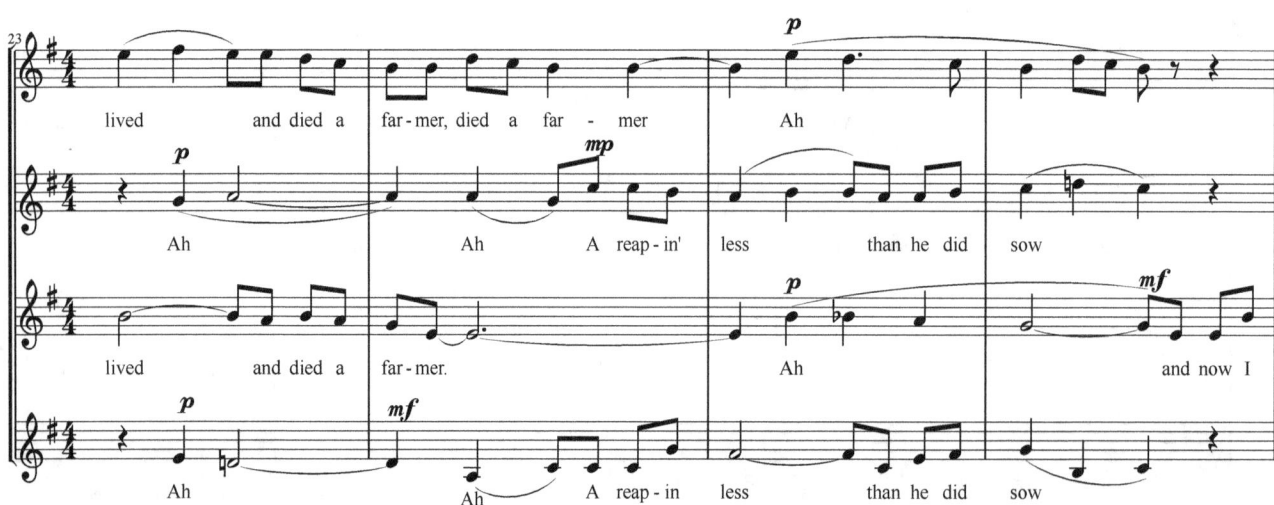

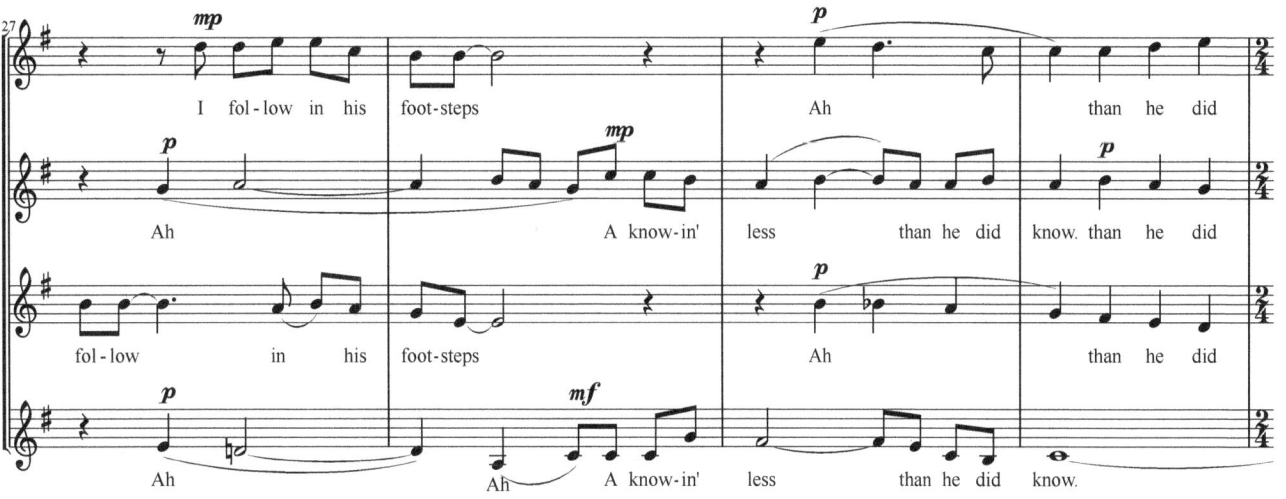

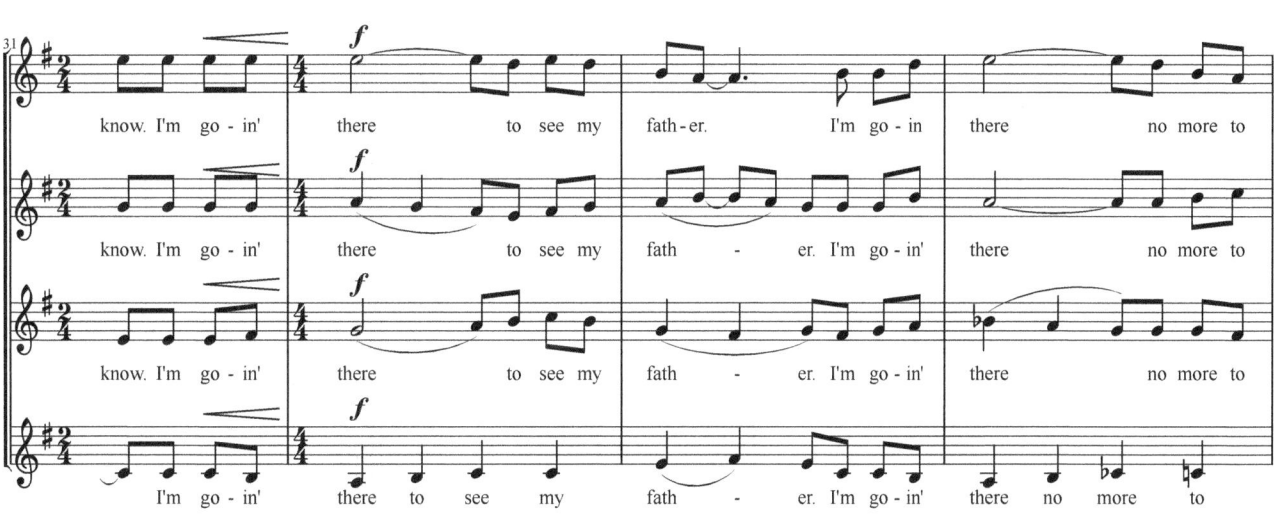

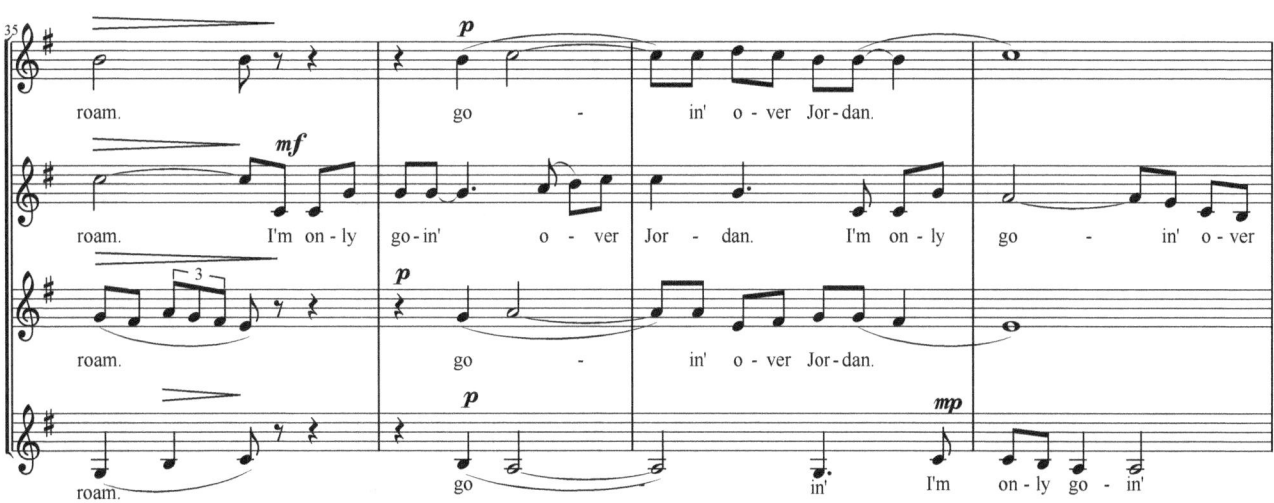

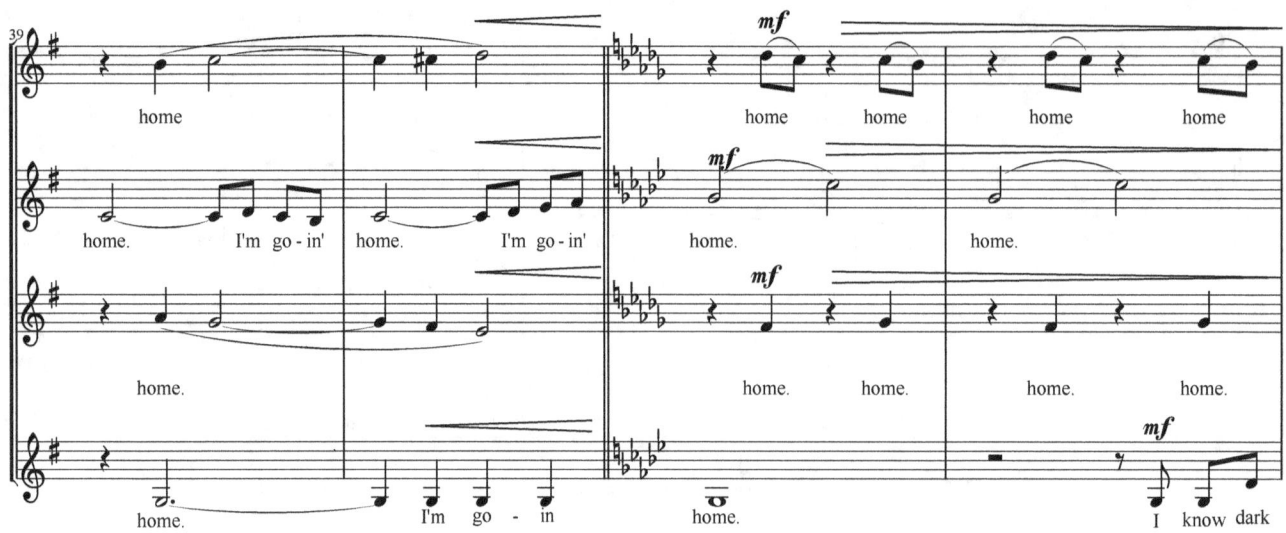

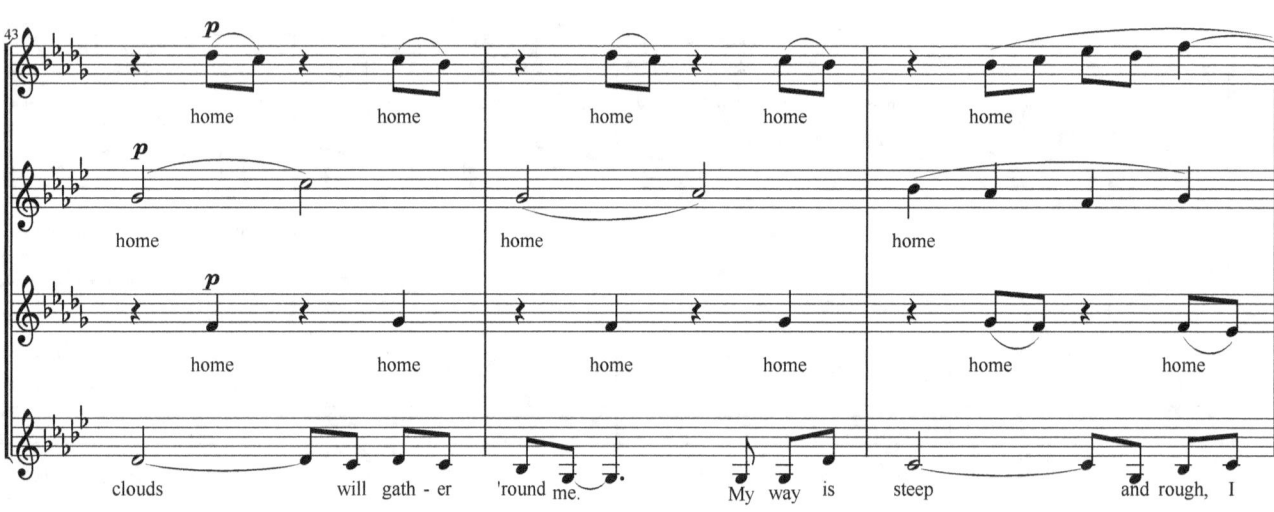

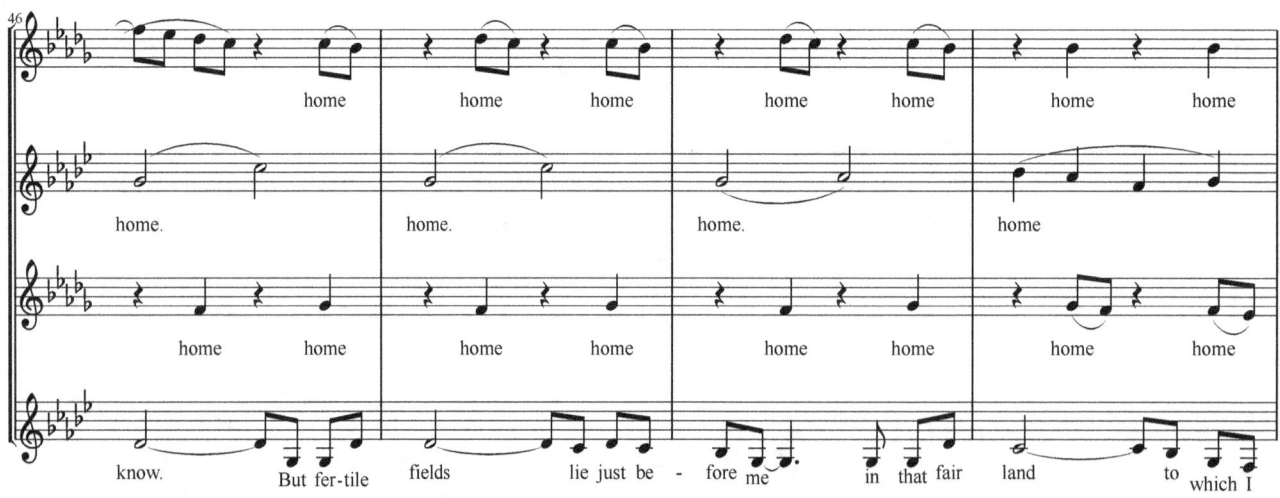

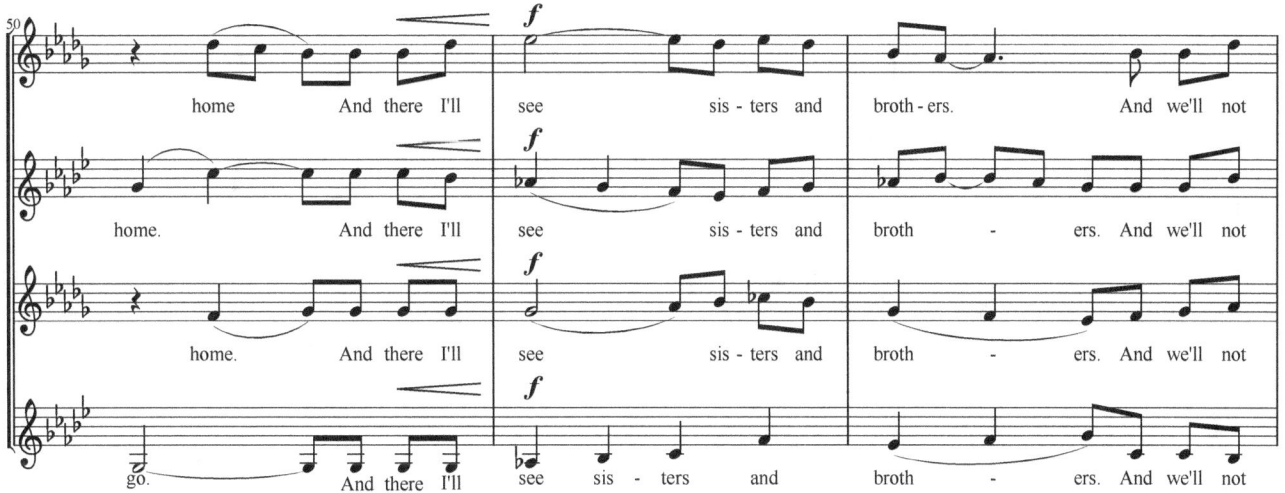

home And there I'll see sis - ters and broth - ers. And we'll not
home. And there I'll see sis - ters and broth - ers. And we'll not
home. And there I'll see sis - ters and broth - ers. And we'll not
go. And there I'll see sis - ters and broth - ers. And we'll not

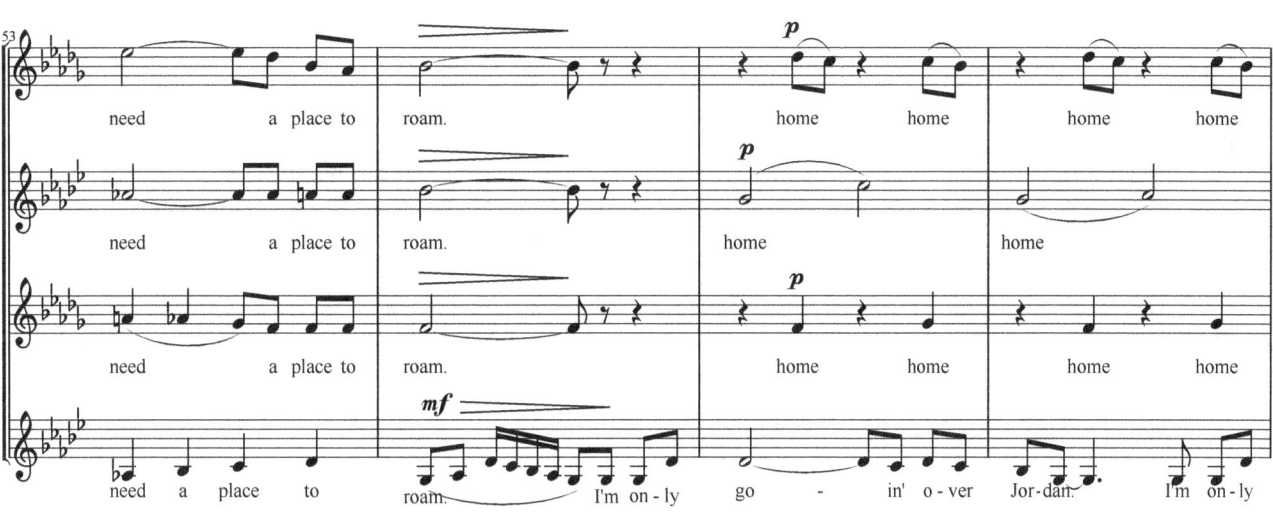

need a place to roam. home home home home
need a place to roam. home home
need a place to roam. home home home home
need a place to roam. I'm on - ly go - in' o - ver Jor - dan. I'm on - ly

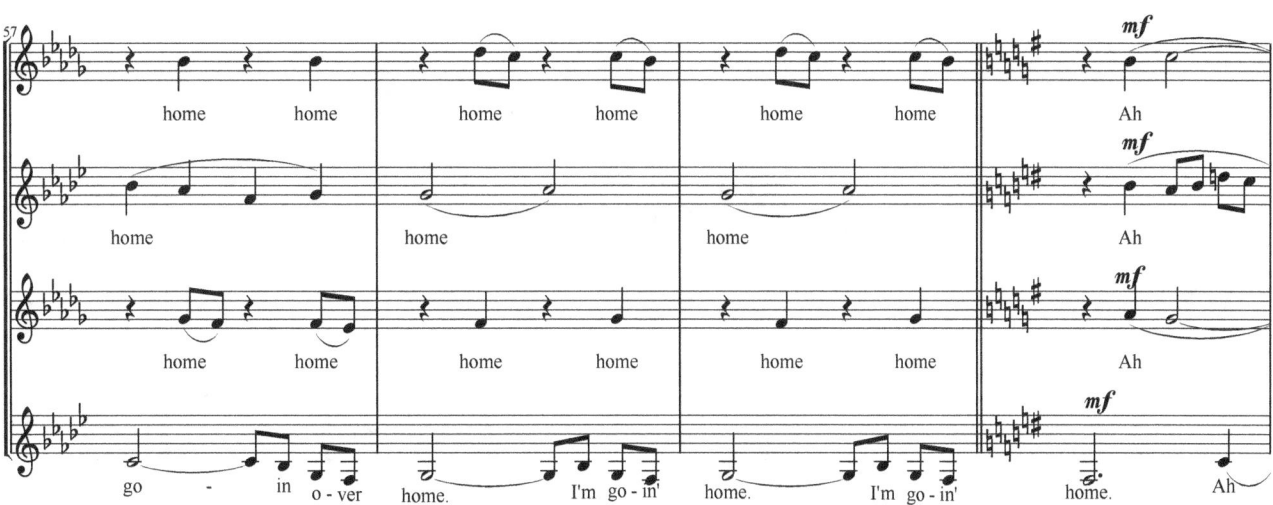

home home home home home home Ah
home home home Ah
home home home home home home Ah
go - in o - ver home. I'm go - in' home. I'm go - in' home. Ah

103

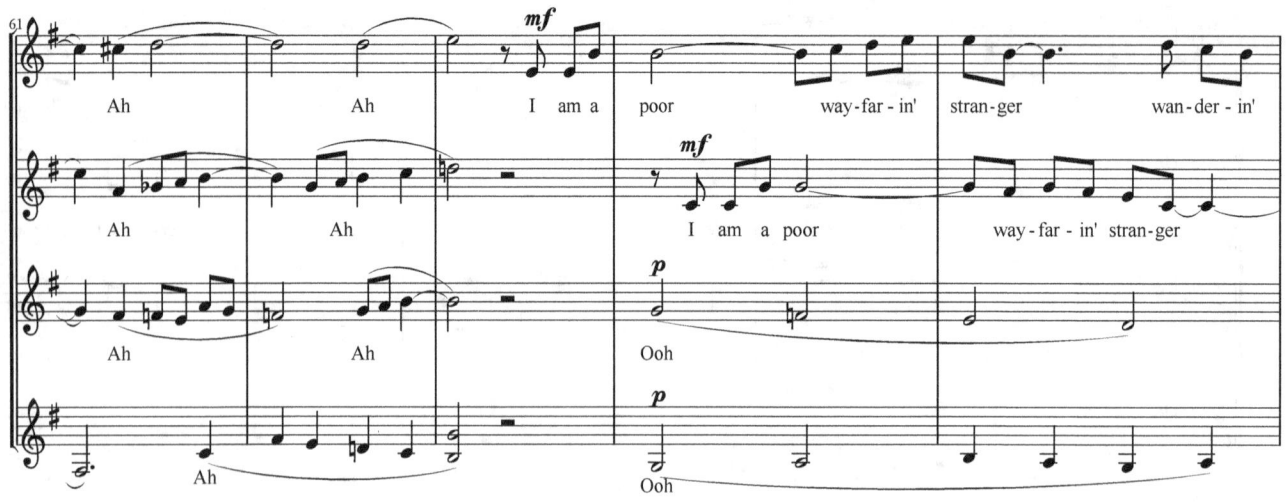

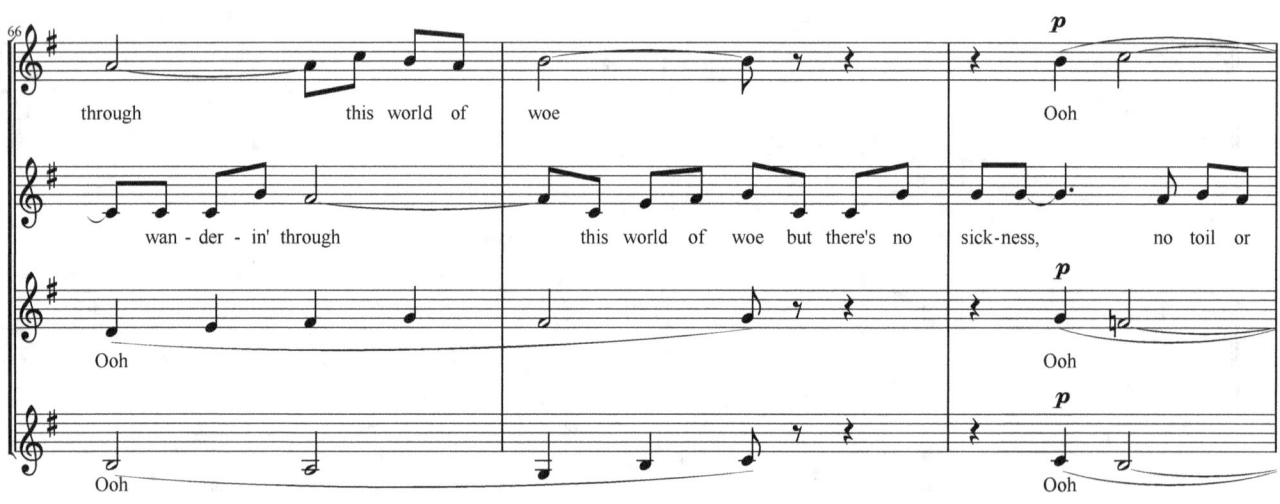

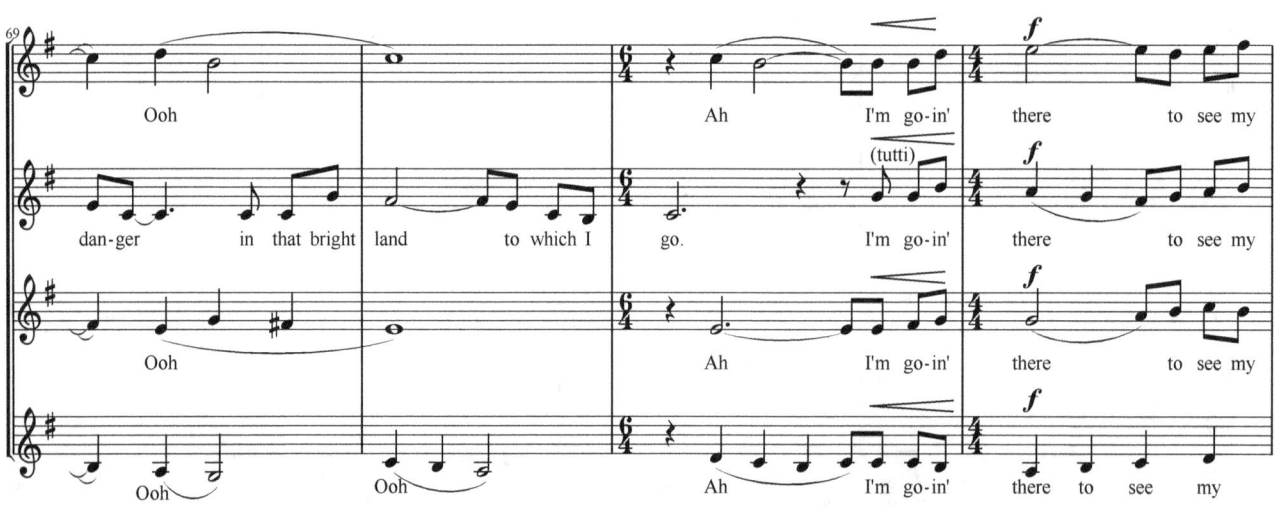

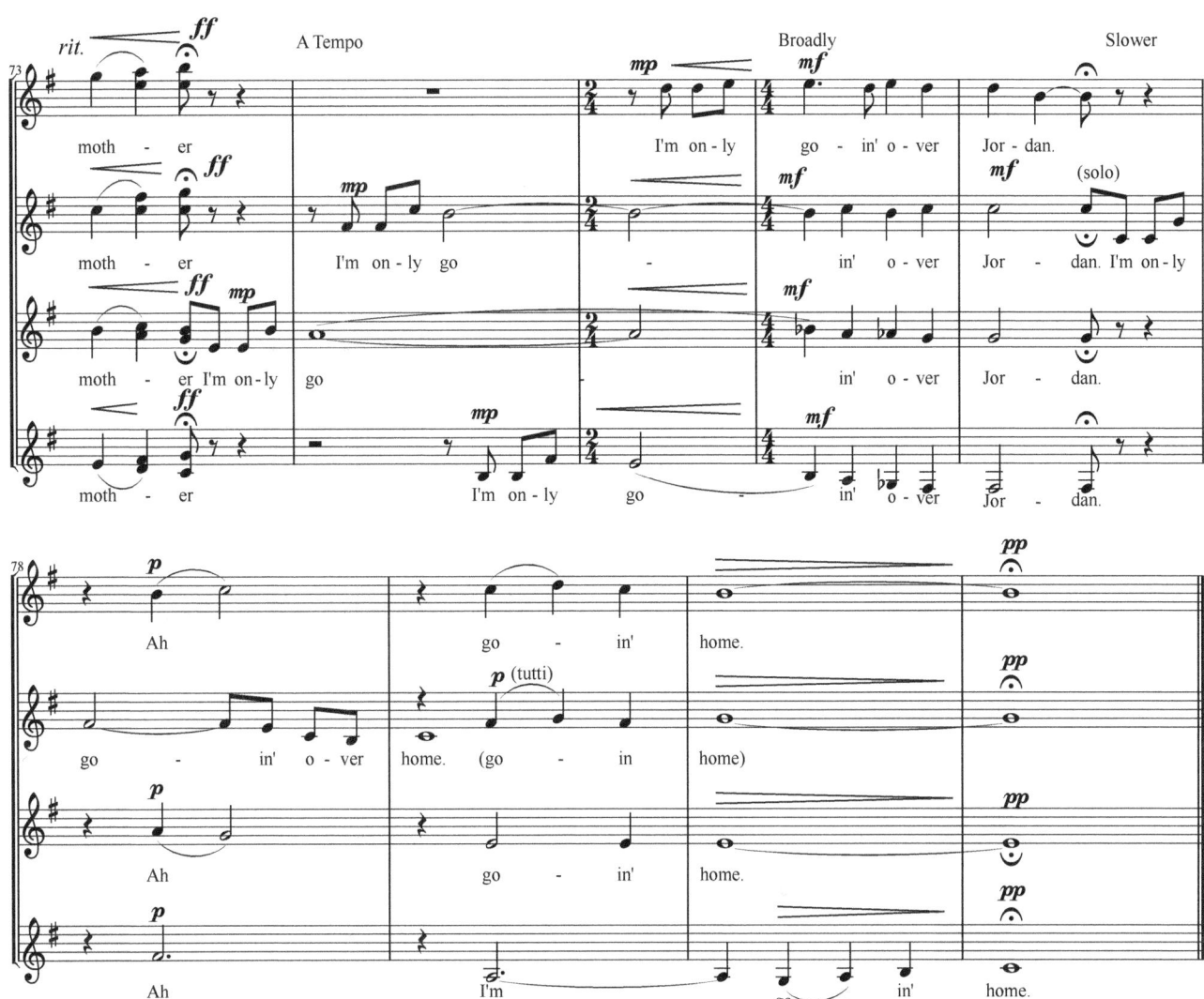

About The Composer

Dr. Kenneth Langer was born in the Pittsburgh area in 1959. He began playing trumpet in the 5th grade and decided in high school to make music his career.

Dr. Langer earned a Bachelor's Degree in Music Education at James Madison University in Harrisonburg, Virginia; a Master's of Music Degree at Radford University in Radford, Virginia; and a Ph.D. In Music Theory and Composition at Kent State University in Kent, Ohio. Since that time, he has taught music at several small colleges.

He has also been the full-time Director of Music and Arts at the Eno River Unitarian-Universalist Fellowship in Durham, North Carolina and the Assistant Conductor and Resident Composer at the Montpelier Unitarian-Universalist Church in Montpelier, Vermont.

During his twenty years of writing over 150 original works of music for various genres including brass, chorus, strings, orchestra, wind ensemble, and woodwinds; he has received numerous awards for his compositions including being named Vermont's Composer of the Year in the year 2000 and winning placement in several international composition contests. He has commercially published well over 30 compositions.

Dr. Langer currently lives in the Boston area with his family where he works as the Head of the Music Program at Northern Essex Community College in Haverhill, Massachusetts.

Publishers

Music For Brass

Nichols Music Company (Ensemble Publications)
P.O. Box 32 Ithaca, NY 14851-0032
www.enspub.com

Solid Brass Music
P.O. Box 2277 Rome GA, 30164
www.solidbrassmusic.com

Cimarron Music Press
15 Corrina Lane Salem CT 06420s
www.cimarronmusic.com

Wehr's Music House
www.wehrs-music-house.com

Music For Chorus

Yelton Rhodes Music
1236 N. Sweetzer Avenue #5 West Hollywood CA 90069
www.yrmusic.com

www.ingramcontent.com/pod-product-compliance
Lightning Source LLC
Chambersburg PA
CBHW081239180526
45171CB00005B/471